SARAH·ORNE JEWETT

A Writer's Life

SARAH·ORNE JEWETT

A Writer's Life

◆

ELIZABETH SILVERTHORNE

THE OVERLOOK PRESS
WOODSTOCK • NEW YORK

First published in 1993 by
The Overlook Press
Lewis Hollow Road
Woodstock, New York 12498

Library of Congress Cataloging-in-Publication Data

Silverthorne, Elizabeth
    Sarah Orne Jewett : a writer's life / Elizabeth Silverthorne.
        p. cm.
    Includes bibliographical references and index.
        1. Jewett, Sarah Orne, 1849-1909—Biography. 2. Authors, American—
19th century—Biography. I. Title.

PS2133.S56   1993
813′.4-dc20
[B]
                                                                    92-24589
ISBN: 0-87951-484-1   CIP

Dedication

Like Willa Cather in *O Pioneers!*,
I dedicate this biography:

To the memory of
SARAH ORNE JEWETT,
in whose beautiful and delicate work
there is a perfection
that endures

◆
Contents

PREFACE   9

ONE: "sister to a giddy-minded bobolink"   19

TWO: Beginnings   37

THREE: Widening Circles   57

FOUR: *Deephaven*   71

FIVE: The Queen of Sheba   87

SIX: 148 Charley Street   103

SEVEN: "A White Heron" and Other Tales   121

EIGHT: "To know the world..."   138

NINE: Country of the Pointed Firs   159

TEN: *The Tory Lover*   181

ELEVEN: "The lilac bushes still green"   197

AFTERWORD   213

SELECTED BIBLIOGRAPHY   217

INDEX   232

◆
Preface

THE WORLD TODAY is finally catching up with some of Sarah Orne Jewett's main concerns. Although her life and her writing were firmly rooted in the nineteenth century, she espoused causes that have become major crusades on the eve of the twenty-first century. In her own life she was modern and independent, and her characters were too. She championed freedom of choice for women in their careers and in their life styles. As a consequence, there has been a recent flood of writing about her in connection with women's studies.

A second area in which she pioneered was ecology. In essays, in short stories, in books, and in her personal correspondence, she protested the destruction of American forests, the pollution of natural resources, and the devastation of wildlife habitats caused by careless industrial practices. She also advocated the conservation and preservation of the architectural past and deplored inappropriate architectural renovations, such as the restoration of First Church in *The Old Town of Berwick*.

Another reason for renewed interest in Sarah Orne Jewett's writing is the realization that she conserved a slice of early American history by doing for the natives of Maine what

Marjorie Kinnan Rawlings did for the natives of Florida. Both writers preserved folklore, speech patterns, and folkways and at the same time revealed the nobility often found in the lives of ordinary people. Like Marjorie Rawlings, Sarah Jewett had a deep Wordsworthian reverence for nature and believed materialism was destroying the essential bond between man and nature. Both women also had an intense interest in the lives of the people around them and in their backgrounds, and each appreciated the deep pleasures of simple things.

Unlike Marjorie, however, who came to Florida from a sophisticated, urban background, Sarah grew up in the setting in which her best stories are laid. She walked, rode on horseback and in carriages, swam or rowed over every foot of it and could truthfully say "every bush and tree seem like my cousins."

In quiet country villages and in the seemingly placid lives of country people, she found tragedy and comedy, romance and adventure. In "A Late Supper" she tells her readers about the tiny town of Brookton: "Life is as important and exciting there as it is anywhere; and it is like every other town, a miniature world, with its great people and small people, bad people and good people, its jealousy and rivalry, kindness and patient heroism."

A number of readers have acknowledged the impact of Sarah Orne Jewett's works on their lives and on their writing, not the least among them Theodore Roosevelt, who recognized that his reading was important in developing his social awareness. In an article in *Outlook* (October 12, 1912) entitled "How I Became a Progressive," he said he received "instruction from the works of Mary E. Wilkins and Sarah Orne Jewett." Willa Cather frequently expressed gratitude for Sarah Orne Jewett's advice and guidance, and in the introduction to the Mayflower edition of *The Best Stories of Sarah Orne Jewett*, said, "If I were asked to name three American books which have the possibility of a long, long life, I would say at once, *The Scarlet Letter, Huckleberry Finn*, and *The*

Country of the Pointed Firs. I can think of no others that confront time and change so serenely." Truman Capote, in the introduction to *Other Voices, Other Rooms*, named the American authors who had been most valuable to him, including in his list Hawthorne, Poe, James, Twain, Cather, and Jewett. "Each of them," wrote Capote, "have contributed to my literary intelligence."

Since her death in 1909, there have always been those who refused to leave Sarah Orne Jewett lying in a bin labeled with a fading "local colorist" or "regionalist" tag. Her evocative prose and quiet humor, the refreshing and hopeful qualities of her writing have never failed to find a select, appreciative audience. Her work has naturally enough been better known in the North, and especially in New England, than it has been in other parts of the United States, but one purpose of this biography is to try to remedy this unfortunate situation.

Her first biographer, Francis O. Matthiessen, whose *Sarah Orne Jewett* appeared in 1929, twenty years after her death, had the advantage of being able to interview a number of her contemporaries, including her sister Mary Rice Jewett and her nephew Theodore Eastman. In 1960 John Eldridge Frost's biography appeared, providing data and details missing in Matthiessen's work, but neither biographer consistently attempted to relate her life to her work.

In the more than thirty years that have passed since the Frost biography, many letters and manuscripts have come to light. Especially significant is the recently acquired collection of letters (dating from 1872 to 1881) in the Special Collections section of the library at Colby College, Waterville, Maine, written to Theophilus Parsons, which reveal the influence he and his espousal of Swedenborgianism had upon her.

More than any other person, the late Richard Cary of Colby College has researched and published substantial information relating to Sarah Orne Jewett and her writing. His documentation and annotations are meticulous, and I am indebted to his scholarship for answering many questions and for providing many identifications of people and places.

Through the years, literary scholars and critics have continued to dissect and sometimes to disparage Sarah Orne Jewett's writing. Since the 1980s interest in her work and in her life has escalated, as more people have come to realize that the times have finally caught up with Sarah Orne Jewett. Lately a spate of books and essays have exalted and sometimes battered her work with Freudian, feminist, and Marxist interpretations.

Gwen L. Nagel, a Jewett scholar, has provided two helpful works: (Gwen L. Nagel and James Nagel, comps.) *Sarah Orne Jewett: A Reference Guide* is a valuable chronological bibliography, and her *Critical Essays on Sarah Orne Jewett*, published in 1984, is a useful collection of modern criticism with an insightful introduction.

Josephine Donovan, in *Sarah Orne Jewett*, explores the themes of city versus country and isolation versus community in Jewett's writing. Donovan has also been one of the leaders in the exploration of Jewett's intimate relationships with Annie Fields and with other women, which have recently become an area of heated controversy.

In my biography I have tried to go beyond what has been done before to bring Sarah Orne Jewett to life, to relate her life to her work, and to show the importance of her contribution to American literature. She often said that like Plato, she believed that the best thing that could be done for the people of a state—that is, a country—was to make them acquainted with each other. This she did consistently in her work, and if I have succeeded in making the readers of this book acquainted with Sarah Jewett, it is because I have received so much generous help and encouragement.

Dorothy Healy, curator of the Maine Women Writers Collection at Westbrook College, Portland, Maine, kindly shared the material in her Jewett archives and showed me the original edition of *An Island Garden*, by Celia Thaxter, with the paintings by Childe Hassam in all their pristine beauty. Marie Donahue, corresponding secretary of the Old Berwick Historical Society, gave me personal tours of the Jewett Home in South Berwick, the house next door, where Sarah grew up, and the Jewett family plot in the South Berwick Cemetery, and guided me to the Hamilton House.

At Colby College, Waterville, Maine, Patience-Anne W. Lenk, curator for the Special Collections of the Miller Library, went out of her way to give me access to their fine collection of Jewett material. Dianne Gutscher, curator of Special Collections of the Hawthorne-Longfellow Library at Bowdoin College, Brunswick, Maine, and Elizabeth Singer Maule, curator of Manuscripts and Special Collections at the Maine Historical Society headquarters in Portland, Maine, were also very helpful. And I am grateful to Lorna Condon, associate archivist at the Society for the Preservation of New England Antiquities headquarters in the Harrison Gray Otis House in Boston, for her expert assistance in using the material there.

I also appreciate the help of Rodney G. Dennis, curator, and Jennie Rathbun and the staff at the Houghton Reading Room at the Houghton Library at Harvard University; to Bernard R. Crystal, head of the Manuscripts Division of the Libraries at Columbia University, New York; and to Sarah H. Spurgin of the Reference Department, Columbia University. I also owe thanks to the staffs at the Dimond Library at the University of New Hampshire, Durham, New Hampshire, and at the Aldermann Library at the University of Virginia, Charlottesville, Virginia.

In the three years spent in researching and writing this biography, I have been bewitched by New England, and I am grateful to my fiends and relatives who have patiently listened to my ravings about its charms.

Heaven only knows the story of the lives that the gray old New England farmhouses have sheltered and hidden away from curious eyes as best they might. Stranger dramas than have ever been written belong to the dull-looking, quiet homes, that have seen generation after generation live and die. On the well-worn boards of these provincial theatres the great plays of life, the comedies and tragedies, with their lovers and conspirators and clowns; their Juliets and Ophelias, Shylocks and King Lears, are acted over and over and over again.

from "A Landless Farmer"
—SARAH ORNE JEWETT

SARAH·ORNE
JEWETT
A Writer's Life

CHAPTER ONE

◆

"sister to a giddy-minded bobolink"

S ARAH ORNE JEWETT once told a friend that she looked
upon her grandparents' generation as the one she belonged to: "I who was brought up with grand-fathers
and grand-uncles and aunts for my best playmates." In addition to the constant influence of her grandparents, she had
an innate sense of history. She never saw an old house, a moss-
covered cellar hole, a tumbledown stone wall, or a crumbling
wharf without imagining what it had been like in earlier
times, surrounded by the bustle and strife of those who had
built it.

Although her own life (1849–1909) spanned only the
second half of the nineteenth century and the beginning
decade of the twentieth, in her mind and heart and in her
writing she took as her province all of the history that had
preceded her in her small area of New England. She believed
strongly in the indelible imprint of inherited characteristics,
and she acknowledged the deep impression on her life and
on her writing of three men whose genes she carried. These
patriarchs were her paternal grandfather, her maternal grandfather, and her father—whose influence was the greatest of
all three.

Theodore Furber Jewett, Sarah's paternal grandfather,

ran away, as a boy, from an apprenticeship to sail on a whaling ship in the Pacific and was left, with two companions, for almost a year on an uninhabited island to guard ship stores and hunt seals. At twenty-four, as a ship's captain, he defied the Act of 1809 against shipping to English and French ports and was captured by an English privateer and confined in the infamous Dartmoor prison. After the War of 1812 ended, he became a ship owner and a merchant and married four times. For many years Captain Jewett kept and extended his interests in shipping. He built ships and bought large quantities of timber from the north and the east to send down the river from South Berwick and on to sea. He grew rich in the West Indies trade, and after he died, her inheritance from the fortune he made enabled her to remark that she did not need to write for her "bread and butter." He left his granddaughter another legacy as well—his love of sailing ships and of the sea and his yarns of sea life and faraway places.

In 1839, Captain Jewett had moved his family from Portsmouth, New Hampshire, to the village of South Berwick, Maine, which is situated on the Piscataqua River, a tidal estuary that forms the lower border between Maine and New Hampshire. Just below South Berwick, the Salmon River joins the Piscataqua and the two flow down to Portsouth and the Atlantic Ocean. One of the oldest permanent settlements in New England, the area has a romantic history that Sarah Orne Jewett would use in many ways in her writing.

Captain Jewett bought the John Haggins house—or mansion, as John "Tilly" Haggins called the fine Georgian house he built in 1774. Haggins, a prosperous merchant as well as the owner of mills, slaves, and farms, was typical of the wealthy gentry that built elegant homes in the Piscataqua region and called themselves the River Society. But the Embargo Act of 1807, which prohibited all commerce with foreign nations, and the War of 1812 crippled the area economically and socially, with the Civil War completing the devastation and leaving South Berwick to gradually become a quiet backwater village. Sarah Orne Jewett grew up listening to her forebears' stories of the glory days of the colonial maritime community, and many of her stories reflect her sympathy for the River Society gentry and her regret for a way of life that was fast fading even as she was born.

According to legend, it took three ship's carpenters a hundred days to build and carve the dentelated cornices, the carved balusters and newel posts, the fluted columns and paneled wainscoting of John Haggin's house, which was located in the center of South Berwick. When Captain Jewett bought the house, he furnished it with some of the merchandise he traded in: French flocked wallpaper and tapestries, carved furniture, and exotic bric-a-brac. To these he added fine American furniture, including tables and chairs, highboys, chests on chests, and Adams mirrors, plus a library of leather-bound books. In this house Sarah was born and in this house she died.

With Captain Jewett at this time lived his third wife and his son William, a ship chandler who ran the family store, known as the W.I. (West Indies) store. The aging captain felt keenly the loss of two of his sons. The eldest had died of tuberculosis, and the youngest (only twenty-three) had sailed out of Boston in charge of the *Berwick*, one of the captain's own ships, and been lost in a collision with a Danish ship 250 miles off the Cape of Good Hope. Captain Jewett's other son, Theodore Herman Jewett (Sarah's father), was a delicate boy who loved books and had no interest in a sea life. He entered Bowdoin College in Brunswick, Maine, at fifteen. One of his professors described him as a "most loveable young fellow, somewhat quiet and diffident, but very winning in his manner, a very great favorite both with the faculty and his classmates."

Deciding on medicine as a career, Theodore Jewett sought an education in his profession that went far beyond the apprenticeship method common in the first half of the nineteenth century. After graduating from Bowdoin, he attended medical lectures at Hanover and Boston, studied with Dr. Winslow Lewis of Boston, worked in Boston's charitable institutions, and spent a year at the United States Marine Hospital in Chelsea. After taking a medical degree at Jefferson Medical College in Philadelphia in 1839, he planned to go to Europe to learn a specialty and then to locate his practice in a large city in the United States, but poor health plagued him, and after he suffered several alarming hemorrhages from his lungs, his father begged him not to leave the country.

Consequently, Theodore Jr. settled in Exeter, New Hampshire, not far from South Berwick, where he worked with Dr. William Perry, an eminent physician and surgeon and community leader. Dr. Perry, who was to become Sarah's maternal grandfather, was an extraordinary man, with several of his accomplishments bringing him recognition in the *Dictionary of American Biography*. In 1814, after receiving an M.D. degree from Harvard, he set up practice in Exeter, where his professional skill earned him a reputation that brought patients flocking to him from great distances. He continued to perform difficult operations into his late eighties, and at ninety-two he operated successfully for strangulated hernia. Keenly interested in insanity, he delivered two lectures on the subject to the state legislature, urging the building of an asylum for the insane, and it was largely through his efforts that an asylum was eventually built at Concord. His interest in chemistry led him to conduct a series of experiments to find a substitute for "British gum," an expensive imported sizing used by manufacturers of cotton cloth. He found that a suitable starch could be made from potatoes, and he built a mill to produce the starch for the Lowell cotton producers.

Strong-minded and original in his thinking, William Perry was looked up to by his fellow citizens, who sought and respected his opinion on civic and religious affairs. After she was grown, Sarah wrote an essay about this stern Scottish Covenanter, who had given up his rights in the family farm in order to attend Harvard; yet as a child she was sometimes irked by his extremely high standards. After a visit to him and her sweet-faced, gentle grandmother in Exeter, Sarah recalled driving with him to the railway station in his old two-wheeled gig with her little trunk at her feet, a blue ribbon fluttering from the handle for better recognition. In a last effort to impress upon her the risks of rebellious behavior, he gravely warned her: "You must remember that there will come a day when you will call upon the hills to fall upon you and the rocks to cover you."

Dr. Perry took an intense interest in his grandchildren's upbringing and he shared with Sarah, as she grew older, his knowledge and love of good horses. Until he was in his late eighties he delighted in racing spirited horses in wide open spaces. He also supplied her with books and made sharp comments about the reports he insisted she make on her reading.

"He was always showing me where good work was to be done and insisting on the moral qualities that led to achievement," Sarah recalled. Grandfather Perry was full of ambition for his grandchildren, telling them that only laziness and lack of understanding of the possibilities of life kept them from being useful and good and even great. Sarah gave him credit for stirring her out of her tendency to daydream and also for influencing her moral values. "Make the best of yourself!" he would exclaim. "Act—act! Go and *do it* if you think you are right!" He was, Sarah said, a rock against which "drifting seas of indifference and hedonism dashed in vain." He mellowed as he aged, taking pleasure in being with young people, and rejoicing in their least flicker of success. Sarah liked hearing him reminisce about his early life, and when he died in 1887, at the age of ninety-nine, she thought he might have been the last living person who could remember having heard the news told of Marie Antoinette's execution.

When he was thirty William Perry had married Abigail Gilman, so through her grandmother Perry Sarah was connected with the Gilmans, a notable family in New England history. In 1638 Edward Gilman of Hingham, England, had sailed with 133 religious refugees—including his wife, three sons, and two daughters—for America. At Hingham, Massachusetts, "Edward the Emigrant" (as his descendants called him) established himself and founded the Gilman dynasty. Some years later he moved to Exeter, then the capital of New Hampshire, where he acquired valuable real estate and sired governors, judges, lawyers, and business tycoons. Nicholas Gilman, Sarah's great-great-uncle, was a member of the first Congress and one of the signers of the Constitution. Gilmans were active in the Revolution and afterward they remained important citizens of the new republic. Throughout Sarah's life the Perrys and Gilmans of Exeter visited back and forth with the Jewetts of South Berwick, as did other branches of the Gilman and Perry families who lived in other places in New England.

When Theodore Jewett settled in Exeter to practice medicine with William Perry, he found that his mentor had an attractive daughter named Frances. Five years Theodore's junior, she was well educated, well read, and certainly well brought up by her father's strict code. Propinquity and preference did their work; Theodore and Frances fell in love and were married in 1842. Their first daughter, Mary Rice Jewett, was born in June of 1847.

Shortly after that, Captain Jewett persuaded his son to leave Exeter and move with his family to South Berwick to practice medicine. Accordingly, the young couple and their daughter Mary came to live in the fine old colonial house in the center of town. Here their second daughter was born on September 3, 1849. She was named after two grandmothers, and her full name, Theodora Sarah Orne Jewett, was duly inscribed in the family Bible (the Theodora soon dropped from use).

After she was grown, Sarah commented that one may travel, literally, at home and "always be learning history, geography, botany or biography." Few have traveled in their own regions with deeper insight or keener powers of observation than Sarah Orne Jewett. Berwick (or Old Berwick), South Berwick, and North Berwick were once a part of Kittery, but in 1713 they were incorporated as Berwick, the ninth town in Maine. South Berwick, separated from Berwick and incorporated in 1814, was rich in memories and associations by the time of Sarah's birth.

It was a beautiful setting to grow up in, with high hills and pine forests, distant mountain views, and fields of wildflowers. The two large rivers that joined just below the village made a magnificent stream bounded by tall pines and hemlocks along its high banks and in other spots by green fields sloping gently to stands of graceful willows along the edge of the water. The sound of the falls made a constant background music for the activities of the inhabitants of the village.

Indian tales and names are entwined with the lore of the area. The main branch of the Piscataqua ("river of right angles") led to Newichawannock Falls ("my place of wigwams") and to Quampeagan ("great fishing place"), where Indians came to catch and dry their fish. Tradition says that at one time it was possible to walk across the water on the salmon that became wedged together in their desperate attempts to leap the impossibly high falls at Quampeagan, the old name for South Berwick. Indians in the area were friendly to the early English settlers and encouraged them to settle in the region. Sarah came to know some families who still lived on land their ancestors had bought from Indians, and she examined with interest the "queer, barbaric" signatures on the deeds.

Even though the Jewett house was large, it became a little cramped when Dr. Jewett and his wife and two daughters were added to the Captain and his wife and grown son, William, plus several servants. To ease the situation, Dr. Jewett built a substantial but smaller house next door. While she was a tiny girl, just beginning to explore the world, Sarah's realm was bounded by the low fences that enclosed her grandfather

Jewett's house and her own house. It was easy to squeeze through the hedge of shrubbery that separated the two yards, and to Sarah they were equally her playground. From between the palings or by climbing up on the gates, she could see on one side the houses across the street with their neat yards and on the other side she could watch riders on swift horses, carts drawn by plodding oxen, and people going in and out of the post office and the shops with their red chimneys and over-hanging gables.

Before she knew their names, Sarah loved the flowering shrubs and the flowers that bloomed in succession in her two yards. White and yellow daffodils heralded spring, followed by lilacs, larkspur, Canterbury bells, and London pride. She knew where to find ladies-delights under certain bushes and a stray-away called ambrosia. Tiger lilies and some of the rosebushes grew higher than her head, but she stood on tip-toe to pick crumpled petals of cinnamon roses to make her-self a "delicious coddle" with cinnamon and damp brown sugar.

Sarah's feeling of kinship with nature and her habit of personifying everything in it developed early. From the grown-ups around her she knew that the dandelions were interloping invaders, but she liked their audaciousness, and they remained favorites all of her life. Outside the fence grew French pinks, which she thought were treated as if they were "poor relations of the other flowers." Young Sarah felt sympathy for them, admiring their fresh, sweet, resigned look, as if they were making the best of their lives, "remembering that they had sunshine and rain and could see what was going on in the world, if they were outlaws."

Her stern step-grandmother Jewett deplored Sarah's im-pulsive behavior and rightly considered Mary a more tractable child. Sarah felt a closer kinship to the long-dead real grand-mother for whom she was named—especially after she grew up and discovered letters that revealed tantalizing tidbits of information about the first Sarah Orne (or Sally, as everyone called her) in the attic of grandfather Jewett's house. Sarah traced a brief romance between her grandmother and a Frenchman who sailed into Portsmouth on one of the captured French ships during the French and Indian Wars. Among the letters was an exquisite watercolor of a carnation (which she guessed Sally had picked for him) and a note begging that "charming Sally" would think of "poor Ribere," who could never forget her. Presumably the romance ended when Ribere was freed to return to France at the end of the war. In the same trunk there were also the love letters written by grandfather Jewett to Sally while he was away at sea. They had married when Sally was eighteen, and after bearing him two children, she died at twenty-five. It was through Sally's French ancestry that Sarah believed she inherited her *gaieté de coeur* or happy disposition—a characteristic also of her father.

Sarah described Mary Jewett, the woman she was taught to call "grandmother," as a "proud and solemn" woman. To her grandmother's dismay, Sarah loved to escape her authority by running off into the fields like a wild thing, feeling "own sister to a giddy-minded bobolink." Neither was her grandmother pleased when Sarah acted out her belief that mud puddles were made for stomping in. And her hobbies of building dams and collecting bugs also brought down disapproval on her head. When four-year-old Sarah discovered a first bud on a cherished tea-rose bush in her grandfather Jewett's yard, she plucked it and ran in great excitement to show the prize to her grandmother. Opening her small fist to display the stemless bud in all its beauty, she was so shocked by her grandmother's severe scolding that she felt bowed down with guilt and shame for days.

The next year her grandmother died. It was Sarah's first encounter with death, and she never forgot the experience. Sitting alone on the steps of the side porch of her house, she could see lights being carried hurriedly from room to room of the great house next door. Her Victorian grandmother was ceremoniously taking leave of the family members one by one. A servant came for Sarah, but she refused to go—curious as she was to know what "dying" meant, she was afraid to be alone with her grandmother. As she sat on the doorstep, the December sky grew dark and cold, and she began crying softly to herself. Someone loudly rang the bell of the street door of her own house again and again, and she became terrified. It seemed to her that a messenger from an unknown world had come to the wrong house to call her grandmother away. Her family, coming back at last to find her alone and forlorn, comforted her. Two days later, with the resilience of children, she found that the funeral, with its pomp and ceremony, gave her "vast entertainment," for it was the first grand public occasion in which she had a part.

During Sarah's early childhood, her grandfather Jewett was still engaged actively in buying large quantities of timber from the north and east and shipping it down the Piscataqua River and on to sea. The up-country people who brought timber to South Berwick conducted their business chiefly by barter—lumber was exchanged for flour, rice, barrels of molasses, sugar and salt, cotton cloth, raisins, and spices, tea, and coffee, plus a little cash to pay taxes and parish dues.

When the long trains of yoked oxen pulling sleds loaded with timber came into sight at the head of the village street, Sarah ran to meet them, hoping to be allowed to climb aboard and ride triumphantly through town. Before many years passed, however, she realized that the great timber pines were irreplaceable and began to feel "sorry at the sight of every huge lopped stem of oak or pine that came trailing along after the slow-stepping, frosted oxen." But she delighted in lingering in the busy country stores listening to the talk of the timber merchants. She absorbed their way of speaking, their descriptions of neighborhood affairs, and their tall tales of impossibly large tracts of impossibly huge timber pines.

On the other side of the business, she came into contact with sailors and ship captains. Her young ears were tuned to pick up news of a ship's coming into port, and she listened eagerly to the exciting tales of the bronzed captains who dined heartily with her grandfather. They brought gifts of filberts, oranges, and great red jars of olives, and they told fascinating tales of their voyages: of great storms, of winds that blew them "north-about," and of good bargains to be had in Havana or Barbados. She knew the names of her grandfather's ships as well as she knew the names of members of her family, and she thought of the ships as other children of the family who were away from home visiting exotic places and having exciting adventures.

As effortlessly as she soaked up geography, Sarah absorbed history as she listened to the grownups talk. They still recounted details of the siege of Louisbourg, recounting how the English finally took permanently out of French hands that strategic fort that guarded the waters off Nova Scotia. Sarah learned that her father's ancestors had been "honest but mistaken Tories" during the Revolutionary War, and that her mother's family, the Gilmans, had "nobly" fought for independence. There were many stories about John Paul Jones, who had recruited men for his flagship, the frigate *Ranger*, in the Berwick area. One member of that crew, in his old age, became her father's patient. Sarah often heard tales of Lafayette's visit to South Berwick, and the "last war," the War of 1812, was fresh in the minds of the adults, who spoke as if it had just happened yesterday.

In 1855 several important events happened in six-year-old Sarah's life. In the spring, Uncle William Jewett married, and his bride, twenty-five-year-old Aunt Augusta, became the mistress of the big house. Sarah soon grew to love her lively new relative. Visiting Aunt Augusta's home in Kittery that summer, Sarah made her first scientific discovery. At low tide, she walked under the wharf picking up little pale green and brown and purple mussels, but to her disappointment, she found the colors faded as they dried. Once she left a heap of her carefully chosen shells wrapped in newspaper in a bureau drawer in her bedroom and forgot about them. After tracing the source of the disagreeable odor that ensued, the grownups merely laughed and insisted that she not do that again. Sadly, her kind new aunt only lived a few more years.

It was also in 1855 that Sarah began her formal education. In 1853 two young sisters had opened a "Dame School" in South Berwick, only a few doors from the Jewett home. The Misses Raynes' school offered individual instruction to from fifteen to thirty boys and girls. Mary Jewett, serious and studious, made high grades, but Sarah's grades were only average, for her mind tended to stray off into daydreaming about things that were important to her. Her first composition, written at age six, shows her love of nature, her powers of observation, and her inability to cope with punctuation:

On Rosees

There are A great manny kinds of Rossees of which are Dammask Blush cinnamon and Red we have A great manny of the Red around our door in the summer time and i am very fond of them my sister and I have small garden and there is A rosebush in each there is also the Archduke Charles it is A small rose but it is very pretty

Sarah O Jewett
So Berwick
Me

The final important event in Sarah's life in 1855 was the birth of another sister, Caroline Augusta, on December 13. Sarah developed a close and loving relationship with her younger sister, although she was not close enough in age to be the companion and playmate that Mary was. The sheds and barns and John Haggins' coach house provided them with play places if the weather outside was disagreeable. There were always two or three horses in the stables to visit, and it was fun to take imaginary rides in the sleighs and carriages and wagons. Upstairs in one shed a ship's foresail spread on the floor where apples lay drying made a fine place to play dolls.

Dr. Jewett encouraged Sarah's natural inclination to run free out of doors and to engage in sledding and skating and all sorts of summer sports. As an adult, reading the lives of such precocious scholars as Margaret Fuller and John Stuart Mill, Sarah felt great pity for them and for anyone who could not look back on such a simple, natural childhood as she enjoyed. "Just think of having no memory of one's dear playthings, and those long sunshiny pleasant days when the whole world was new to us," she said.

At age sixty-nine Captain Jewett married for the fourth time. His bride was his brother's widow, Eliza Sleeper Jewett. This step-grandmother had a much closer relationship with Sarah than her predecessor had. Sarah liked to run over to the big house for visits and treats of fresh-baked cookies or cakes, and she enjoyed her new grandmother's stories. Sarah later said she used some of them as springboards for her first stories—including "The Shipwrecked Buttons" and "Mr. Bruce," as well as others in *Play Days*.

From their mother Mary and Sarah learned proper Victorian manners. Caroline Frances Perry Jewett had ability—or "faculty," as New Englanders called it—in whatever she turned her hand to. Her household ran smoothly, meals were good and on time, clothing and linens clean and in ample supply, flower and vegetable gardens well tended and productive. She trained her girls to be gracious hostesses and considerate visitors, well versed in all the subtleties of correct behavior; so although Sarah loved to run free and wild in the fields and byways, she knew how to conduct herself in parlors.

Among Sarah's treasured memories were visits to a friend of her mother's who lived in one of the old, stately South Berwick homes. Miss Elisabeth's father had been a Boston

Cushing, but the family had moved to South Berwick in 1795, when the town, according to Miss Elisabeth, "though small, was as proper a place to live in as Boston." Madam Cushing, Miss Elisabeth's mother, had ruled society like a duchess and had been a friend of Lafayette's during the Revolutionary War. On one of his return visits to the United States, he made a special effort to go to South Berwick to see her, an important event in the history of the village.

Miss Elisabeth was more reclusive than her mother, but she welcomed the visits of little Sarah, who put on her best manners and made her conversation as proper as she knew how. Sitting on a tall ottoman, her feet "off soundings" in regard to the floor, she felt both perilous and important. She and Miss Elisabeth discussed the weather, Sarah's school, and of course the details of Lafayette's visit to the Cushings. A maid served pound cake on a silver tray and tiny glasses of wine, and Sarah ate the cake with her gloves on, being careful not to crumble it. As she took her leave, she tried to make her manners as distinguished as those of her hostess and walked sedately down the walk between the boxwood hedges.

Probably Elisabeth Cushing and the Cushing home were part of the memorabilia Sarah had in mind many years later when she remarked to Willa Cather that her head was full of old women and old houses. The independence and dignity of elderly women and their insistence on maintaining their own standards and way of living in the face of change, old age, and even serious illness is a recurring theme in her sketches and stories. Almira Todd and her mother, Mrs. Blackett, in *The Country of the Pointed Firs*, are examples of the self-reliant older women in her stories. So, too, is Betsey Lane in "The Flight of Betsey Lane," who, even though she is an aged inmate in a poorhouse, manages to fulfill a dream and bring some joy into her own life and that of other inmates. Even the loss of mental ability does not deter Miss Chauncey in *Deephaven* from living the life she chooses in the decaying house she still imagines to be the elegant manor of her youth.

As she did with nearly all her early acquaintances, Sarah kept in touch with Miss Cushing, watching her become shriveled and a little addled, so that when a new Methodist church was built near her home she asked, "It that a ship I see? When are they going to launch?" Visiting the Cushing house to pay her condolences to a nephew after Miss Elisabeth died at ninety-two, Sarah was moved by the sight of the ottoman on which she sat during her childhood calls and by the sight of her tiny friend being carried down the walk between the tall boxwood borders that had been her pride.

Sarah liked being sent on errands to the houses where she was sure to be invited to wait while the mistress of the house gathered a bouquet of fresh flowers for her to take home to her mother. These bouquets were flat, with the taller flowers carefully placed behind the shorter ones and invariably accompanied by a message that the sender had not taken time to arrange them.

Instinctively, young Sarah cherished the fast-fading world inhabited by the grandparents and the great-aunts and uncles she visited. Later she would refer to them as "not the wine that one can get at so much the dozen now." She and Mary frequently visited their aunt Anne and cousin Marcia, who lived in a huge old house on the river just opposite Portsmouth. Although she was terrified of a big Newfoundland puppy who ran and jumped at her when she was small, Sarah loved her visits to this aunt, who was a model of courtesy and would never let them go away empty-handed. In her story "Lady Ferry" Sarah used this old house as her setting and captured in the frightening events of the plot something of her terror at the sudden appearance of the dog.

During the summers, Sarah and her sisters spent long weeks with their Perry relatives in Exeter. Sarah wrote to her friend Sara Norton some forty years later, "I have had to go to Exeter several times lately, where I always find my childhood going on as if I had never grown up at all, with my grandaunts and their old houses and their elm trees and their

unbroken china plates and big jars by the fireplaces. And I
go by the house where I went to school aged 8 in a summer
I spent with my grandmother, and feel as if I could go and
play in the sandy garden with little dry bits of elm-twigs stuck
in painstaking rows. There are electric cars in Exeter now,
but they can't make the least difference to me."

Sarah's favorite companion and childhood friend was her
father. The people in South Berwick and on the lonely farms
of the countryside and in the cottages on the nearby seashore
loved Theodore Jewett for his kind heart and for the cheer
he brought into their troubled lives. Probably only a few
realized that he was exceptionally well trained for a horse-
and-buggy doctor or that he kept up with the latest advances
in medicine. The medical profession, however, did recognize
his expertise. For some years he held the Professorship of
Obstetrics and Diseases of Women and Children at the Medical School of Maine and was one of the consulting surgeons
of the Maine General Hospital at Portland, and at one time
he served as president of the Maine Medical Association. He
wrote several articles for medical journals, and his essay on the
practice of medicine, which he delivered at a meeting of
the Association in 1878, was for many years considered one
of the ablest essays ever written on the subject.

To young Sarah he was the loving friend with whom she
had a special relationship. Perhaps because he had suffered
from delicate health himself as a child, he understood her
tendency to "droop" when she was confined indoors for long
periods of time. In a practical sense, too, he considered sunshine and fresh air a good treatment for the arthritis (diagnosed as rheumatism) that chronically affected Sarah. As soon
as she was old enough, he began to take her with him on his
rounds. "The best of my education was received in my father's
buggy and the places to which it carried me," Sarah once told
an interviewer. A knowledgeable botanist and zoologist, Dr.
Jewett taught his receptive little daughter to look closely at
the details of animal and plant life. From him she learned

the names of the trees, flowers, birds, and beasts they passed as they made their slow rounds to call on his patients in out-lying farmhouses and seaside cottages. He also passed on to her a knowledge of the healing powers of some of the plants they saw, such as the odd witch hazel shrub, with its branches that twisted and pointed in all directions. He showed her the feathery, golden clusters of witch hazel blooms that only ap-peared after the leaves had died in the fall. In "A Winter Drive" (in *Country By-Ways*) she mentions the astonishment she felt as a child the first time she saw witch hazel flowers blooming in the snow. And her father would have made her aware of how the witch hazel lotion was used as a tonic and healing astringent for a number of medical problems after it had been distilled from the bark and leaves.

Sometimes Sarah watched as her father treated his pa-tients, and in this way she picked up rudimentary bits of medical knowledge. At other times she wandered around visiting with whoever had time to talk with her, coming to know "many delightful men and women of real individuality and breadth of character." As they ambled along to the next call, her father told her of the struggles of some of his pa-tients and of their hopes and their sorrows. It was an unusual education for a child and an invaluable one for a writer-to-be.

After she learned to read, her father's own delight in books kindled her enthusiasm for them and influenced her taste in reading, but it was his passion for learning from direct obser-vation that had the greatest influence on her writing. She gratefully acknowledged that her father never lost a chance to make her observe—flora and fauna, the sky, the ocean and rivers, buildings, and above all, people. He seemed early to have sensed that writing was to be important in her life. After she began to experiment, he told her repeatedly, "Don't try to write *about* people and things. Tell them just as they are!" In her best writing this is what she learned to do, and it was advice she often repeated to other would-be writers.

All her life, Sarah kept in contact with her father's old

patients and their descendants in the Berwicks, York, Wells, and Eliot. In *A Country Doctor*, Sarah tried to draw a portrait of her father in the main character, Dr. Leslie. She always said, however, that it was an inadequate picture compared with "the gifts and character of the man himself." In the story, Dr. Leslie takes his frail and sickly ward, Nan, with him on his rounds:

> Presently, instead of having a ride out into the country as an occasional favor, she might be seen every day at the doctor's side, as if he could not make his morning rounds without her; and in and out of the farm houses she went, following him like a little dog, or as Marilla scornfully expressed it, a briar at his heels; sitting soberly by when he dealt his medicines and gave advice, listening to his wise and merry talk with some, and his helpful advice and consolation to others of the country people.

Another book, *Country By-Ways*, Sarah dedicated "To T.H.J., my dear father; my dear friend; the best and wisest man I ever knew; who taught me many lessons and showed me many things as we went together along the country by-ways."

◆

CHAPTER TWO

Beginnings

IN 1861 twelve-year-old Sarah entered Berwick Academy, where her elder sister Mary had been a student for two years. Berwick, established in the late eighteenth century as a college preparatory school for boys, had a reputation for turning out students who became successful graduates of Bowdoin, Dartmouth, and Harvard. Women began to enroll in the academy in 1828, and once, in totting up its distinguished alumni, Sarah wrote that there were in addition to college presidents, governors of states, and eminent businessmen, "many women, who, in their ever widening public service or beautiful home-making and home-keeping lives, have been among the true leaders of civilization in their time."

The academy stood on the crest of Powderhouse Hill, its two gables conspicuous above the treetops. The large schoolroom, which could be divided into smaller classrooms, was light and airy, as was the auditorium, with its open beams. But the interior of the well-designed school and its well-planned curriculum held little attraction for Sarah. "I remember," she wrote, "a good deal more about the great view toward the mountains, or down river, and the boys and girls themselves, or even the ground sparrows and the field strawberries that grew in the thin grass, than I do about learning my lessons."

She was drawn to the classmates who had an aura of exotic places about them, and she envied the experiences of two captains' daughters from Down East Maine, who had traveled with their fathers in the merchant service. Since whispering was forbidden during school hours, Sarah pointed to places on her geography maps with a questioning look and was answered by a shake of the head or by a nod, which sent her off into daydreams about the adventures these young girls might have had in Lisbon or Bombay or Le Havre.

Also in her class were three handsome young Cuban boys who stayed in the academy boardinghouse. Francisco, Eduardo, and Venancio generously shared the guava jelly they received from home and also the small, sweet cigarettes, which the students, including Mary and Sarah, smoked in secret hideaways. To the other students, and especially to the imaginative Sarah, the laughing, quick-tempered Cubans symbolized Cuba itself and all its exciting history, filled with rich sugar plantations, buccaneers, and pirates.

A young Dane, who had come into Kennebunk with one of the shipmasters, enrolled as a temporary student at the academy. Sarah teased the cheerful, rough young sailor into telling her stories of his seafaring life. He had simple-hearted ways and a longing for his faraway northern home, and she fancied he was like a character in one of her favorite bittersweet Hans Christian Andersen stories.

During one semester, academy records show that Mary Jewett was never tardy and never absent and received one hundred merit marks. Sarah Jewett, during the same period, was tardy five times and absent twelve times and received eighty merit marks. Since the school was only a few minutes' walk from their home, perhaps Sarah was tardy because she dallied to observe a bird or examine a flower or to play in the snow. Some of her absences were for her genuine illnesses, but others were undoubtedly on days when she accompanied her father on his rounds—an activity they both considered equally as valuable as a day of schoolroom discipline and drill.

Although Sarah found formal education dull, she reveled in the world of books. Just as she had free range of her grandfather Jewett's grounds and house, she was free to browse in his library as well as in her father's. Her curiosity led her to pry into everything from the *Arabian Nights* to her father's medical books. And despite the fact that many of the leatherbound histories and sermons on her grandfather's shelves were heavy going, Sarah recalled, "In my youthful appetite for knowledge, I could even in the driest find something vital, and in the more entertaining I was completely lost."

As they went from patient to patient, her father shared his knowledge of books with Sarah, eventually leading her to read and appreciate his favorite authors: Laurence Sterne, Henry Fielding, Tobias Smollett, Izaac Walton, and Cervantes. Her mother, also an avid reader, introduced Sarah to important women writers such as Jane Austen, George Eliot, Margaret Oliphant, and Elizabeth Gaskell. Unwittingly, Sarah was studying classics in literature. She remained a lifelong admirer of Jane Austen's works and enjoyed rereading them as an adult. Margaret Oliphant, a Scottish novelist who wrote about provincial English society, provided examples of what could be done with material found in a very small and select sphere, as did Mrs. Gaskell's sketches of life among the women of the quiet country village of Cranford. Both Oliphant and Gaskell mixed humor into loving but sharply realistic portrayals of the lives of their old-fashioned characters—a technique Sarah Orne Jewett learned to use with great success.

The humor in several of her stories comes from her stance that women are naturally more artful than men; and as Richard Cary points out, they usually bag their men in superannuated courtships before the men know they are being stalked. One of the best of these tales is "A Winter Courtship," in which the driver of the passenger-and-mail covered wagon is neatly maneuvered by the Widow Tobin into a declaration during the seven-mile journey between Sanscrit

Pond and North Kilby. Mr. Briley, who fancies himself to be in the tradition of the pony express drivers, carries under his seat a heavy pistol (unloaded), which he imagines the mere sight of will be enough to frighten the boldest robber. The widow has "a sudden inspiration of opportunity" during the chilly trip. She moves up front to sit beside Briley so they can share the two buffalo robes, and adroitly steers the conversation. By exploiting his Walter Mitty delusions and then by subtly making him realize the comforts of having a helpmate like herself, a good cook and housekeeper, she accomplishes her goal. "Mr. Briley had been taken on the road in spite of his pistol," the author concludes.

The book that Sarah singled out as being the most influential of all her youthful reading was not written by Europeans but by a New Englander like herself. Harriet Beecher Stowe's *The Pearl of Orr's Island*, published in 1862 (when Sarah was thirteen), is set on a real island off the coast of Maine, and it contains characters and a dialect that Sarah knew well. It awakened her to the idea that she too might use the countryside and the people she knew so well in writings of her own. Years later, Sarah wrote to her friend Annie Fields that she had been reading *The Pearl of Orr's Island* again and found the beginning just as "clear and perfectly original and strong" as it had seemed to her on her first reading. But she lamented that the melodramatic sentimentality into which the book lapses made it "an incomplete piece of work," although she still found a divine touch in it "here and there."

Ironically, even though she recognized at such an early age the value of Mrs. Stowe's realistic portrayal of places, characters, and setting, in her own early works Sarah too floundered in melodrama and sentimentality before she found her true voice. Her first published short story, "Jenny Garrow's Lovers," which is riddled with clichés and wooden characters who suffer through melodramatic situations in far-off England, does not in any way foretell the realistic, evocative art with which she would capture the essence of her beloved Maine in later years.

Sarah's love of the outdoors and of outdoor sports was as important to her as her love of books, and this remained true all her life. Whenever it was possible, she spent her time in the open air, and when inside she liked the feeling of open doors and windows. Her father encouraged her craving for vigorous exercise, and during her years at the academy she grew into a tall, slender, attractive girl with large, expressive brown eyes and rosy cheeks from her frequent outdoor activity. She loved horseback riding and became adept at an early age in handling boats, managing sails and oars with ease. Like many other Victorians, she and her friends thought nothing of walking many miles on country hikes. In summers Sarah enjoyed playing on the beaches and in the water at York and Wells. In winter she eagerly joined in the sports of the season—skating, sledding, and sleigh riding, unless she was kept inside by the wretched colds to which she was prone or by a bout of her "rheumatism."

As she grew older, Sarah liked to go on solitary "rambles," often with Joe or Crabby, family dogs, as her companions. She also liked to go off alone on horseback rides. On her horse she looked for straight, sandy strips where she could have a "hurry." Her rides often covered impressive distances, and sometimes she stopped to visit patients of her father's or other friends, such as the village dressmaker or the old woman who had nursed her through a childhood ailment. Afterward she would contentedly splash homeward through mud puddles with her long skirts pulled up.

Sarah was also fond of going on solitary rowing expeditions on the river. Most of the people in the area who rowed or sailed kept their boats on the large, smooth pond above the dam, but when Sarah went there, she felt confined by the two dams above and below the pond. She preferred rowing on the lower or tidal river, where it seemed as if she could set off for Europe or anywhere on the high seas with no barrier between her and all foreign ports. When the tide went out, there were rapids that took skill to navigate safely, but when the tide was in the river became a slow and dignified stream. She never felt lonely on the river, being perfectly content to spend the morning in the company of a muskrat acquaintance that she admired as a busy creature who knew how to live well.

In warm weather it sometimes took her a whole afternoon to go a few miles, there were so many reasons to stop along the way. She knew every cove where little fish and frogs had their playgounds and swallows darted along the surface of the water scooping up insects. She knew where to go to gather deckloads of cardinal flowers and where to pick water mint to chew on. A great fish hawk dropping through the air and rising with an unlucky fish glittering in its claws was enough to start her thinking of the great chain of being in nature. In spring the soft tinge of early green contrasting with the long, shining brown furrows of freshly turned earth pleased her. If the farmers who called to each other across their fields sounded cheerful, so, she thought, did the frogs and bobolinks who also called to each other. In summer, after a hot day, Sarah liked nothing better than a moonlit night on the river with fireflies everywhere and a whiff of sea salt coming up with the tide. Fall was not a time for drifting with the current, but a time to pull the boat briskly past the oaks and maples dressed in their bright new fashions and to observe the ducks flying away from the coves. In winter the ice-covered river bordered by the black pines and hemlocks "staring across it at each other" became a skating rink, although icy winds blowing over it often drove one to pleasanter pastimes such as drinking hot chocolate by a blazing fire.

Sarah's time at Berwick Academy spanned the years of the Civil War, and the students naturally had a burning interest in the progress of the battles. In speech class they declaimed on patriotic themes and put on public debates. Those representing the South declared their convictions and then dramatically covered their heads with veils, perhaps to illustrate the withdrawal of the rebellious states from the union.

During the war years Dr. Jewett was away from home more than usual, fulfilling his duties as surgeon of the Board of Enrollment for the first district of Maine at Portland. The people of the small rural town were united in their feeling that they were fighting to preserve the union, and over two hundred men from the little village went to fight for their country. As the years passed, funerals were held for boys that Mary and Sarah had known as playmates in earlier years.

Sarah's knowledge of slavery was largely hearsay. She knew that most of the prominent families in her part of New England, near tidewater, had possessed African slaves in the previous century. Listening to the stories of her adult relatives and their friends, she was convinced that the slaves were content, loyal, and affectionate toward the white families "they adopted as their own." She often visited a little sandy hill— called Cato's Hill from the fact that its sunny bank was a favorite retreat of an ancient slave of one of the old families in South Berwick. Cato was from Guinea, and Sarah enjoyed hearing the old-timers tell tales of his "droll ways and speeches." At the peak of her writing career, she wrote two stories with Southern settings that reveal the kinship she felt with aristocratic Southerners and show sympathy for the losses they suffered during the Civil War. In her last novel, *The Tory Lover*, a slave brought from Africa, Old Caesar, who had been born a prince in his own country, and Old Rodney, born in the bush and stolen by a slaver's crew, are portrayed as faithful family servants, quirky but sincerely devoted to their white families.

When Richmond, the Confederate capital, fell, classes at Berwick Academy were dismissed, and the whole student body marched, two by two, to the beat of a drum down the main street of the village "as proudly" Sarah recalled, "as if we were Grant's army itself." At that time she had no way of knowing that the end of the war signaled radical changes in her region and an end to the simple life of her childhood. Expanding railroad networks, rising immigration, burgeoning industrialization, and invasion by hordes of summer visitors were to change forever the provincial character of the area. Sarah would come to lament particularly the loss of shipping and all the romance of seafaring. "A harbor, even if it is a little harbor, is a good thing," she wrote in *Country By-Ways*, and she anguished over "the destroying left hand of progress."

In 1865 the war was over, and Sarah's formal education was finished. At sixteen she was free to enjoy a carefree life of entertainment, recreation, and travel securely supported by a network of loving family and friends. Her friends were of all ages and ranged from friends of her parents to her classmates and to people like Edith Haven Doe, who was seven years older than Mary, and a close friend of both Mary's and Sarah's. Edith was married to a successful New Hampshire lawyer and mistress of the extensive Doe estate in Rollinsford, about a mile from South Berwick. There was constant, almost daily, visiting between the two homes, picnics with the Doe children and Jewett dogs, walks, rides, drives, trips to the beach, and frequent exchanges of books and magazines, food and plants.

Sometimes Sarah accompanied her father to Portland or Portsmouth when he had medical business to attend to in those towns, and she also traveled to Boston and New York with family members. On Sarah's eighteenth birthday she and her father and Mary and Carrie went with other relatives from Portsmouth out to the Isles of Shoals on a steamer. Her gifts included books, material from Mary for a dress, and twelve dollars from her Uncle William to buy an Etruscan gold pin she had seen in Dover and expressed a "fancy" for. But the gift she treasured most was a China teacup from her father.

A few days after her birthday she wrote in her journal,

"I do believe that if any one should ask me how old I am and I didn't think, I should say 'ten.'" The reading she listed, however, was quite adult. It included Whittier's poems, Professor Draper's essay, "Intellectual Development of Europe," and articles in the *North American Review* and *Harper's*. In addition to having a strongly developed sense of history, she had a sense of her place in it. "I think it would be funny," she wrote, "if a hundred years from now some girl like me should find this diary somewhere and *wonder* about me." She decided to call her imaginary reader of 1967 "Phebe" and to address the journal to her. She warned Phebe "I am a very '*sinfle*' bad girl, and it is very much for your interest that you live in the time you do instead of the age in which you might have come across me." But the maxim she passed along to Phebe, and the one she actually tried to live by, was "Be virtuous and you will be happy."

She advised Phebe to keep Sunday "in a moral manner," a pattern by which she had been raised. Often the family went to the First Congregational Church (where Sarah became a Sunday school teacher) three times on the Sabbath. Apparently she listened to the sermons carefully, for she commented on them—not always favorably—in her journal.

She was wholeheartedly involved in the things that normally interest girls her age. In her diary she described her "very swell" new jacket: "nearly white, trimmed with brown velvet, silver buttons and frogs to button it." She relished going to Portland to be in the wedding of her beloved cousin Nelly Gilman. The "thousands of dollars worth of presents" dazzled her, and she noted that Nelly received "everything in silver that I ever heard of and a large table of vases and lots of carvings and pictures—and books and everything beautiful." She found the room that was the setting for the wedding lovely, with its great trails of smilax around the pictures and brackets and heaps of tuberoses and orange blossoms and ropes of white rosebuds. And she called the wedding feast of "foreign fruits and ice cream of different kinds and all kinds of wines and roasted birds and scolloped oysters and chicken salad and all kinds of cakes big and little" the most "splendid collation" she had ever seen. The music was so "exquisite" it almost made her cry.

A six-week visit to her Perry and Gilman relatives in Exeter included reading "quantities" of books, going to innumerable teas and dinners, and visiting Hampton Beach. She especially enjoyed a masquerade party at which she was Highland Mary and decided she liked Scottish things, particularly Scottish songs. Because of the presence of Phillips Exeter Academy, it was easy to get up parties at a moment's notice, but although Sarah reported to Phebe that the parties were "jolly," she didn't mention any young man to whom she felt especially attracted.

The time spent with young people her own age received less space in her diary than the descriptions of days passed in company with her Aunt Mary Long (Mary Olivia Gilman Long), the *grande dame* of the family. During long carriage rides her aunt entertained her by recounting the family history. One afternoon, after a cozy tea together by the fire, they spent the rest of the day ripping up an old-fashioned yellow silk counterpane that had belonged to Sarah's great-great-granduncle Nicholas Gilman, the one who had been a member of the First Congress and a signer of the Constitution. Noticing that the cotton wadding inside the quilt was "just like silk," they speculated about who in England had made it.

At home in South Berwick there were parties and dances, too, as well as church suppers and sociables. The Jewett girls belonged to a young people's social club, and sometimes there were dances in their home when it met there. Charades, euchre, and croquet were popular amusements also. In the fall Berwick Academy provided a number of entertainments such as amateur theatricals and lectures (including one by Dr. Jewett on the atmosphere). In her late teens Sarah began her lifelong habit of writing long, chatty letters to distant friends and relatives. She also began keeping a commonplace book* of extracts from her reading, and she continued to make sporadic diary entries. Her hobby of collecting bugs was replaced by an interest in collecting the autographs of famous people of the past.

Underneath the pleasant surface life of a young girl growing up in the second half of the nineteenth century, Sarah had, from the time she was fourteen, a covert existence in which she tried seriously to launch herself as a writer. She decided to try a magazine she read regularly, *The Flag of Our Union*, a weekly that sold for ten cents a copy. Her submission was accepted, and Sarah Orne Jewett's first published short story, "Jenny Garrow's Lovers," appeared on January 18, 1868, under the pseudonym A. C. Eliot. The setting is England, and the feverishly melodramatic plot includes a lovers' quarrel, a missing person, death, false imprisonment, and a supposed murder. The female narrator (a persona Sarah would use in many of her stories and sketches) is the most realistic character, although she intrudes gratuitously on the action and at the end pops up to inquire brazenly, "How do you like my story?"

Later that same year a poem by Alice Eliot appeared in *Our Young Folks*. With the exception of Mary, none of the family knew at this point of Sarah's forays into the world of writing. At the post office she inquired furtively for mail addressed to A. C. or Alice Eliot, names posted on a list as if the addressee were a stranger in town.

Each trip she took farther from South Berwick intensified in Sarah a love for seeing new places and meeting new people. In the summer of 1868 Dr. Jewett took Mary and Sarah on a trip to Canada. After a slight bout of seasickness the first day, Sarah enjoyed the trip immensely, vowing that when she had made her fortune she would have a house at St. Andrew and a yacht "and some Indian canoes and an Indian

---

*Many people kept commonplace books in the nineteenth century, filling them with quotes and memoranda about events, for reference.

to paddle." She was heartbroken at having to leave Calais and loved the names of the streets—King, Queen, Prince William, Regent—in St. John and the "perfect" music of the British army band. Even the experiences of being bitten by fleas and enveloped in thick fog didn't squelch her enthusiasm. In her journal she rhapsodized over everything that caught her interest: the beauty of Passamaquoddy Bay and the Bay of Fundy, the architecture in the towns, their history, the grand scenery, and the differences in the people of French and English descent—plus every new sensation.

There were times when Sarah acted like a typical self-centered adolescent. In late 1868 she went to Cincinnati to stay with her Aunt Sarah and Uncle John Perry and remained there until April of 1869. Her New Year's entry in her diary for January 1, 1869, complains of the weather and the New Year's Day callers: "If all the New Year is to be like this day! Yah! It was foggy & horrid and I was blue...We 'received calls' and had a number of worthy people I hadn't the least interest in." Occasionally she was temperamental, admitting in her diary to being "cross." On one day she stayed in her room, biting her lip and her hand, because she was "mad," but usually she was outgoing and enthusiastic and tried hard to be a good houseguest. She enjoyed her Uncle John's sense of humor and liked the family evenings of reading aloud from such books as Kingsley's *Water Babies* and *Oliver Twist*. She tried to improve her mind by reading on her own—essays by Thomas Macaulay and Charles Lamb, Tennyson's poetry, Dickens' *Great Expectations*, and *Under Two Flags*, by Ouida (Marie Louise de la Ramée). Ouida may have had a negative influence on Sarah's early writing, for although the enormously popular writer had great narrative power and emotional energy, her stories are unrealistic and crammed with super-human heroes who display miraculous beauty, courage, and strength.

While in Cincinnati Sarah took art and dancing lessons and enjoyed visiting art galleries, attending concerts, and

going to the theater. Her favorite plays were *Queen Elizabeth,*
As You Like It, and *Marie Antoinette,* which seemed to her
almost "too real and too touching," since she had always had
a great affection for the unhappy queen. Sarah herself acted
in an amateur performance of a comedy called *Ici on parle*
français. No sooner had she recovered from her inevitable
winter cold and cough than a problem with a tooth sent her
to a dentist, who, she complained in her journal, hurt her
"shockingly." The toothache may have been caused by eating
large quantities of candy, for which she had a weakness.

With her aunt she made formal calls on the Brahmins of
Cincinnati and went to the Congregational church twice on
Sunday and to prayer meeting on Wednesday. Always open
to new experiences, she welcomed opportunities to visit
Catholic, Episcopal, and Jewish services with various friends.
Among the children of her aunt's friends she found a circle
of friends with whom she lunched at Keppler's, attended club
socials, parties, and dances, and went for drives in barouches
and for long walks. Sometimes these activities proved too
strenuous for her, as when after a day of walking across the
river to Covington, Kentucky, and around the city for several
miles, she had to spend the next day lying on a sofa recover-
ing her strength, or when, after a night of "dancing every
dance," she was completely exhausted.

Sarah wrote long letters to her family about her activities
and received long letters about home affairs from them,
especially from Mary, who kept her posted on the activities
of their mutual friends and on the family pets. Aside from
letters, the only other writing Sarah mentions working on
during her long stay in Cincinnati is a story called "An
Apology" for her aunt's reading club. She noted with satisfaction that her story was received by the members with "great
applause."

With characteristic enthusiasm, Sarah formed several intense teenage friendships among her new acquaintances,
sealed with vows of everlasting devotion. Cicely Burt was her

best friend, and Sarah was thrilled when Cicely gave her a gold ring to remember her by. For some months after Sarah returned to South Berwick they corresponded faithfully, but when Cicely became engaged Sarah noted with disenchantment that Cicely was "altogether too spoony, and it seems so funny!"

Sarah did not record in her diary the name of any of the young men with whom she danced or went to parties while in Cincinnati, except for noting matter-of-factly that a Dr. Freeman, who had a fast horse, took her for a ride and gave her a box of candy. In South Berwick, the Jewetts entertained frequently, and with three attractive daughters in the house, there were gentlemen callers. But none of them elicited a hint of romance in Sarah's letters or diaries. One entry refers to a call by Charlie Walker, who is "handsome," but he is not mentioned again. There were, of course, young men included on trips to nearby beaches and on picnics and other outings, but excursions with her father, such as the day in August of 1869 when the three sisters climbed a hill with their father to witness an eclipse of the sun, are described much more enthusiastically.

If, as seems likely, Sarah measured her youthful male companions against the standard of her father, they undoubtedly fell far short. Dr. Jewett was highly intelligent, knowledgeable about people and things, witty, and especially empathetic with his middle daughter. From early childhood he had been her closest companion, and it would have been surprising if she had not developed an Electra Complex in some degree. Both Mary, who also remained a spinster, and Sarah had more freedom of choice than many other middle-class women of their day. Each had independent means plus a secure place in a loving family, and neither had to fear that she might end up living in an attic bedroom of relatives who had taken her in out of pity or a sense of duty. And from an early age Sarah seems to have had a definite feeling that marriage would be a handicap to her career as a writer.

Friends, however, were a different matter. Seemingly there could not be too many. The number of friends with whom Sarah kept in close touch through letters and by visits increased with every passing year. In late 1869 Sarah and Mary visited relatives in Boston and became part of a circle of friends there. Edith Doe introduced them to the Gordons, and Grace Gordon became a valued friend, as did Ella Walworth. With them and half a dozen others, they went for carriage rides and attended art exhibitions, concerts, and luncheons. On Sundays they attended Trinity Church to hear the famous Phillips Brooks preach. The six-foot-four Episcopalian minister had a commanding presence and great eloquence and was noted for writing the hymn "O Little Town of Bethlehem," which he had composed for a Sunday school class. Sarah noted in her diary that he preached one of the most satisfactory sermons she had ever heard. She also enjoyed immensely seeing Edwin Booth star in a performance of *Hamlet*. And one day she and Ella Walworth took Turkish baths for a lark and afterward felt they were "beautiful to behold."

After the excitements of Cincinnati and Boston, Sarah found life in her little village somewhat limited. Except for gardening, she was not fond of domestic tasks, although she joined in helping with the sewing. A village seamstress sewed for the Jewetts, but the women of the family took pleasure in creating some of their own garments, stitching by hand or on a treadle sewing machine, an invention that had become increasingly popular and available following the Civil War. In the evenings one of the three girls, often Carrie, played the piano while the others sang. Sarah had a talent for whistling tunes and sometimes did it to amuse the others.

Reading aloud often provided evening entertainment, and the sisters particularly enjoyed *Little Women*, which appeared in two parts in 1868 and 1869. Sarah especially identified with the rebellious Jo. She liked to laugh and could be something of a tease, occasionally playing mild practical jokes such as dressing up a bolster in Mary's clothes and putting it on her bed while she was out. At other times Sarah's arthritis and bad headaches made her out of sorts and moody, but she had learned to avoid inflicting her spells of ill humor on others by withdrawing to her room or by going on a ramble with one of the dogs, Joe or Crabby. She had infinite patience and empathy with wild creatures, and when she was given a young hen hawk she managed to tame it although it was a "very cross" animal.

There were old friends in South Berwick like Mary Hayes, with whom Sarah liked to go sketching in the fields or in the woods or to pick mayflowers or wild strawberries. All her life she continued to cultivate and nourish these early friendships as carefully as she cultivated and nourished her garden. But she did not need companionship to enjoy herself. She never felt lonely on her long solitary walks, which she preferred to take between roads by climbing over the low stone walls and shaky pasture fences in the South Berwick countryside. Every walk was a tour of exploration and discovery. Her favorite recreation of horseback riding took her on even farther expeditions, sometimes to Guptill's Woods, near the village, or to Rollinsford Point or along the Old York Road, where there were abandoned ruins of houses and farms to explore and wonder about.

Like a detective looking for clues, Sarah searched for evidence of what life had been like for the former tenants of the overgrown spots. She hunted among the weeds and grasses for lilacs or roses or syringa blooms that showed the owner loved flowers and tried to cultivate them. And she read inscriptions on crumbling gravestones to see if members of the families had died untimely deaths, perhaps by accidents, or if the whole family had been demolished at once by an Indian raid or by some dreadful disease.

After noticing one particular straggling orchard of ancient apple trees and deducing from the very large cellar nearby that there had been a large house on the site, she adopted the old farm as her own "little kingdom." In "An October Ride" (*Country By-Ways*) she described her discovery of the place and her subsequent visits to it after she had learned a little of its history. She was delighted when she found an old-timer who knew about the last occupant of the place—a thrifty, proud old woman who had been a famous weaver and spinner. Sarah imagined this old survivor sitting in the twilight of a summer evening listening to the thrushes calling in the woods, living her peaceful, lonely life, thinking of those she had lost.

In this same sketch, she used another experience that had occurred on one of her solitary jaunts. It happened one afternoon when she was caught in a sudden storm and sought shelter in a ruined building that had been a parsonage. Having heard stories that it was haunted, she eagerly took advantage of the chance to explore it, and after satisfying her curiosity, she built a fire in the fireplace of the study from sticks and corn shucks. There she happily passed the hours of the storm, picturing other times and other people who might have enjoyed fires in the still handsomely wainscoted but thoroughly leaky room. As she left through the broken gate, she felt sure hers would be the last fire so enjoyed in the old house.

Many of the experiences, feelings, and ponderings recorded in the very personal essays in *Country By-Ways* were taken from accounts written up much earlier in her journal. And in many of them she preserves some fast-fading bit of history. In "River Driftwood" she again displayed her penchant for catching a glimpse of the past by observing something in the present. As she rowed by herself on the Piscataqua River, she amused herself by looking out for the last two gundalows that sailed from the landing wharves, where forty years before there had been twenty. The gundalow (sometimes spelled gondola) made her think of Egypt with its pyramids and sphinxes, for the low, heavy craft with its tall lateen sail had actually been copied from a Nile boat by an old sea captain many years earlier. As her grandfather told her, it had proved its worth as a practical vessel to catch the uncertain breezes that came in flaws and gusts between the high, irregular riverbanks of the Piscataqua.

It is obvious from the way she wrote up these and other experiences in her journal that Sarah realized she might want to use them sometime in her writing. For no matter what else occupied her time, the writer in Sarah was active, and she set her sights high. One of the periodicals she read regularly was the *Atlantic Monthly*—only about a decade old but already recognized as one of the pre-eminent magazines in the country. James T. Fields was then chief editor, and William Dean Howells his assistant. The *Atlantic* rejected her first manuscript, "Uncle Peter's Tragedy," with a letter saying the characters were not good enough for the amusing plot and suggesting she try something in which the chief characters were young ladies rather than young men. Sarah promptly sent them another manuscript, which also came back, but with a note of regret and encouragement: "If your story were only a little better, or a good deal worse!"

Undaunted, Sarah sent them a third submission, and on August 17, 1869, she wrote in her diary, "At night I came as near being utterly satisfied & happy as I can. My story is accepted & I had a very nice note from the *Atlantic*." Her writing was done unobtrusively, often late at night; she was still writing under the pen name A. C. Eliot, and Mary was still the only one who knew of her attempts at publication. With this significant success, Mary persuaded Sarah to tell the other members of the family—a step Sarah immediately regretted. "I wish with all my heart I had never told any body; it seems as if it no longer belonged *all to me*," she lamented. But she was gradually becoming more open about her literary efforts. In September she finished a story called "The Shipwrecked Buttons," which *The Riverside Magazine for Young People* accepted. The story is reminiscent of Hans Christian Andersen's stories personifying inanimate objects—

it is about some buttons that are abandoned by the children who have been playing with them by sailing them in a pan of water. The animated buttons tell their story before they become shipwrecked and drown. Their viewpoint is that of any small creatures who are at the mercy of careless, indifferent larger ones.

Just before Thanksgiving "Mr. Bruce" appeared in the *Atlantic*, and Sarah read it aloud to the family. That evening she modestly noted in her diary, "Father and all think it very nice." "Mr. Bruce" is a lighthearted story about a New England girl named Kitty. One day when her father brings home unexpected company, including an Englishman named Mr. Bruce, Kitty blithely takes the place of the maid, who is out. The following year Mr. Bruce is surprised to meet Kitty in Baltimore in her normal role as a pretty young socialite. After the complications are cleared away, they make plans to marry. Jewett scholar Richard Cary has called "Mr. Bruce" "a rompish fling at urban social comedy obviously beyond her [Sarah's] aptitude." The structure of the story is clumsy, being told by Elly, who got it from Aunt Mary, who passed it along in the words of her friend Margaret, who got it largely from Kitty's letters. The stiff, ultrasophisticated characters in their gilded settings are a far cry from the natural, human characters in their native settings that make her later sketches and stories so praiseworthy.

Nevertheless, its acceptance by the *Atlantic* (who paid her fifty dollars for it) was an indication to Sarah and to other readers that the story had merit as entertainment. And it was quite an accomplishment for a girl of nineteen. When Horace Scudder, editor of *The Riverside Magazine*, read "Mr. Bruce," he sent Sarah his congratulations and expressed surprise at finding that the writer, whom he had thought to be a young girl just starting to write children's stories, was a contributor to the foremost magazine in America. He did, however, venture a word or two of constructive criticism on the story. Sarah wrote to thank him, acknowledging that she could write better if she put more effort into it. She compared herself to Jo in *Little Women*, who had a habit of "falling into a vortex," and commented, "It's a dreadful thing to have been born very lazy, isn't it, Mr. Scudder? I might write ever so much; it's very easy for me, and when I have been so successful in what I have written, I ought to study—which I never did in my life hardly, except reading. And I ought to try harder and perhaps by and by I shall know something and can write really well."

Sarah was twenty as 1869 ended, and on the last day of the year she wrote in her diary that it had been the happiest year of her life because:

> My friends are dearer than ever; I have tried harder to be good, and I have had success in writing and in other things, and my afflictions have been few and far between and my pleasures many. E. W. [Ella Walworth] is my best friend. I hope I can say these same things next year.

CHAPTER THREE

◆

Widening
Circles

A S SHE PASSED from adolescence to young adulthood, Sarah's restless and sometimes rebellious nature brought on black moods and moments of deep despair when her desire to be "good" seemed frustrated. Her New England conscience smote her when passion or coldness or selfishness overcame her on occasions when she expected herself to feel loving kindness. In letters and in her diary, she railed at herself for her laziness and excoriated herself for being so self-centered. At times—perhaps when nagging headaches or dragging colds or arthritic pain made her energy burn low—she mentioned suicide, but she quickly dismissed the idea as being an act that would be too distressing to those who cared for her. After a visit to her Aunt Helen in Portland, she despaired of ever becoming the sincere, useful person she perceived her aunt to be and wrote despondently in her journal, "I wish I could be ill or die, for then they [her family and friends] would not mind it so much and it would not seem my own fault."

Many nineteenth-century women her age escaped the confines and duties of their homes by exchanging them for the confines and duties of marriage, but Sarah remained at home, chafing under real and imaginary restraints. Her efficient mother and efficient sister Mary ran the household, but there were small domestic tasks she was expected to share. In a conscious effort to improve her behavior, she kept account of it in her journal. One entry notes that she had had only nine "bad days," which she called an immense improvement, since "it is so easy for me to be cross and say wicked things." She promised herself, "From this day to do pleasantly all the little things which people ask me to, which are so apt to come just at the wrong time. Not only to do them without scolding or 'making a time' but to do them as if I wished to and had rather do it than not!"

She frequently read the Bible, especially the Psalms and the New Testament. In South Berwick the family attended the Congregational church, but many of Sarah's relatives were Episcopalian, and she owned a copy of the *Book of Common Prayer*. The beauty of the ritual of the Anglican service attracted her, and when visiting in larger cities, she frequently attended Episcopal churches. It was at Trinity Church in Boston that she had fallen under the spell of the charismatic Phillips Brooks. On November 27, 1870, both Mary and Sarah were baptized and confirmed at St. John's Episcopal Church, Portsmouth. Sister Caroline was confirmed a few years later. Like many Victorians Sarah relished long-winded sermons if they had food for thought in them, but she was quick to condemn those she found "boring" or "stupid." A preacher whose sermons she praised as "magnificent" was Henry Ward Beecher, pastor of the Congregational Plymouth Church in Brooklyn, New York. Beecher, the brother of Harriet Beecher Stowe, achieved renown as an original, witty, and eloquent speaker. The deepest religious influence, however, on the impressionable young Sarah's mind came from a Harvard law professor. In August 1872, while she was visiting at Wells, Maine, Sarah met seventy-five-year-old Theophilus Parsons, professor of law at Harvard and a leader in the controversial Swedenborgian New Church.

Emanuel Swedenborg (1688–1772), a brilliant Swedish

scientist and inventor, drew plans for forerunners of airships, submarines, and magazine-loading guns. He was the son of a bishop and nobleman, a member "extraordinary" of the Swedish State Council of Mines, and an authority in the fields of geology, metallurgy, mathematics, astronomy, and anatomy. But in April 1745 he had a vision of Jesus Christ that caused him to abandon abruptly all his wordly learning and devote his enormous energy for the remainder of his life to theological concerns. He wrote a large number of essays and books setting forth his "heavenly doctrines," which he claimed were based on Bible teachings as they were interpreted for him directly by the spiritual world. He rejected the idea of Christ as the Son of God, saying rather that the Lord had allowed himself to be born into the human world through a mortal woman in order to bring man back to an understanding of God's original purpose in creating the world. Man's misuse of his free will, Swedenborg taught, had disturbed the true order of creation. He felt that God's "essence" could be understood by two of its primary qualities—love and wisdom. Soon after his death, some of Swedenborg's followers founded the Church of New Jerusalem, based on his views. His theological writings have been translated into many languages, and his ideas have been an inspiration for such writers as Balzac, Baudelaire, Emerson, and Yeats.

In his lectures and writings, Professor Parsons fervently expounded the theology initiated by Swedenborg. Sarah paid Professor Parsons a graceful compliment by making a metaphor of their first meeting, when he had lent her his spyglass and pointed out things far away at sea to her. Ever since that day, she told him, he had continued to open her eyes and mind to things she might have overlooked if left to herself. Parsons lent Sarah books and tracts and articles on New Church beliefs, and they began a correspondence that lasted until his death ten years later. Sometimes they visited in Cambridge or in Rye, New Hampshire, where Sarah often visited her aunt's home at Little Boar's Head.

The collection of letters written between 1872 and 1881 to Theophilus Parsons (recently added to the archives in the Special Collections section of Colby College), reveals the significant influence he had on her. In her personal life his influence was beneficial, but on her writing, it was, at least for a time, more harmful than helpful. She felt free to discuss her doubts and religious waverings with him, telling him she was an "instinctive" doubter who was always "aware of all the opposite side" of any question. Before long she was sending him copies of her sketches and short stories and asking his opinion on everything from her writing and her relationships with friends to explanations of Bible stories she was teaching in her Sunday school classes: What was the meaning of the parable of the loaves and fishes? What was the meaning of certain symbols connected with Jonah? Why was the punishment so severe for the children who were eaten by bears for calling Elisha names?

When Sarah remarked in one of her letters that she had thought of Swedenborgianism as another "sect," Parsons gently corrected her. The nature of men, he reminded her, may be divided into the affectional (emotional), intellectual, natural, and spiritual. In all of its forms, he said, Christianity has appealed to and nourished the spiritual-emotional side of man, but only in the form of Swedenborgianism has it offered food to the spiritual-intellectual side of his nature. Out of their exchange of letters and long interviews, and from the reading matter he sent her, she formulated a plan for living in which being helpful and compassionate were daily aims to be achieved by thinking carefully through what it was best to do in every situation. She found particularly appealing the tenet of New Church doctrine that taught that each person could and should do his own thinking and reach his own conclusions about what was the best way to live his life.

By 1874 the closing of her letters had progressed from "Yours sincerely" to "With ever so much love" or "Always your loving, Sarah." She mentioned less frequently getting into a "puzzle" or a "tangle" over things. "Sometimes," she told him, "I wonder why I have such a very good thing for my own as your friendship—just an *almost* good-for-nothing girl— but then luckily the rain and the sunshine do not choose out the very best of the flowers—and help [only] them to grow stronger." Under his guidance she felt she was able to live more serenely, and she discussed with him her need to find a focus and an identity in her life. In her 1873 New Year's greeting to him she said confidently, "I shall be so much better in the year to come because I have known you."

Swedenborg's belief in the redemptive powers of divine and human love became a part of her creed. She reported to Professor Parsons that she knew he would be glad that she was much more interested in her neighbors than ever before and that she was reading aloud to a woman who could no longer read herself. The woman, a former teacher of Sarah's, was a difficult person, but they "got on famously." She came to find a sense of Swedenborg's teachings "under everything else," and it amused her that her father objected (as did many others) to the mysticism in Swedenborgian ideas, although she felt sure he believed almost exactly as she did. Once she told Parsons gleefully that after a sermon in which a minister expounded on New Church ideas, everybody in the congregation was excited, including her father, who came bounding up the pew, exclaiming how good the sermon was, before the benediction was finished.

Sometimes Sarah professed to believe in the New Testament concept, often advanced by Phillips Brooks, that the best way to come to God is as little children, trusting him as a weary child trusts a father to know best. As a matter of fact, however, she couldn't help analyzing every phase of her religious beliefs, a practice encouraged by the New Church philosophy. She was pleased when she realized that the Lord's Prayer says "lead us not into temptation, *but* deliver us from evil" and not "*and* deliver us from evil," thus defining temptation as the evil we need to escape. Her own interpretation of temptation/evil was "doubting God and being careless about pleasing Him, and all our temptations to neglect our duty and to be selfish, and thoughtless and inconsiderate of the people about us."

Exposure to New Church philosophy, Sarah told Parsons, had made her more deeply humanitarian. "I realize," she said, "more than I ever did before that the best thing in the world is to be helpful." One of the people she helped was a girl named Lily, the daughter of South Berwick's Methodist minister. A sensitive, morbid, scholarly man, he was misunderstood by many of his parishioners and actively disliked by a number of them. As a consequence the whole family was unhappy. Sarah, mindful of her own recent adolescent conflicts, became Lily's confidante, visiting her almost daily and writing her long letters of advice and encouragement when the family was transferred to another parish.

Parson's influence on Sarah's writing was not as fortunate. Thanks to his advice to put something "positive," "something to be really learnt" into her stories, many of her early stories and poems have patently unsubtle morals attached. And his passionate commitment to doing good and teaching others to elevate their principles had for a time the effect of leading Sarah to moralize excessively in her stories, especially in those written for children. It is unfair, of course, to blame Parsons entirely for her sermonizing. Many Victorian parents approved and even insisted that stories for their children have strong moral values, and her stories and poems suited their wishes. They also suited the editors of the best juvenile magazines being published, including *Our Young Folks, Wide Awake, Merry's Museum*, and *St. Nicholas*, as well as *The Riverside Magazine for Young People*, in which they were published. Her work also appeared frequently in the children's section of *The Independent*, a semireligious magazine, and when its editor, William Hayes Ward, a Berwick friend of the family, advertised her as one of their "crack contributors," she told Parsons she was feeling *"very grand"* and crowed, "Isn't that a step ahead!"

Because Sarah had read widely and possessed innate good taste, she soon became aware that moralizing did not make for good literature. Calling herself a "preachy Pinny" (a family nickname), she vowed in her journal that she would get her messages across without being overtly pious. And she quoted Charles Lamb's criticism of an author whose books were "stuffed with scripture—too parsonish." For a time, however, she found it a resolution easier said than done. Her diaries and journals are filled with religious quotations and her own sermonettes, and although her intelligence made her realize that preachiness should be avoided in fiction, it was a difficult habit to break.

As Sarah matured, she gradually acquired more patience with herself as an imperfect human being. Among the many inspirational quotations she copied into her journal was "Our ideals partially realized, are powers for good in our lives." The friends that Sarah was closest to in Newport and Boston were equally earnest and sincere about religion, and many of them were deeply interested in New Church ideas. Although they enjoyed sports, concerts, plays, teas, dinners, and other pleasures during their long visits to one another, they also spent much time in reading, in memorizing psalms and sermons, and in talking about how to live the best life. Sarah told Professor Parsons she was dependent on her friends and happy to be so. In her journal she compared some of them to flowers:

Georgie [Georgina Halliburton] is my wild rose, a bright little wild rose, not the pale kind—tender-looking—wilful-looking—brave-looking little fellows! Kate [Birckhead] is like a very tall white hyacinth (and Ellen [Mason] is like a pink one) and Kate is also like spring violets the very fragrantest sweetest ones and knowing her is as good as having them bloom all year round! Georgie says I am most like a little bright red poppy—which at this time is dreadful to think of—for what would one say to see my friends & myself in a bouquet together! 'That staring horrid poppy in with the roses! Throw her away!'

In addition to those mentioned in this passage, Sarah had close and cherished relationships with Grace Gordon and Ella Walworth. She and her friends provided therapy for one another by freely confiding their worst problems and faults and by encouraging and praising one another. They exchanged inspiring poems, biblical quotations, and quotations from sermons they had heard or read, and they expressed their feelings for one another in sentimental letters and poetry.

This network of friendships, sustained by frequent correspondence and long visits, was also strengthened by trips taken together to such places as Philadelphia, Cleveland, Chicago, and Green Bay, Wisconsin. The great prairies of the West reminded Sarah of "reading the same page of a story book over and over" and made her wish for her New England hills. She did, however, find a visit to a settlement of Oneida Indians fascinating and described to Professor Parsons a visit to an Episcopal church in which all of the congregation were Indians, looking just like those in her picture books. While on a trip to New York in the spring of 1873, she narrowly escaped being killed when she fell and was run over by a horse on Broadway. For a long time she was bruised and sore from the accident. She felt weak and her head bothered her so much that for weeks she could not write letters, and it was months before she felt normal again.

Just about the time she felt well again, Dr. Jewett became very ill, and for a while it was feared he would be blind. Terrified, Sarah told Parsons it was the first time she had known what real sorrow was. When her father was finally out of danger, she went to Wells Beach for three weeks to regain her emotional and physical strength.

In her early twenties, although Sarah had achieved some success with her writing, her feelings of restlessness and discontent still occasionally threatened to overwhelm her, and she had not been able to settle down to taking writing seriously as a vocation. She tried activity as an antidote, going for fast, tomboyish rides on her horse or for furious rowing sprees on the river. She took German and music lessons and read voraciously. "I know I ought to do a great deal and I grow so sorry and discontented when I find myself so useless, and continual carelessness and thoughtlessness pulling me back. The days come and go, and I tell myself over and over again the same story of coming short of the mark," she complained to Parsons.

When an idea interested Sarah, she often took it as a starting point for a short analytical essay in her journal. She wrote such a mini-sermon about people who say, "I cannot change that, [some behavior] it has always been my nature." Our natures, she argued, are given us to cultivate. Comparing difficult, thorny natures such as her own to stony ground, she declared that with great care and attention both can be brought to produce a harvest that is all the more precious for the trouble it took to create it.

Her sense of humor, always a saving grace, kept her from being weighed down by her earnestness. Once, when her father read a story she had written about a little girl who was neat and orderly and always finished whatever she began, he commented dryly that guideposts "never travel over the roads they point out," and Sarah found the implied comparison very funny. On another occasion she amused Mary by pointing out an apple tree that reminded her of her own life. From lack of pruning it was a mass of suckers and unprofitable little scraggly branches. "I wish," Sarah told her sister, "I grew in three or four smooth useful branches instead of starting out here, there and everywhere, and doing nothing of any account at any point."

Sarah realized, without conceit, that she had the ability to write well, and she was ambitious to use that gift, sensing, perhaps unconsciously, that through it she could center her life. Following publication of "The Shipwrecked Buttons," by Alice Eliot, in January of 1870, *The Riverside Magazine for Young People* printed "The Girl with the Cannon Dresses," by Sarah Orne Jewett, in August 1870. Sarah did have feelings of shyness and a desire to keep her identity secret until she felt secure in her success, and these were the likely reasons for her use of pen names, although she never did explain it. Her pen names included Alice Eliot, A. C. Eliot, and Sarah O. Sweet. Nor did she explain where the Eliot came from, although some have speculated that it was derived from George Eliot, whose writings she liked, or (more probably) from the nearby town of Eliot, Maine, where she frequently visited.

Although "The Girl with the Cannon Dresses" is written for children, it is also a successful story that can be enjoyed by adults. It clearly marks a turning point in Sarah's writing toward the direction she would follow in her best work for the remainder of her life. The story, a simple tale of friendship between an older and a younger girl, used the country characters and rural landscape she knew so well, and it thereby achieved a reality lacking in her earlier stories. The protagonist is a dominant, self-confident female character, who appears in many of Sarah's later stories in a number of guises. "Dresses" also marks the beginning of her use of the Wordsworthian themes of nature as a beneficent guide and nurturer as well as a giver of gifts to please our senses. It has the theme of country versus city, one that Sarah would use repeatedly in her writing.

Since the end of the Civil War, she had been disturbed by the fact that the swarms of summer visitors did not understand the Maine natives. Years later in an interview in the Boston *Journal* she remembered:

When I was, perhaps, fifteen, the first "city boarders" began to make their appearance near Berwick; and the way they misconstrued the country people and made

game of their peculiarities fired me with indignation.
I determined to teach the world that country people
were not the awkward, ignorant set those persons
seemed to think. I wanted the world to know their
grand, simple lives; and so far as I had a mission when
I first began to write, I think that was it.

Remembering Plato's maxim that the best thing that can
be done for the people of a State is to make them acquainted
with one another, she set herself the goal of doing just that.

Sarah was fortunate to live at just the right time to come
under the guidance of some of the most distinguished editors
of the nineteenth century. These mentors, all noted writers
themselves, included James Russell Lowell, William Dean
Howells, James T. Fields, Thomas Bailey Aldrich, and Horace
E. Scudder. With each of them, and with their families, she
eventually formed close friendships. Scudder (1838–1902),
biographer of Lowell, edited *The Riverside Magazine for
Young People* from 1867 to 1870 and the *Atlantic Monthly*
from 1890 to 1898. He bought Sarah's material for *The Riverside Magazine* while she was still in her teens and gave her
the encouragement and guidance she thirsted for. She told
Scudder she welcomed his criticism, since her friends were
not "unexceptionable authorities on literary questions." She
acknowledged that her early success in getting her "nonsense"
printed before she had learned her craft was a disadvantage
and confessed that at times her talent frightened her more
than it pleased her. She was aware of her limitations and told
Scudder, "It seems to me I can furnish the theatre, and show
you the actors, and the scenery, and the audience, but there
is never any play! What shall be done with such a girl?" Instinctively she knew where her strengths lay, and on those
occasions when she allowed the advice of unwise friends and
critics to lead her into attempting stories with complicated
plots, she invariably was less successful than when she displayed her rural characters going about their business in their

natural setting; in other words, when she followed her father's injunction to "tell them just as they are."

Sarah once remarked that when she first began sending out her material, she had "no friends at court." It was the policy of many magazines for the editors to sign their letters to unknown writers generically as "the editors." Consequently, in her first reply to William Dean Howells, Sarah simply addressed him as "the editor with the nice handwriting." Howells (1837–1920), editor of the *Atlantic Monthly* for ten years, is often called "the dean of American letters." He knew and influenced such writers as Henry James and Mark Twain, and he was quick to realize the potential of the fledgling author Sarah Orne Jewett. This was the editor who accepted "Mr. Bruce," the first of her stories to appear in the *Atlantic*, a strong champion of literary realism as opposed to the romanticism so prevalent in the late nineteenth century. Howells proved a beneficial guide to Sarah at the start of her literary career, and after they were better acquainted, Sarah became a frequent caller and dinner guest at the Howells' home on Berkeley Street in Boston, and they exchanged visits during the summers, when the Howells moved to their summer cottage at Kittery Point, near South Berwick.

When Sarah sent Howells a sketch titled "The Shore House," he praised its freshness and realism but suggested to her that the characters were good enough for her to say "a great deal more of them." A little disappointed that Howells could not accept the sketch as a familiar essay about the Maine shoreline and inland area she was so familiar with, Sarah repeated Howells' advice to Scudder, commenting, "I am certain I could not write one of the usual magazine stories. If the editors will take the sketchy kind and people like to read them, is not it as well to do that and do it successfully...?" Eventually Howells gave in and "The Shore House" appeared in the September 1873 issue of the *Atlantic*. The *Nation's* literary critic praised it as agreeable reading, "more like talk than reading, and talk of a very fresh, unaffected kind."

Several more sketches of a similar nature followed. Van Wyck Brooks, in *New England: Indian Summer*, perhaps captures best the appeal of her finest sketches: "light as smoke or wisps of sea-fog, charged with the odours of mint, wild roses and balsam." And it was Howells who told her, "Your voice is like a thrush's in the din of all the literary noises that stun us so."

The house featured in "The Shore House" resembles the Jewett home in South Berwick, and the town of Deephaven is like South Berwick and York and other south Maine coastal towns. After the *Atlantic* published several other sketches, including "Deephaven Cronies" and "Deephaven Excursions," Howells began urging Sarah to revise them and collect them into book form. The idea of writing a full-length book both attracted and frightened her. In the end, she accepted it as a challenge.

CHAPTER FOUR

◆

Deephaven

ONE OF THE HIGHTLIGHTS of the Boston social season of 1875 was Ella Walworth and George Little's November wedding, during which Sarah and Mary stayed at the Walworth home and helped Ella entertain her many guests. Among these was Anna Laurens Dawes of Washington, D.C., daughter of the Senator from Pittsfield, Massachusetts. Immediately after the wedding, Anna and Sarah began to exchange long letters and visits. In her letters to Anna, Sarah told her new friend of her struggles with what she called the "Deephaven Papers." Although she was taking her work more seriously now and devoting big chunks of time to it, interruptions, many of them connected with her religious activities, frequently pulled her away from it.

Even though she was a member of St. John's Episcopal Church in Portsmouth, Sarah was active in the Congregational church in South Berwick when she was at home. One day when she had settled in for a good afternoon's work with her papers spread out and "all sails set," she was called out by a friend to go with her to make parish calls on the new people who had recently come to work in the mills and factories in the village. During another week there was a church fair to prepare for, and Sarah told Anna, "you probably know what that means in a small town?" She was much interested in her Sunday school class of young adult women and tried to instill in them her goals for herself: "to become a brave good woman"; to "be a Christian through and through"; and to be "tireless in trying to do right." She volunteered to recatalogue and add to the Sunday school library, a job that took her three weeks but brought her great satisfaction.

Family, friends, and relatives also took up her time and attention. Somewhat reluctantly she attended the Centennial in Philadelphia during the heat of summer in 1876 with members of her family. And when her father, who didn't get to make the trip, wanted her to go with him to see the Centennial in October, she couldn't refuse. They stayed with the Ornes, cousins of Sarah's, and she enjoyed the show better in the cooler weather. On a visit to Boston she enjoyed tea parties, luncheons, dinners, and theatricals with an ever-widening circle of friends.

On a visit to friends in Concord, she saw a good deal of the Ralph Waldo Emersons, and particularly enjoyed getting to know Ellen, Emerson's daughter. Sarah had a great reverence for Emerson and for his disciple and friend Thoreau, who died when she was thirteen and with whose writings her nature descriptions are often compared. She had read many of Emerson's essays, probably including the one on Swedenborg, and she naturally felt a kinship with a man who could say, "What is a farm but a mute gospel?" and "What is a weed? A plant whose virtues have not yet been discovered." In her compilation of Sarah's letters, Annie Fields says that one day she received a poem about Emerson in which Sarah tells of meeting the philosopher: "I met great Emerson, serene, remote/Like one adventuring on seas of thought" in the midst of a noisy, crowded street. By the time she became intimate with the family in the late 1870s, Emerson was quietly sinking into a peaceful senility.

Sometimes poor health caused Sarah to lose time from

her writing, and she learned—and sometimes ignored—the fact that too long and hard a stint of work would invariably be paid for with an onset of arthritis, severe headaches, or respiratory ailments. Nevertheless she plowed ahead. "I have never worked so steadily for so long," she told Parsons. She found the rearranging and rewriting and adding of new material to her sketches the most difficult writing she had ever done. At times when she felt low-spirited and tired, she wondered if her writing would seem as dull to everybody else as it did at that moment to her.

Choosing a publisher turned out to be a dilemma—Professor Parsons suggested one publishing house and her editor, William Dean Howells, suggested another. After interviews with the directors of both houses and encouragement from both of them, she decided to trust her manuscript to the house Howells had suggested, James R. Osgood and Company of Boston. Reluctantly informing Parsons of her decision, she reminded him, "The *Atlantic* is after all the mainsail of my craft, and Mr. Howells has always been the kindest of friends to me." The choice turned out to be a good one. James Osgood proved to be another supportive editor, and Sarah stayed with the firm through a series of name changes as it evolved into Houghton, Mifflin and Company.

In January of 1877 Sarah reported to Parsons that she had a new beginning and a new last chapter and "ever so many bits to put in all the way along." With a last furious sprint she met the deadline for the final draft of the 240-page book. In early April, when she received her advance copies of *Deephaven*, she wrote enthusiastically to Mr. Osgood: She loved the design, especially the little triad of gilt cattails that appeared on the spine of the book. Practically, she suggested sending an advance copy to her uncle, John Taylor Perry, editor of the Cincinnati *Gazette*, who, she said, "ought to speak a good word for Deephaven...!" Eagerly she collected notices of the forthcoming book as they appeared in various journals and asked friends such as Anna Dawes in Washington to watch out for and send along any notices of it in their local periodicals.

Deephaven is dedicated to Sarah's parents and "also to all my other friends, whose names I say to myself lovingly, though I do not write them here." The bond holding the sketches together is that everything and everybody in Deephaven and in the surrounding countryside is seen through the eyes of two young girls, visitors from Boston. Helen Denis, the narrator, tells the story and with her friend, Kate Lancaster, provides continuity. Helen, a Jewett persona, rhapsodizes over the virtues of her friend Kate in much the same vein that Sarah used in her diaries when describing the girls on whom she had teenage crushes.

Both girls in the story are twenty-four, the same age as Sarah when she wrote the first of the Deephaven sketches for the *Atlantic*. Like their creator, they are reluctant to think of themselves as "irreparably grown-up," and consider it a lark to have a whole summer to play house in the stately house Kate's mother has inherited from an aunt. The aunt, Katherine Brandon, for whom Kate Lancaster is named, was the *grande dame* of the village, and as the summer visit progresses, the girls come to learn what her life was like.

Before they arrive in Deephaven, the girls look forward to building sand castles, collecting shells, and playing in abandoned boats. Before the visit ends, they have enjoyed these pleasures and many more, but they have also come to know a great deal about the rise and decline of Deephaven and its inhabitants. They discover that the old aristocracy is dead or dying and there is no new "class of country people who preserve the best traditions of culture and of manners, from some divine instinct." The imaginary village of Deephaven is as realistic a place as Jefferson is in Faulkner's novels. But Sarah resisted the efforts of some of her readers to identify Deephaven with any specific place and felt it necessary in the preface to the second edition to state that it was a "fictitious village which existed only in the mind." Although it can't be located on a map, Deephaven is a composite of South Berwick, York, Wells, and the countryside surrounding these towns at the southern tip of Maine.

Part of its charm for the proper Bostonian girls lies in its isolation and in the quaintness of the residents, whose lives are immersed in the past. The village itself is "utterly out of fashion"—twelve miles from the railroad, with a harbor steadily filling up with a sandbar. Alongside the wharves lie schooners and a brig that are slowly going to pieces. In fact, the whole town looks to the girls to be "more or less out of repair," a lazy little English seaside town rather than a busy nineteenth-century American town. The pecking order of the society also shows vestiges of its English heritage, the decaying gentry (of whom Kate's grand-aunt was the leader) being treated with respect by the middle and lower classes, who are well aware of their shortcomings.

Brandon House, like the spacious Jewett home in South Berwick, is a cupolaed mansion full of treasures. From the paneled hallway to the garret harboring ancient chests and boxes, the girls explore. In the best chamber they discover an immense canopied bed, massive chairs, a ceiling-high mirror, and pink and maroon wallpaper captured from a French ship a hundred years before. Also reminiscent of the Jewett house are the curios garnered by seafaring ancestors, such as a knick-knack cabinet filled with Chinese carvings.

During their long visit, Helen and Kate become as intimately familiar with the natural world around Deephaven as Sarah was with her own woods, fields, coves, and cliffs in the South Berwick area. Lonely farmhouses, tiny fishermen's cottages, rocky coasts, the smell of bayberry bushes, pitch pines, the "delicious saltiness of the sea," and the inspiring view from the lighthouse are faithfully distilled from Sarah's direct observations and memories dating back to her childhood rides in her father's buggy and visits to relatives.

The characters, too, are amalgams of individuals who had flickered through her life. Arthritic old sea captains who sun themselves "like turtles" on the wharves derive from the aging captains who came to visit her grandfather when she was a small child. The girls discover it is "etiquette" to call all of them captain, although they suspect that some of these beached seamen appropriated the title after reaching a certain age. The old sailors try to outdo each other in telling harrowing tales of adventure on the high seas and argue about the tonnage of some vessel that fell prey to dry rot or barnacles fifty years earlier. They ostracize Captain Lant, who deserted seafaring to take up farming and who now signs his letters "condemned as unseaworthy." Captain Sands spends his days in a warehouse filled with memorabilia of his seafaring days—old figureheads, fantastic shells from the South Seas, and a swordfish's sword embedded in a ship's plank—none of which he will part with, to his wife's despair. Both Lant and Sands are visionaries, with an interest in dreams and the supernatural, prefiguring Captain Littlepage in *The Country of the Pointed Firs.*

Danny, a young fisherman, is based on George Hatch, with whom Sarah went out fishing at Wells. George told Sarah about having a cat on board a schooner, and from there, Sarah told Anna Dawes, she enlarged on his history at her "own sweet will." In *Deephaven* Danny tells the girls a pathetic story in which he reveals that the only creature he has ever had a close relationship with was a cat he had rescued. He has a dream of owning a snug little house and farm but accepts the fact that he is probably better off fishing than farming. He feels "first rate" in a trig-built topsail schooner "painted up *nice*, with a stripe on her and clean sails and a fresh wind with the sea a-shining." Danny's loneliness also came from Sarah's imagination, as the real George Hatch had a son and a wife, who were also Sarah's friends.

As is characteristic of most of Sarah's writing, there are more memorable women than men in *Deephaven*. Self-sufficient wives, widows, and spinsters abound. Mrs. Kew, wife of the lighthouse keeper, grew up in the hills of Vermont and is an "upcountry" woman at heart, but she finds contentment and relieves the confinement of her life through observing nature and reading. Many readers have concluded that the descriptions of the lighthouse are probably based on the well-known Nubble Light, on Neddick Point.

Another indomitable character is Mrs. Patton, known as the Widow Jim, who has survived a disappointing marriage with a drunkard, who left her nothing but debts and a dent in her forehead from a stone bottle he hurled at her in a drunken rage. She has created a full life for herself and gained a reputation among the villagers as a woman with "faculty." She is skillful at needlework, knowledgeable about herbs, and an excellent nurse. When her patients fail to survive, she acts as "commander-in-chief" at their funerals. To eke out her living, the Widow Jim does housecleaning and helps at entertainments. The visiting girls come to depend on her for local lore and the pedigrees of the inhabitants.

Mrs. Bonny, whom the girls visit in her isolated shack, is a forerunner of Sarah's titanic women and the prototype of Almira Todd in *The Country of the Pointed Firs*, a character notable for her vast knowledge of natural lore and her indomitable independence. Dressed in men's clothing and boots, several layers of aprons, a tight cap, and "steel-bowed" spectacles, she lives exactly as she pleases. She has a razor-sharp tongue and consumes huge amounts of tobacco. Her chickens wander through her shanty at will while she spends her time enjoying wildflowers and the magnificent view from her doorstep. As she shows the view to her visitors, she comments proudly, "Real sightly, aint it?"

Sarah acknowledged that the only character in *Deephaven* that she took from real life without modification was Mrs. Chauncey, who is based on a woman Sarah had visited and found in the same situation as this demented Deephaven aristocrat. Living alone in the once elegant mansion of her once wealthy shipbuilding family, Mrs. Chauncey believes that she is still the lady of the manor, an empty decaying shell of a house, which, to her eyes, has retained its ancient grandeur. Oblivious of dangling cobwebs and dangerously decaying floors, she entertains Helen and Kate by recounting details of her splendid coming-out party and invites them to stay for tea—a tea that exists only in her imagination. Mrs. Chauncey refuses to accept the idea of death, commenting, "They say everyone is 'dead' nowadays. I do not comprehend the silly idea!" When the girls ask her to read from the Bible for them, she opens the great book at random and reads, "In my father's house are many mansions." Watching a leaf drift in through a broken space in the wall, she repeats slowly, "In my father's house are many mansions; if it were not so I would have told you."

Sarah's descriptions of the girls' encounters with a squalid circus troupe and a pitifully ineffective lecturer, plus the chapter about Miss Chauncey and one called "In Shadow," are examples of Sarah's mastery of naturalistic realism and stand to refute the charge that she wrote only bland stories about the light and lovely side of life. "In Shadow" reveals a devastating portrait of rural poverty. When the girls visit a lonely little farmhouse in a rocky cove, the man explains that although he and his wife have worked as hard as possible, sickness and the "poorness" of their land have defeated them, and they can "never seem to get forehanded." The neatly dressed children are pitifully thin. When the girls pay a return visit to the desolate farm in late fall, they find a funeral in progress and learn that after the wife died, the man took to drink and is now being buried. The children will be farmed out to unwelcoming relatives. A neighbor says of the family's bad luck, "'twas against wind and tide with 'em all the time." And Helen, Sarah's spokesperson, wonders "how we can help being conscious in the midst of our comforts and pleasures, of the lives which are being starved to death in more ways than one."

When Professor Parsons criticized *Deephaven* for not having enough "moralizing" in it, Sarah thanked him for his

advice but said, "I like best to have the moral in the story—
to make the *character* as apparent as I can. I always feel when
I say anything directly as if it were awkward and that if the
story itself doesn't say it, it is no use to put it in afterward."
She admitted that this idea might not always work and went
on to point out the theme and the moral she hoped to convey
in *Deephaven.*

She wanted, she explained, to help people look at commonplace lives from the inside instead of the outside "to
see that there is deep and true sentiment and loyalty and
tenderness and courtesy and patience—where at first sight
there is only roughness and coarseness and something to be
ridiculed." She hoped the moral was apparent. "Such a life
as I told about in *Deephaven* is so much pleasanter and more
real than what one calls 'society life.'" So many girls, she told
the professor, cared so little for outdoor life and its pleasures
and saw so few of its beauties, and she pointed out to him
that Kate had said that they might easily have had a dull
summer—only they *chose* not to have it. "I meant to teach
that if I could." Obviously the young writer did not depend
on anyone to do her thinking for her, not even her beloved
professor.

Deephaven received favorable reviews in many periodicals, with the notable exception of the *New York Times* (April
28, 1877), whose literary critic scoffed that it was a dull tale
and concluded, "It is by some mistake, doubtless, that it got
into print at all." The London *Saturday Review* called it "a
collection of tolerably clever social sketches of New England
life and character." A less blasé reviewer praised the author's
"Raphaelite fidelity and minuteness of detail" and "her
delicacy of touch" in the *Eclectic* (June 1877). *Literary World*
(June 1877) found the book "overhung by a kind of glowing
haze, which softens every outline" and described it as a choice
book of its class.

Just what class *Deephaven* belonged to puzzled reviewers
and librarians. According to nineteenth-century criteria it was

not a novel. It only encompasses one summer and fall; there is no neat chronology about the tales; the book does not trace the development of its characters through birth, life, and death. On the other hand, it is clearly not just a group of essays or a mere collection of character studies. The descriptions vibrate with realistic details, and yet the author insisted that her setting and characters were fictional. At various times she called it her *Deephaven* "papers," "tales," or "sketches"— terms that baffled some critics and inveterate pigeonholers. Most bibliographies group the book with her novels.

In May 1877 Sarah wrote to Anna Dawes that the success of her first book frightened her and made her feel inadequate. "It has not been wholly pleasure, this success which I seem to have—though there is so much pleasure." Reviews of her book by strangers in periodicals were difficult to relate to and seemed "vague" to Sarah, but the praise of friends "warmed her heart." In the *Atlantic* her editor and friend William Dean Howells wrote of the "Conscientious fidelity" and art of the book, "while over the whole is cast a light of the sweetest and gentlest humor." And Sarah was especially pleased by a letter from John Greenleaf Whittier. She had long admired the Quaker poet's poems about New England country people—poems such as "Maud Muller," "Snow-Bound," and "Barefoot Boy." In turn, Whittier had been impressed by her sketches as they appeared in the *Atlantic*. Now he wrote to tell her he had read *Deephaven* three times and had given it as gifts to several friends. "I know of nothing better in the literature of the kind," he said, adding, "I heartily congratulate thee on thy complete success." Sarah had been introduced to Whittier in the offices of her publisher, James R. Osgood, in the winter of 1876. Despite the more than forty years difference in their ages, the lifelong bachelor and the lifelong spinster soon discovered they were soulmates. Letters, frequent visits, and poetical tributes to each other reinforced their friendship, which lasted until Whittier's death in 1892.

With her first royalties from *Deephaven* Sarah bought a

saddle horse, a chestnut thoroughbred. She named the mare Sheila, but pronounced the name "Shy-la", as the horse had the habit of occasionally shying as well as indulging in unexpected jumps. These quirks didn't bother her owner, who found her new "friend" beautiful, amusing, sensible, and brave. Sheila soon learned to follow her around, knowing her pockets contained treats of apples and sugar. Describing her horse in the autobiographical sketch "An October Ride," Sarah says, "I glory in her good spirits and I think she has a right to be proud and willful if she chooses." She praises Sheila's quick eye and ear, her sure foot, and her slender, handsome chestnut head. "I feel as if I had suddenly grown a pair of wings when she fairly flies over the ground and the wind whistles in my ears," she writes. Eventually Sarah got a new phaeton for Sheila to pull—a light little gig that "she whisks along joyfully" Sarah told Anna Dawes.

Sarah's publisher was eager to ride the crest of *Deephaven's* success by quickly launching another book, and James Osgood urged her to gather up her children's stories to make up a volume to be called *Play Days*. Accordingly, Sarah settled down to collect and revise the children's stories that had been published in such magazines as *The Independent* and *St. Nicholas* since as early as 1870. *Play Days: A Book of Stories for Children* (1878) contains fifteen stories for readers from eight to twelve. It is prefaced by her poem "Discontent," which was first published in *St. Nicholas* in 1876. This poem illustrates a theme running through many of the stories: that one should make the best of one's situation and not make oneself miserable pining to be something one is not. In "Discontent" a robin scolds a buttercup that wishes to be big and tall like the daisy with a white frill around her neck. He reminds her that although the swallows leave him out of sight, he is happy, and he admonishes her to "Be the best buttercup you can / And think no flower above you."

Other conventional nineteenth-century themes—such as

charity, industry, honesty, and self-reliance—run throughout the stories, but Sarah's charming style and her deft use of humor and pathos offset her tendency to underscore her morals too heavily. Some of the humor comes from the fact that several of the stories are fantasies in which stuffed owls talk and pepper shakers come to life ("The Pepper-Owl"), buttons express their feelings ("The Shipwrecked Buttons"), and a cat tells a tale about some spools who take revenge on a cat that has pestered them ("The Yellow Kitten").

The misery of nineteenth-century urban poverty is shown in the pathos of the plight, in "Nancy's Doll," of Nancy and her aunt, who live on the edge of starving and freezing to death in extreme privation in a tenement house. Nancy is shy and lame, and her only wish is to own a battered old doll she sees in a secondhand shop window. But it costs seven cents—far beyond her means. The outcome illustrates the typical welfare system of the nineteenth century: two wealthy women take pity on Nancy and give her family money. Then they nurse Nancy through an illness and arrange to provide medical care that promises to cure her lameness.

Like Hans Christian Andersen, Sarah blended stark realism with fantasy in her children's stories. The shipwrecked buttons drown because of the carelessness of their owners. And in "The Best China Saucer" there is a disagreeable little girl who is dirty and rude and whose essential meanness is symbolized by the grotesque necklace of live flies she wears around her neck.

"Patty's Dull Christmas," a favorite of Professor Parsons, illustrates the point made by Patty's father that "the greatest happiness comes from doing good for others." Overcoming her reluctance to spend Christmas with her elderly aunts in Boston, Patty puts her father's dictate into practice and has a wonderful time.

Horace Scudder, Sarah's first editor and her friend, wrote a review of *Play Days* for the *Atlantic Monthly*. He praised it for its "temper of gentleness and good-breeding" and for its originality, but pointed out the thinness of plot of some of the stories and expressed the hope that Sarah would "cultivate the power of invention." The London *Saturday Review* called the book "a collection of lively stories of and for children." When people remarked on the realistic personality of some of the children in the stories, Sarah modestly said, "That did not take any work. It is just a child I knew once, lifted out of those days and feloniously transferred to my book. I ought to be arrested for kidnapping, because it is nothing else."

Among Sarah's friends was Mrs. William Chaflin, wife of the former governor of Massachusetts; Chaflin also served from 1877 to 1881 in the House of Representatives. In early 1878 Sarah went to Washington for an extended visit with the Chaflins, who introduced her to a number of writers and people associated with the literary world and kept her in a whirl of activity from morning until late at night. She told friends that on one busy day, in which she helped receive ninety callers in the afternoon, attended a reception hosted by President Lincoln's son, entertained dinner guests, and went to a White House reception that evening, she felt like a "used-up Society girl." When she left Washington, she had a strange feeling that she was finished with the carefree life of her girlhood. The feeling was prophetic.

For some years Dr. Jewett had had warning signs of increasing heart problems but had continued to work even as his condition worsened. In August of 1878, Sarah wrote to Anna Dawes that her father had come home a few days earlier "feeling wretchedly and looking worse" but added that he was better and was planning to go to the mountains with her mother for a little vacation. Mary went along with their parents to spend several weeks at Crawford House in the White Mountains. Dr. Jewett was in high spirits. On September 19 he greeted an old college classmate with a quotation from his commencement speech many years earlier. The two friends had a pleasant reunion and after breakfast the next morning were chatting on the porch in front of the hotel. After a few minutes, the doctor suddenly took his friend's hand and said, 'I'm quite poorly. I must get home. I shall take the next train." He turned and as he crossed the hotel entrance, he fell forward and died almost instantly.

In South Berwick Sarah received the news by telegram. She wrote to Professor Parsons:

> My dear father died suddenly yesterday at the mountains. It is an awful blow to me. I know you will ask God to help me bear it. I do not know how I can live without him. It is so hard for us.

The professor, who had seen the news in the morning paper, immediately wrote a comforting letter. He understood as much as anyone how deeply her life had been interwoven with that of her father and what a terrible shock she was experiencing. In addition to his friendship he offered her all the consolations of his deeply felt religious beliefs. Her strong religious faith did help Sarah, and she also worked through her grief by writing about it in her diary. Even harder to bear than the first feelings of despair was the crushing sense of irremediable loss. "It clings to one so, and lies so heavily on one's heart and such a Sorrow is the thing that says good morning and good night and follows one all day long," she wrote.

Typically, she tried to analyze her emotions. "I learned a great deal when Father died," she noted. For the first time she had learned what despair and grief and sorrow really meant. At first the suddenness of the tragedy stunned her and bewildering agony and positive physical pain left her numb and unable to react. She went through all the funeral preparations in a trance. But after it was over everything came back to her as if the event were burned into her mind, and she remembered what people said and did. Sometimes the sight of something that had belonged to her father or the remembrance of something he said or the simple longing to touch him again was almost more than she could bear.

She found comfort in going into her father's office to read his diary and sort over his papers, books, and medicines. Her faith enabled her to write in her journal, "I am certain already that through my father's death a larger life has come to me as well as to him." But it was through her writing—in two poems about her father—that she expressed her sense of loss most poignantly.

In the first poem (both are titled "To My Father") she speaks of the changes his death brought to her life "With all its pleasures stolen suddenly." This poem ends with the expectation that his will be the hand that will lead her through Heaven's gates, since "Heaven's peace you bring who ever brought me earth's / And some fair day I too shall fall asleep." The second poem to her father was written in April 1879, when she heard a bluebird sounding the first notes of spring. As always, the song made her think happily of summer's flowers to come. But then remembrance filled her heart: "It was mistaken in its winter's end / I think I never was so grieved and sad,"

> And in my mind there was no longer room
> For any thought but of that dearest friend
> Who taught me first the beauty of these days—
> To watch the young leaves start, the birds return,
> And how the brooks rush down their rocky ways,
> The new life everywhere, the stars that burn
> Bright in the mild, clear night. Oh! he has gone,
> And I must watch the spring this year, alone.

◆

CHAPTER FIVE

The Queen
of Sheba

IN NOVEMBER 1878, a couple of months after Dr. Jewett's death, Carrie was quietly married to South Berwick's druggist, Ned (Edwin C.) Eastman, a handsome and popular young man-about-town. Carrie was a semi-invalid all of her life and was seldom strong enough to join her sister in the vigorous outdoor sports Sarah loved, but she made her own special place in the village. She was deeply compassionate and showered gifts of food, flowers, books, fuel, and money on the ill and needy and paid them cheerful, sympathetic visits. Although she scarcely left the South Berwick area after her marriage, she was greatly loved by the villagers whose lives she touched.

The next year after their marriage Carrie and Ned had a son, whom they named Theodore Jewett after Dr. Jewett. "Stubby," as he was nicknamed, brought laughter and joy to the family, and his aunts became his willing slaves. As he grew up, Sarah was the one who went skating and sledding and riding with him and talked football with him as well as books. She and Mary took great pride in him and monitored his education every step of the way.

During the year following her father's death Sarah found it difficult to do any new writing, but she could and did rework some stories, which were published as *Old Friends and New* by Houghton, Osgood and Company in 1879. Six of the stories had been published in magazines, but the seventh, "Lady Ferry," had been rejected by the *Atlantic Monthly*. In their use of suspense and supernatural elements such as ghosts and unexplainable happenings, both "Lady Ferry" and "A Sorrowful Guest," perhaps the least successful of the stories in the collection, resemble somewhat Hawthorne's stories, which Sarah had read growing up.

"A Bit of Shore Life," the best story of the lot, is often compared to the stories of a contemporary of Sarah's, Mary Wilkins Freeman, who wrote tales set in the grim underside of rural poverty. It depicts the cheerless lives of elderly women who have a morbid interest in sicknesses and deaths, and indulge in petty disputes, which are sometimes handed down from generation to generation. "Is it because their world is so small, and life affords so little amusement, and pleasure, and is at best a dreary round of the dullest housekeeping?" the narrator (another Jewett persona) asks. Deeply affecting is the scene in which the narrator stops to take in a country auction of the effects of an elderly widow. Her son, John Wallis, who has made a fortune in the city, is bent on "rescuing" his mother from her life of hardship by taking her to the city to live with him. John insists she get rid of all her dingy artifacts, but old Mrs. Wallis, although grateful to her son, is distraught at the idea of parting with her keepsakes, even her mended and cracked china, and at leaving the home where the doors have been worn smooth by the touch of her hands.

There are bits of autobiography in "A Bit of Shore Life." Just as in real life Sarah was mourning the cutting down of her beloved woods where she had played as a child and found peace and solace as a young woman, the narrator in the story mourns the loss of the great pines she has grown up with: "There will never be such trees for me any more in the world. I knew where the flowers grew under them, and where the ferns were greenest, and it was as much home to me as my own house." The story is graced by a sprinkling of delicate lyrical passages, such as this description of early morning by the sea: "The world was just then like the hollow of a great pink sea-shell; and we could only hear the noise of it, and the dull sound of the waves among the outer ledges."

Two stories in the collection, "A Late Supper" and "Mr. Bruce" (which had been one of her first published stories ten years earlier), are farces. Both involve improbable coincidences, but "A Late Supper," in its blend of pathetic and comic elements, is the more successful story. In it, another of Sarah's strong spinster heroines, Miss Catherine Spring, acknowledges that although in her single life she may occasionally be lonely, "it is, after all, a great satisfaction to do as one pleases." But then her security is menaced by the treachery of big business: the railroad stock she invests in fails to pay its dividends, and she is afraid she is going to have to sell her home. In the meantime, unexpected guests arrive for dinner, and she runs over to the neighbors, on the other side of the railroad tracks, to borrow some cream, only to find a train stopped on the tracks blocking her way back home. She attempts to take a short cut by crossing through the train, but before she can jump down on the other side it starts up, and she is caught on the moving train in her housedress, holding her cream pitcher. There is nothing to do except ride on to the next stop and catch a local back to her village. During her inadvertent ride she encounters a woman and her aunt to whom she reveals her financial predicament. That evening she arrives back home in time for "a late supper," and a few days later receives a letter from the women she encountered on the train asking if they can board with her for the summer. The story ends happily as Miss Catherine's home is saved, and she can even afford to take in a homeless orphan to live with her.

It is easy to see why "Miss Sydney's Flowers" pleased Professor Parsons. Only good writing and felicitous analogies save the moralistic story from being overwhelmed by preachiness. The reclusive Miss Sydney, who has loved only her flowers, learns late in her life to be unselfish and caring and finds a better life as "the seeds of kindness and charity and helpfulness began to show themselves above the ground in the almost empty garden of her heart."

Various reviewers of *Old Friends and New* liked different stories for different reasons. The London *Saturday Review* called it a "miniature collection of brief and graceful stories." The literary critic of *Harper's* was somewhat condescending: "Brief, making no severe exactions upon the time or the feelings, gay without levity, and pure without prudery or affectation, they are very genial recreative aids." *Literary World* praised the stories for their "simplicity, keenness of insight," and "exquisite descriptive power," and cited the author's "observing eye" and "breadth of sympathies." Horace Scudder reviewed *Old Friends and New* for the *Atlantic*, praising Sarah's portrayal of her spinster characters for "their dignity and homely truthfulness" and for letting the reader "smile quietly with her at their quaintness." But as usual he complained about her lack of plot, saying the stories "remain chiefly sketches, studies, episodes."

On December 3, 1879, Sarah attended a reception given by the *Atlantic Monthly* to honor Oliver Wendell Holmes, the seventy-year-old autocrat who had given the periodical its name and much of its fame. Among the distinguished guests at the party were William Dean Howells, Thomas Bailey Aldrich, Mrs. Julia Ward Howe, Charles Dudley Warner, John Greenleaf Whittier, and Mr. and Mrs. James T. Fields. All of these eminent literary figures were, or soon would be, friends of Sarah's—and they would remain so for the rest of their lives. But the Fieldses would play the most important role in her life.

At the age of fourteen James Fields began his career as a clerk in a Boston bookshop. Six years later he became a junior partner in the bookselling firm of Ticknor, Reed and

Fields, which became Ticknor and Fields and then Fields, Osgood and Company. As a publisher, Fields encouraged such talented writers as Longfellow and Hawthorne, and as a bookseller he established the Old Corner Bookstore, which became a Boston institution and a place for members of the literary world to congregate. Fields succeeded James Russell Lowell as editor of the *Atlantic Monthly*, retaining ownership of the periodical after retiring as its editor. While still a relatively young man he was renowned as a literary mogul who sought out and encouraged some of the best American and British writers of the nineteenth century. Fields married his second wife, Annie Adams Fields, in 1854, when he was thirty-seven and she only nineteen.

The daughter of a doctor, who served as a member of Boston's school board, Annie Adams attended the George B. Emerson School for Girls in Boston, where she studied mathematics, science, English literature, and languages. Annie was an excellent student and learned to translate from German, Italian, French, and Greek. Emerson School for Girls emphasized the importance of exercising the body as well as the mind and inculcated in its affluent young women a strong sense of responsibility for helping those less fortunate than themselves.

The Fieldses had no children, and Annie became a vital partner to her husband, translating for him when they traveled abroad, offering valuable judgments on manuscripts submitted to him, and entertaining business associates and friends from the worlds of literature and art. Under the hospitable roof of 148 Charles Street in Boston, Charles Dickens, Matthew Arnold, and William Makepeace Thackeray read from their works and occasionally did some writing. There they met other renowned travelers as well as famous natives such as Longfellow, Emerson, Hawthorne, Whittier, Oliver Wendell Holmes, Edwin Booth, Winslow Homer, and John Singer Sargent and other distinguished Americans in arts and in public life. In *Not Under Forty* Willa Cather says of Annie

Fields, "No woman could have been so great a hostess, could have made so many highly developed personalities happy under her roof, could have blended so many strongly special-ized and keenly sensitive people in her drawing-room, without having a great power to control and organize." Annie Fields also used this organizing ability in helping to found the Associated Charities of Boston, an organization in which she served as director and vice president and for which she worked diligently all her long life. When Boston began to simmer in the summer heat, the Fieldses retreated to their cottage on Thunderbolt Hill at Manchester-by-the-Sea, on the North Shore of Massachusetts. In 1874 they had built Gambrel Cot-tage on the crest of the hill. A steep, curving driveway led to the house, which had a piazza running its full length. From this porch one looked over the green lawn and beds of bright hollyhocks, past the tops of maple and pine trees to the shin-ing blue Atlantic. An ocean breeze constantly cooled this secluded retreat. It was Annie who had dubbed the village Manchester-by-the-Sea, after the English fashion of naming waterside towns, and the name stuck. Gambrel Cottage also became a mecca for the Fieldses' numerous friends and literary acquaintances, including the budding young author Sarah Orne Jewett. After a visit to Gambrel Cottage in the summer of 1880, Sarah wrote to the Fieldses, "I left a bit of my heart behind me in Manchester-by-the-Sea."

Toward the end of the 1870s James Fields became increas-ing ill and feeble and then died unexpectedly in April 1881. Annie Fields was devastated; she and her husband had truly been partners in life. After the prescribed mourning period for wearing black, Annie wore widow's lavender for the rest of her life in memory of her husband. But she would survive him by thirty-four years, and she was too dynamic a person-ality to sink into mourning. Sarah's own shattering experience of her father's sudden death made her especially able to sym-pathize with Annie; she worried over Annie's health and made long visits to 148 Charles Street and to Manchester-by-the-

Sea. Both women found solace in reading and writing. Within a year of her husband's death, Annie had published his biography and rewritten a volume of her own verse, "Under the Olive." Annie was deeply interested in Sarah's writing and understood her need for a quiet time and place to work, wherever they might be together. Each encouraged the efforts of the other, and their time together was highly productive.

Sarah's publication for 1881, *Country By-Ways*, a collection of familiar essays, is dedicated to:

T. H. J.

My dear father; my dear friend;
The best and wisest man I ever knew;
Who taught me many lessons and showed me many things
As we went together along the
Country by-ways.

The essays were published by Houghton, Mifflin, and five of them describe discoveries Sarah had made in her rambles in the Berwick area by carriage, on foot, on horseback, and by river transportation.

"River Driftwood" tells of her adventures on the Piscataqua River and includes the history of the river and anecdotes about the people who have lived along its banks and depended on it for food, for transportation, or for making their livelihood. "How many men have lived and died on its banks," she writes, "but the river is always young." Regretfully, she observes that there is no more seafaring, no more sound of shipwrights' hammers in "this inland town of mine." It has become only a station on the railways and grown so little "it is hardly worth while for the trains to stop." There are the mills and factories, and the village "earns its living and enjoys itself," she admits, but she insists "it seems to me its old days were its better days."

"An October Ride" begins with high praise for her horse

Sheila and describes their visits to her "secret farm," where she imagines the life of the long-dead owners and meditates under the influence of her Swedenborgian studies about the meaning of life: "I wonder what I am; there is a strange self-consciousness, but I am only a part of one great existence which is called nature. The life in me is a bit of all life, and where I am happiest is where I find that which is next of kin to me, in friends, or trees, or hills, or seas, or beside a flower, when I turn back more than once to look into its face."

"From a Mournful Villager" begins with a lament for the extinction of New England front yards and the disappearance of the fences that protected the sanctity of their carefully cultivated gardens. This sketch includes Sarah's memories of the delight she felt as a child playing in the gardens of her grandfather's and father's houses.

"An Autumn Holiday" recounts a walk through fields and lanes that took Sarah to visit two old friends who tell her a long comic story of an old militia captain who "got sun-struck" and thought he was his own sister Patience, who had died some years ago. When he insists on wearing dresses and bonnets, the neighbors pity him even as they laugh at him and call him "Miss" Dan'el Gunn, but they accept his aberration and humor him as his doctor instructed, even though the storyteller says, "he did make a dreadful ordinary-looking woman." The old women in the story ply their young visitor with gingerbread and milk as they click their knitting needles and entertain her with other tales that reveal the idiosyncrasies and the merits of their country neighbors.

The fifth autobiographical sketch in *Country By-Ways*, "A Winter Drive," describes a chilly drive Sarah took in the Mount Agamenticus area near South Berwick with faithful John Tucker, the Jewetts' hostler and jack-of-all-trades for many years. Her theme in this sketch is the value of trees and the sadness she feels at their loss, especially those she has known well. "Happy is the man who has a large acquaintance [among trees] and who makes friends with a new tree now and then as he goes through the world," she writes. Trees, she contends, are as individual as people; no two trees are exactly alike any more than any two persons are exactly the same. Continuing the comparison, she observes that some trees are tall and proud and inclined to begrudge others their right to live and thrive. But most of the trees she is acquainted with have better natures, offering shelter to countless families of birds and squirrels and small wild creatures. Her own favorite tree is an ancient pitch pine that she believes has seen much and grown wise with age.

Commenting on the sadness of seeing sick and dying trees, she predicts that someday there will be tree doctors and surgeons who will be able to keep them healthy and cure them of some of their ailments. Coming into a great clearing where tree choppers are working, she watches a man "creep carefully like a great insect" along the trunk of a fallen tree and begin to lop off its branches. And she imagines that the scattered trees left standing have a shocked and fearful look "as if some fatal epidemic had slain their neighbors."

Reviews of *Country By-Ways* were generally positive. The *Nation* praised it for giving the reader the "same restful feeling with which one listens to a strain of sweet music repeating itself again and again." An anonymous review in the *Atlantic* (could it have been Horace Scudder again?) speaks of her ability to catch and hold "some flitting movement of life, some fragment of experience" and compares her sketches to "delicately executed water-color landscapes" but concludes by asking for more: "a larger work, one not limited by 'too narrow a range.'" More than one reviewer compared her to Thoreau in her powers of description, and others mentioned her skillful use of dialect and her sly humor.

Among the many distinguished literary people introduced to Sarah by Annie Fields was Henry Wadsworth Longfellow. He was past seventy, feeble and often in pain, when Sarah and Annie visited him in the famous Craigie House in Cambridge. When he died, on March 24, 1882, Sarah wrote Annie a comforting letter, reminding her that on their last visit he had been well and eager to talk with them about books and people. Acknowledging that it is the change brought about by death that is hard to bear, Sarah tried to console Annie by reminding her, "A man who has written as Longfellow wrote, stays in this world always to be known and loved—to be a helper and a friend to his fellow men." And she made a beautiful metaphor to comfort Annie: "His work stands like a great cathedral in which the world may worship and be taught to pray, long after its tired architect goes home to rest."

Sometime after Longfellow's death, his brother Samuel sent Sarah a clipping of one of her poems that he had found among his brother's keepsakes. The poem, "On Star Island," written following a visit Sarah and Annie made to the Isles of Shoals in July 1880, described an abandoned village on Star Island and especially the forsaken church there, which both women had found moving. Sarah's poem, which ends:

> I saw the worn rope idle hang
> > Beside me in the belfry brown.
> I gave the bell a solemn toll:—
> > I rang the knell for Gosport town.

was published in *Harper's*, and Longfellow must have read it and cut it out to save shortly before his death.

One of Longfellow's daughters, the Alice he wrote of in "The Children's Hour" ("Grave Alice and laughing Allegra / And Edith with golden hair"), became Sarah's good friend. Alice introduced Sarah to the pleasures of vigorous outdoor sport at Mouse Island in Boothbay Harbor and to the soothing effect of the beauty of the area. Through the years Sarah visited Alice there and at Craigie House frequently.

Theophilus Parsons also died in 1882. As she matured and acquired other father figures in her life, such as Whittier and her various editors, Sarah turned to Parsons less often for guidance, but she remained grateful for the role he had played in her life. She continued to believe in New Church ideas that he had introduced her to and discussed them with Annie, also lending her books on Swedenborgianism. In a letter to Parsons shortly before his death, Sarah told him that in writing *Country By-Ways* she had discovered some bits of truth for herself, adding, "Nobody has helped me to think more than you have." It may have been coincidence or a sign of Sarah's maturing, but the stories she wrote following Parsons' death show a sharp decline in didactic sermonettes.

For the next ten years of her life her chief father figure would be John Greenleaf Whittier. As Sarah and Whittier became better acquainted through frequent meetings in Annie Field's lively drawing room and at her hospitable dining table, the salutations of her letters progressed from "Dear Mr. Whittier" to "My dear Friend" and the closings from "Yours sincerely" to some variation of "Yours always most lovingly." Annie and Sarah often referred to Whittier by the way he usually signed his letters: "Truly Thy Friend." Whittier referred to Sarah as "my adopted daughter," and she wrote a poem of adulation, "The Eagle Trees," dedicated to "JGW," suggesting that the great pine trees and high-flying eagles had shared their wisdom with him (*Harper's*, March 1883). Besides their mutual love and admiration for Annie Fields, they had in common their love of an idealized past, their delight in nature in all her moods, the pleasure of discussing their reading and writing—and their ailments, particularly the arthritis both suffered from and sought to find new means of alleviating.

At age twenty-two Sarah had complained to another of her father figures, W. D. Howells, "Everybody is distressingly grown-up and I have 'nobody to play with,'" and on her forty-eighth birthday, she told a friend, "I am always nine years old." She always kept her dolls and constantly recreated the past in her writing. She hated the "demons of change," and her dependence on older males—at first her grandfathers and her father and then her editor friends, Parsons, and Whittier—was very important to her until late in her life, when her need for a parental figure to respond to the emotional child in her was transferred to her sister Mary and her friend and companion Annie Fields, who was fifteen years her senior.

Celia Thaxter, a good friend of Annie's and of Sarah's, had a deep interest in psychic communication and managed to arouse the curiosity of Whittier as well as of Annie and Sarah about the subject. In the late nineteenth century there was a great interest in spiritualism and in mediums who could conduct séances to put the living in touch with the spirits of the dead. An organization interested in an objective investigation of spiritist phenomena, the American Society for Psychic Research, was founded in 1885 and counted William James among its well-known members.

In April 1882 Sarah wrote a long letter to Whittier telling him of a visit she and Annie had made to a medium. Even though Annie found comfort in the belief that her husband and Longfellow were together following the poet's death, Sarah was skeptical and had gone to the séance in a doubting mood. At first she thought the woman was merely quick-witted in putting "two and two together," but after the medium described her father and their relationship and told her things that "amazed" her, Sarah willingly gave up her disbelief. She was greatly cheered by the message from her father that he knew her so much better now than when they saw each other, that he was always with her, and that he loved her ten times more than when he was alive. She also found it pleasant to believe that he and James Fields were together and good companions in the world of spirits. And she accepted "a dear and welcome charge" to watch over and care for Annie Fields. Sarah told Whittier she did not expect either she or Annie would visit the medium again: "One does not think of seeking . . . the teachings of the spirits, only of listening to them gladly when they come." The experience was particularly welcome because Sarah and Annie were planning an extended trip to Europe, and the medium had predicted that it would be a good trip with no accidents, and that she would come home better in all ways.

Sarah and Whittier agreed that a long trip was just the change Annie badly needed. Since her husband's death, she had thrown herself so intensely into her charity work that she was exhausted, and her grief still weighed her down physically and emotionally. Sarah, who was spending increasingly long periods of time at 148 Charles Street, made sure she was there on April 24, the first anniversary of James Fields' death. She helped Annie plan an elaborate itinerary that would take them to England and Ireland as well as Norway, Belgium, Italy, France, and Switzerland. Along the way they planned to visit a number of the celebrated friends that the Fieldses had made over the years. Such grand plans tickled Sarah's fancy, and she began calling herself "The Queen of Sheba" to her mother and sisters in view of the "royal progresses" they proposed.

In mid-May, Annie came to spend two days in South Berwick so she and Mrs. Jewett could get to know each other before the trip. Annie and Mrs. Jewett liked each other, and Annie pleased Sarah by falling "quite in love" with the Berwick country.

The last week in May 1882, Sarah and Annie and Liza, Annie's personal maid, boarded the *Scythia* amid a grand send-off. Several editors and many other friends came to the pier, and Whittier wrote a sonnet, "Godspeed," for the occasion. In it he characterized his two friends, calling Annie "Her in whom / All graces and sweet charities unite / The old Greek beauty set in holier light." Sarah he described as "Her for whom New England's byways bloom / Who walks among us welcome as the Spring / Calling up blossoms where her light feet stray."

Sarah wrote to her mother that although their 500-foot-long vessel sometimes rolled like a "chip" on the Atlantic, she had not been seasick and enjoyed staying on deck all day in the sun and wind and in the evening to watch the moon over the water, hating to go down to her stuffy stateroom. She and Annie read aloud to each other on deck and made friends with other passengers. They saw the "splendid sight" of ships under full sail and shivered in awe as they felt bitterly cold air envelop them when they passed close to two huge icebergs.

They arrived at Queenstown and spent ten days in Ireland, which Sarah found "delightful and strange." The Jewetts had employed several native Irish housemaids from time to time, and the travelers visited some of the maids' home villages, where they were welcomed and shown the workaday side of life in Ireland that foreigners seldom saw. Sarah reveled in visiting thatched-roof country farmhouses, riding a donkey, and warming herself at peat fires. They also did the conventional tourist rounds, staying at the Shelborne Hotel in Dublin and visiting Phoenix Park and Old St. Patrick's Cathedral, where they paid homage to Dean Swift's remains.

Her imagination was stirred by a visit to one of Ireland's most famous tourist attractions—the fifty-million-year-old Giant's Causeway near Portrush in northern Ireland. This area of fantastic basalt rock formations, with columns ranging from four to forty feet, was so popular in the nineteenth century that it had two hotels by the time Anne and Sarah visited the site. (Its popularity has continued, and in 1988 UNESCO declared the Causeway a "World Heritage Site.")

The ruins of once grand castles in the area also fascinated Sarah. One very windy day they crossed a deep ravine by way of a narrow piece of wall to visit the Norman castle called Dunluce, which was perched on a single crag. These ruins inspired Sarah to write a poem, "Dunluce Castle," which was published in *Harper's* (November 1883) and praised by Whittier as "an admirable little poem." Interesting as these ancient monuments were, however, the bitter cold rain and wind straight off the North Atlantic made the travelers grateful to cross over to England.

Thanks to Annie Fields's wide acquaintance in the world of the arts, Sarah met such outstanding English luminaries as the acclaimed actress Ellen Terry and also the American-born actor Edwin Booth, popular in England for his Shakespearian roles. They had a pleasant visit with the poet Christina Rossetti and went on a tour of Oxford with Charles Reade, the English novelist and playwright. Dickens and Thackeray were both dead, but Annie Fields had kept in touch with their children. Sarah, who had read and liked *Old Kensington*, by Anne Thackeray Ritchie, enjoyed meeting the author. Charles Dickens had spent much time at 148 Charles Street while on his American tours, and the Fieldses in turn had visited him at Gad's Hill several times. On the Fields's last visit to England, Dickens had read to James Fields the first chapters of *The Mystery of Edwin Drood*, from pages on which the ink was still drying. And he had taken Fields to an opium den in London to show him the hideous old woman who was the model for Princess Puffer in *Edwin Drood*. Now Annie Fields took Sarah to dine with one of Dickens's daughters and others of his family. An afternoon spent with Tennyson and his family at Farringford on the Isle of Wight thrilled Sarah, who described the aging poet laureate as the "greatest man" she had ever met.

The tourists crossed the North Sea, "as shaky a sheet of water as you ever saw," Sarah told her mother, to spend several weeks in Norway. Sarah picked up a few Norwegian words, drove herself a funny little two-wheeled cariole with rope reins, and helped row over to an island where she and Annie were entertained for two weeks by Mrs. Ole Bull, widow of the violinist, in a fantastical setting. As beautiful as the house was, with its exquisite wood carving and grand pictures and portraits, Sarah was more impressed by the huge climbing roses that might be gathered by the basketful and by the twenty miles of walks laid out about the island through the woods and around the lakes.

Visiting Holland, Sarah found the Dutch people kind and good-natured but thought Dutch the funniest language in the world. She sent Mary a Rotterdam newspaper so she could see words "half a yard long." Sarah wrote that she loved Amsterdam with her "whole heart." She bought cologne for her mother in Cologne and rhapsodized over their beautiful hotel in Heidelberg, but the Rhine and its ruins did not impress her as much as other scenery. After a pleasant stop in a private home in Lucerne, they went on to Interlaken. "I didn't know anything about mountains 'til I reached here," she told her family. She could lie in bed and look up at mountains, at first finding them so dazzling with ice and snow that she couldn't bear to look at them for long. "Nobody knows anything about Switzerland until they see it for themselves," she told her mother.

Venice glowed with splendid pageantry and fireworks when they arrived at the same time as the Queen of Italy. The "Queen of Sheba" gleefully accepted the revels as being on her own behalf. From Venice they went on to take in the history and art of Rome and Paris and then returned to London, where they boarded the *Parthia* for their return trip near the end of October, Sarah's head filled with new experiences, unforgettable scenery, and most of all the exciting new acquaintances she had made.

Her welcome home was warm and sweet, including the servants from both Jewett houses: "Hannah and Annie and John and Hilborn and Lizzie Pray all in *such* a state because I had got home!" Sarah wrote to Annie Fields. After more than six months of daily companionship, she was missing her friend but was looking forward to "no long separation, which is a comfort."

CHAPTER SIX

◆

148 Charley Street

W HEN SARAH AND ANNIE returned from their first European trip, the two women began a pattern of visiting each other that would continue for the rest of Sarah's life. Most of the winter season she spent with Annie at 148 Charles Street in Boston, and a part of the summer she stayed with Annie at the Fieldses' summer place— Gambrel Cottage on Thunderbolt Hill at Manchester-by-the-Sea. During the remaining months of the year, while Sarah was in South Berwick, Annie occasionally came to stay there for a few days.

When James Fields died in 1881, Annie was forty-seven and Sarah thirty-two. Petite and fragile in appearance, Annie Fields has been described by both Henry James and Willa Cather (who met her at age seventy) as having personal beauty and a youthful aura characterized by a merry, musical laugh. Sarah was frequently described by contemporaries as being handsome, beautiful, graceful, and dignified. She was tall and slender (until her figure thickened in middle age) and had large brown eyes, a high forehead, and dark hair. Acquaintances often remarked on the sweetness of her expression and on her radiant cheerfulness. In addition to their huge capacity for enjoying life, both women loved literature and literary people and shared a deep appreciation for the arts. Each was independent in her thinking and ambitious to pursue her own career, but each craved the emotional security of a significant person in their lives—a soulmate in whom they could confide and trust completely.

In her writing Sarah uses the word "mate" in several of its rich and complex connotations. Sometimes she uses it in the sense of fellow, twin, friend, or well-liked companion, as a sailor or an Australian might use it. In "The Queen's Twin," Abby Martin's dream is that she might walk hand in hand through "some pretty field" with Queen Victoria, whom she considers her mate. And in *The Country of the Pointed Firs*, the narrator, seeing Mrs. Todd, her friend and mentor, at a distance, calls her "mateless and appealing." In *Sarah Orne Jewett: An American Persephone*, Sarah Way Sherman points out that "mate" suggests "commonalities of work and love, marriage and friendship." Sarah's father had for many years been her mate in some of those ways, just as James Fields had been Annie's mate.

From an early age, Sarah realized the importance and necessity of friendships in her life, and on the solid rock of close friendships she structured her life. After the death of her father there were men, especially Parsons and Whittier, who partially filled his place, but by far, the majority of her most intense relationships were with women. In her diaries and in her letters to Parsons she tried to describe the importance of these relationships to her. She felt "something transfiguring in the best of friendships," which give us "shining hours" to sustain us and give us courage to persevere in the "fret of everyday life." When she was just emerging from the cocoon of her sheltered life in South Berwick, making friends in Exeter, Newport, and Boston, she sometimes felt overwhelmed by a sense of responsibility imposed on her by her growing network of friends. In accordance with Polonius' advice to Laertes, she "grappled her friends to her soul with hoops of steel," frequent visits and long letters being the components of these hoops. Letter writing preceded manuscript writing in importance, and she sometimes wrote as many as thirty letters in a day. As Willa Cather said of Sarah, "friendships occupied perhaps the first place in her life."

Many of her sketches and stories show marriage as a trap that kept women from fulfilling themselves. Once when Whittier asked her, "Sarah, was thee ever in love?" she answered "No! Whatever made you think that?" and referring to her dislike for domestic tasks, laughingly declared she needed a wife more than a husband.

Her dual residences gave Sarah all the comforts of well-run, well-staffed homes and the best of two worlds. In Boston she enjoyed the excitement of a sophisticated city with choice plays and musical performances, lectures, art galleries, and museums, as well as some of the most outstanding preaching to be heard in the nineteenth century—plus the stimulation of hobnobbing with the literary lions who wandered through the drawing room at 148 Charles Street. In South Berwick she had her family and friends and her beloved rural pleasures and longer, quiet times to write.

The nature of the relationship between Annie Fields and Sarah Orne Jewett has undergone renewed scrutiny and speculation recently, and attempts have been made to interpret it in terms of late-twentieth-century ideology. Some Jewett scholars have adopted Blanche Wiesen Cook's definition of lesbianism ("Female Support Networks and Political Activism: Lillian Wald, Crystal Eastman, Emma Goldman," *Chrysalis*, no. 3 [1977]: "Women who love women, who choose women to nurture and support and to create a living environment in which to work creatively and independently, are lesbians"). While this clearly is an accurate description of Sarah Orne Jewett's relationship with Annie, with several of her friends, and with her sister Mary (and is also true of the relationships among many of her women characters), it has led to confusion and controversy, since it modifies and extends the dictionary definition of lesbianism as a "homosexual relationship between two women." It is doubtful that Sarah or her friends knew the term "lesbian" at all. It was not until ten years after Sarah's death that D. H. Lawrence gave the word "sex" its modern meaning, and intercourse by any name was a taboo subject for a middle-class girl in the nineteenth century.

Using Sarah's poetry ("The Unpublished Love Poems of Sarah Orne Jewett," *Critical Essays on Sarah Orne Jewett*, 1984), Jewett scholar Josephine Donovan comes to the conclusion "that beginning as a young woman and continuing through her life Jewett was involved in several intimate relationships with women. At times these reached a level of passionate intensity." This is a valid conclusion: Sarah's relationships with her close women friends were intimate and intense, according to her nature. Donovan traces Sarah's "affair" with Annie to a poem dated "23 Aug. 1880," which she uses "on the theory that it is addressed to Annie Adams Fields and that it indicated the beginning of their relationship." The poem begins, "Do you remember, darling / A year ago today / When we gave ourselves to each other / Before you went away." And it ends, "And so again, my darling / I give myself to you, / With graver thought than a year ago / With love that is deep and true." If the poem is autobiographical, it seems that Donovan is correct when she says that it is possible the "girl" in the poem is Cora Lee Rice, "an earlier romance," since James Fields did not die until April 1881. Like Shakespeare's sonnets, most of Sarah's verses are not clearly addressed to any certain person, and in her interpretation of them Donovan is careful to use such terms as "probably," "presumably," and "it appears."

In "A Closer Look at the Jewett-Fields Relationship" (*Critical Essays on Sarah Orne Jewett*, 1984) Judith Roman examines the language, and particularly the nicknames and sometimes coy expressions of affection, in the Jewett-Fields correspondence. As Roman and others point out, the use of pet names and cuddling "little language" (similar to baby talk)

so popular with lovers and parents in the nineteenth century
was another means of expressing fondness. The Jewett family
frequently used such nicknames. Sarah sometimes explained
that her own family pet name, Pinny, was given to her because
she was "so tall and thin, like a pin." Mary Jewett was O.P.
for Old Peg. Sarah habitually used pet names for her friends:
Anna Dawes was "Dawsy," Georgina Halliburton "Wags," and
Celia Thaxter "Sandpiper." To Annie, Sarah was sometimes
Pinny Lawson—or P.L.—after Sam Lawson, the lazy and
rebellious but lovable village storyteller in Harriet Beecher
Stowe's *Oldtown Folks.* Sometimes Sarah addressed Annie as
T.L., a more responsible Lawson family member. Other playful names for Annie were Fuff, Fuffy, Fuffatee, and Mouse
or Mousatee.

Roman points out that despite the difference in their
ages, Annie and Sarah's roles were reversible—sometimes one
assumed a parental attitude and sometimes the other. When
Sarah pretended to scold Annie for working too hard or for
not taking care of herself, she used the diminutive nicknames,
but when she addressed her as a guide or mentor, she often
used T.L. Although Annie didn't use pet names as freely in
her letters to Sarah, she frequently addressed her as "My dear
Child" or "My dearest, dearest Child." Roman concludes that
this easy exchange of roles "fostered both freedom and security
for the two women."

The complexity of their relationship has led to various
interpretations by different critics. Ernest Hillhouse Pool, in
an essay "The Child in Sarah Orne Jewett," (*Appreciation of
Sarah Orne Jewett,* ed. Richard Cary, 1973), views Annie
Fields as a parent figure for Sarah and focuses on the childlike
aspect of her personality that needed the emotional security
found in such a relationship.

In *Sarah Orne Jewett: An American Persephone*, Sarah
Way Sherman explores in great depth the similarities of the
Jewett-Fields relationship to that of Demeter and Persephone.
Sherman calls the women "lovers" and says "it appears that

such passionate friendships preserved the tenderness, sensuousness, and security of mother-daughter bonds."

The close alliance of Sarah and Annie was far from unique. The Civil War created a shortage of marriageable men, and since men tended to die at an earlier age than women, there were many single women and widows in the late nineteenth century. For convenience a number of them established joint households and formed partnerships that came to be called "Boston marriages," a term that might or might not imply sexual relationships. Although Sarah was part of a "Boston marriage," unless new evidence is uncovered it will remain impossible to determine with certainty the nature of her sexual activities. A Victorian woman did not discuss her sex life openly, and if there are hidden clues in her writings, they are obviously open to various interpretations. Her close relationships with a number of women clearly influenced her work, and the companionship of these women was vital to her feeling of well-being. When she and Annie were separated, her letters express a longing for them to be together, but so do Sarah's letters to her sister Mary, who was her dearest friend and support when she was in Berwick.

For over a quarter of a century Annie and Sarah cared for each other in sickness, encouraged each other in their work, and loved and supported each other. Their relationship was deep and complex and can only be understood in terms of the atmosphere in which it existed over a hundred years ago. Freudian theories of sexual behavior had not begun to inhibit the expression of natural feelings. In the late nineteenth century women unselfconsciously expressed their fondness for each other freely, both in romantic rhetoric and through physical contact. They also communicated their affection verbally in letters and in poems, using sensual terminology, without the restraining fear of being labeled according to the heterosexual/homosexual mind set of the twentieth century. Popular Victorian writers like Dickens and Thackeray frequently have women characters who "fall in love" with each other and exchange physical caresses. A common expression among these female characters was for one woman to say of another that she "quite doted on her." No doubt these authors (and their characters) would have been astounded if their actions had been interpreted as having sexual connotations.

Early in her life Sarah found the work she wanted to do and came to think of marriage as a handicap to achieving her dreams. She was, however, too warmhearted and ardent to live an ascetic life. After her father's death she needed a sustaining, loving relationship with a companion who could fulfull her emotional needs without the complications of marriage. The widowed Annie Fields had the same need. For twenty-five years she had put the needs of her beloved husband first in her life. Still energetic, with many plans and projects she wanted to devote her time to, she was not looking for another husband. In their rich, fulfilling companionship the two women found security and freedom to pursue their independent goals.

Their relationship was certainly fervent, and as they both often affirmed, it involved a spiritual and intellectual closeness. Whether or not there was a physical dimension will no doubt continue to be a fascinating question for debate by scholars and critics of Sarah's work, but the significant thing about the relationship is that it was ultimately beneficial to them both—in their careers and in their personal happiness.

Sarah's empathetic understanding of Annie's heartache after her husband's death is revealed in a letter she wrote to Whittier in July 1883, telling him she was "dreadfully troubled about Annie," who was feeling miserably lonely at Manchester. Sarah urged Whittier to join her in keeping close to Annie and in loving her "all we can." She pitied their friend, she said, as she would pity a little child that has been run over and hurt, and "yet has to get up and keep on its way." Sarah was torn between being at home in South Berwick, where she felt she "ought" to be, and spending time with Annie, who seemed better contented in her company. Whittier urged them both to come to visit him at Asquam House in Holderness, a summer resort in the White Mountains of New Hampshire. They did go and stayed about a week. The magnificent views of the lakes and mountains and the glorious sunsets (which inspired several poems by Whittier) soothed Annie and made Sarah feel "a great deal better and richer."

At times Sarah acted as a temporary social secretary for Annie, and she often helped her by acting as co-hostess to the hordes of visitors who came to 148 Charles Street. She occasionally attended meetings and benefits with Annie, but in order to have time for her writing she could not afford to become too deeply involved in helping Annie with her pioneering charity work. In turn, Annie encouraged Sarah's writing, introduced her to literary friends, and used her acute editorial skills for Sarah's benefit. So despite all the diversions and temptations of her busy life in Boston, Sarah became increasingly prolific in her writing. Her next published collection of stories, *The Mate of the Daylight, and Friends Ashore* (1884), was dedicated to Annie Fields.

The title story in the collection is notable mainly for the well-drawn portraits of three archaic sea captains, who are tough old barnacles, clinging tenaciously to their ideas and spinning exuberant tales of the sea life they love, much like the sea captains who had held Sarah spellbound with the yarns they exchanged with her Grandfather Jewett.

Another of the stories, "Tom's Husband," is remarkable in that it is an early description of a househusband. It also illustrates Sarah's understanding of the role of the housewife in nineteenth-century New England and her reservations about the married state for women who have special talents that are other than domestic. Mary, who has executive ability, and Tom, who really dislikes managing a business, decide to reverse roles. Mary takes over running the family factory and Tom stays home to keep house. As time passes Tom becomes absorbed in housekeeping trivia, and Mary begins to act more like a businessman, uninterested in the details of daily housekeeping. Disturbed when he realizes he is growing rusty and falling behind the times and is beginning to merge his life in his wife's, Tom calls a halt to the experiment. He wonders if his experience as a housewife has been any more ignoble to him than it is to women themselves. And he has an uneasy suspicion that his wife could "get along pretty well without him when it came to the deeper wishes and hopes of her life."

Feminist Lillian Faderman, in *Surpassing the Love of Men: Romantic Friendship and Love Between Women from the Renaissance to the Present* (1981), calls Sarah Orne Jewett a "conscious, articulate feminist" who illustrates the destructiveness of marriage in "Tom's Husband." On the other hand, Professor Richard Cary thought the story illustrates the idea that "Women entering business in growing numbers do so to the detriment of their 'womanliness.' " And he found the denouement to be "anti-feminist." Sarah herself might have been surprised at either of these stringent interpretations. It seems likely she would have liked better Judith Roman's idea that the story shows the need for flexibility in roles, whether they are "conventional or not"—an idea that Sarah would expand in *A Country Doctor*.

Reviews of *The Mate of the Daylight* were generally good, if not glowing. William Dean Howells commented in the *Century* that he read the collection with "exactly the keen delight with which one would meet her farmer and sailor folk in the flesh and hear them talk." And George Lathrop, in the *Atlantic*, remarked that her stories were notable for their realism, "particularly their regionalism of dialect and ideas." An anonymous reviewer in *Literary World* suggested the author should "now attempt a longer work." As it happened, this was exactly what Sarah was planning.

One day in 1882 (in one of her many undated letters from South Berwick to Annie) Sarah wrote that she had lain in bed reading a handbook of anatomy and finding it very interesting. "Sometimes I think I should like to give up the world...and be a doctor, though very likely I am enough of one already," she told Annie. This was an old dream going back to her childhood—a dream that her fragile health had forced her to abandon long ago. But writers can make dreams come true in their writing, and Sarah set out to do that in *A Country Doctor*, her first conventional novel.

Another long-held dream of Sarah's was to draw an appreciative portrait of her father that would show the humanity of the village doctor as a man who knew more about the people of the community and who did more for their well-being, both physically and psychologically, than any other person. Dr. Leslie's surname Sarah apparently borrowed from another physician, Dr. Horace Granville Leslie, who practiced in Amesbury for many years and had, as Dr. Jewett had, wit, compassion, and a great interest in nature and literature.

The plot of *A Country Doctor* is slight and one-dimensional with no subplots to give it depth. Nan Prince, an orphan, is raised first by her grandmother and after her grandmother's death by kindly Dr. Leslie. Nan decides she will be a doctor, but on a visit to her Aunt Anna Prince, a fairy-tale godmother character, she meets and falls in love with handsome George Gerry. After a rigorous mental struggle, Nan decides to reject the temptation of marriage and devote herself to practicing medicine in her rural village of Oldfields.

A Country Doctor is obviously autobiographical, with Dr. Leslie sharing the compassionate, wise and self-sacrificing character of Dr. Jewett and Nan Prince being in many ways an image of Sarah. Nan is a child of nature who loves to roam the woods and fields, causing one character to say, "She belongs with wild creatures...just the same natur'." Nan leads her classmates into the pasture at recess and makes them late getting back to school, she uses a neighbor's fence boards to make a raft to chase ducks and falls into the river, and she likes to play practical jokes, rigging a tick-tack* on the town

---

*A nail tied to end of a string and run over a bent pin stuck in a window sash. The joker hides out of sight and pulls the string, causing the nail to clack against the window.

gossip's window. When she is a little older, she loves riding her horse on long rambles and taking long nature hikes through the countryside, and she dislikes housekeeping.

From the time she is a small girl, Nan accompanies the doctor on his visits and she, like Sarah, picks up rudimentary medical knowledge and a precocious understanding of human nature and needs as she observes the doctor's patients in some of the most stressful moments of their lives. She also keeps in touch with her father's old patients and goes to visit them after she is grown, just as Sarah did. Dr. Leslie's philosophy in rearing Nan is to let her grow "as naturally as a plant grows, not having been clipped back or forced in any unnatural direction." When she plans to become a physician, he is secretly pleased but determined not to encourage her too much for fear it might not prove to be the right direction for her. He only tells her, "I want you to be all the use you can." He doesn't care whether she chooses "a man's work or a woman's work" so long as she makes the right choice for her.

Evidence of the influence of Dr. Parson's Swedenborgian teachings runs throughout the novel. Like Sarah, Nan has been confirmed in the Episcopal Church, but in keeping with New Church principles, she has a more transcendent view of morality. When her aunt compliments Nan on being familiar with the Anglican church ritual, Nan replies, "I think one should care more about being a good woman than a good Episcopalian." At another point she tells a critic, "People ought to work with the great laws of nature and not against them."

Still another characteristic Nan shares with her author is an "uncommon childlikeness" that misleads her friends at times into underestimating how firm she is in her opinions, although close observers note a streak of "untamed wildness" and self-dependence in her that give her special power.

A central theme of *A Country Doctor* is the right of a woman to choose a role in life that does not fit society's conventional expectations for her. In the late nineteenth century the nature of women and the place of women in society (including the dangers to the family if they became emancipated) were topics of hot debate. Articles about "the woman question," including suffrage, appeared frequently in both scholarly and popular periodicals, and as an omnivorous reader Sarah undoubtedly read many of these. She emphasizes Nan's attractive feminine characteristics as if to refute the contention of writers who insisted that a woman who chose to eschew marriage to work in a field dominated by men would of necessity become mannish and coarse in her behavior. Beginning with the dismay of friends and relatives, Nan encounters obstacles all along her path, getting little encouragement from medical schools or from "society in general." She laments, "If a young man plans the same course, everything conspires to help him and forward him." Nevertheless she determines to pursue the profession for which she has so much natural talent that she comes to think of it as a "calling."

At times this feeling of being called to be a doctor is manifested in Christlike imagery. After a discussion in which her aunt has raised objections and reproaches to her plans, Nan tells her, "Listen, Aunt Nancy! I must be about my business; you do not know what it means to me, or what I hope to make it mean to other people." And the good Dr. Leslie, in thinking of Nan's dedication to her chosen profession, realizes "she had come to her work as Christ came to his, not to be ministered unto but to minister." At the very end of the book Nan has irrevocably turned away from the temptations of love, marriage, and children toward the hardships and uncertainties of the life of a country doctor. In the last scene of the novel Nan is in the country at a spot where her mother had contemplated suicide. Suddenly she reaches her hands upward "in an ecstasy of life and strength and gladness." "O God," she says, "I thank thee for my future."

The *New York Times* praised *A Country Doctor* for its "fine delineations of the manners, habits, and ways of thought of New England people." The *Saturday Review* (London) reported that the book was "saturated with the essence of New England," and many other reviews pointed to the insight and sympathy with which New England character is revealed. Other critics, however, complained of the static "photographic" quality of the story and deplored its "preachiness."

Inevitably critics compared the book with those of two other popular writers: William Dean Howells and Elizabeth Stuart Phelps. Howells' *Doctor Breen's Practice* and Phelp's *Doctor Zay* both explore the subject of women in the medical profession, although in Howells's novel Dr. Breen opts to marry and give up her career, Phelps's Dr. Zay marries on the condition that she can continue her career, and Jewett's Dr. Prince refuses to marry in order to devote herself to her career. Years later, in a letter to Charles Miner Thompson, Sarah acknowledged, "I understand that *A Country Doctor* is of no value as a novel," but added, "It has many excellent ideas, for which I must thank not only my father's teaching, but my father himself." It remained her own favorite of her books.

Recently, there has been a revival of interest in the novel as a valuable piece of social history. In her essay "'Mateless and Appealing': Growing into Spinsterhood in Sarah Orne Jewett," Barbara A. Johns discusses *A Country Doctor* as one of Jewett's stories that posit "a productive future for young single women." Johns points out that these young women do not fit the stereotype of an old maid and are able to "repudiate the traditional, patriarchal restrictions on women and to resist the domesticating promptings of their mothers or aunts." Their independence frees them, Johns says, and they are given flight like the birds, "with whom they are frequently compared." In addition to being a declaration of independence from marriage, the reversal of traditional roles has interested several Jewett scholars, especially as it is shown in one scene: George Gerry and Nan, who have been on a picnic, stop at a farmhouse to ask for water and find that the farmer is in pain from a dislocated shoulder. Nan successfully puts the shoulder back in place while George stands by feeling squeamish. Afterward, he does "not like to think of the noise the returning bone had made."

In "The Rise, Decline, and Rise of Sarah Orne Jewett," Richard Cary points out that "the transcendental trend of the rising generation—rejection of complex, urban material values; hankering after a more instinctual, intimate, ecological, uncomputerized past—perhaps bespeaks Miss Jewett's gently real formulation as a world whose time has returned." Sarah's familiar theme of country versus city, which runs throughout *A Country Doctor*, supports this thesis. Nan's mother is degraded when she leaves the country to live in Lowell, and whenever Nan is feeling discouraged or lonely, she finds comfort in retreating to her grandmother's farm. And finally, the name of the village, Oldfields, where she plans to settle, calls up both the past and rural virtues.

In between her long works Sarah worked consistently at shorter pieces. Between 1878 and 1884 she frequently contributed to the two-column anonymous "Contributor's Club" department of the *Atlantic*. This section—founded by Howells for "opinion on events, manners, and letters which otherwise goes unuttered in print"—resembled the personal essays in Addison and Steele's *Tatler* and *Spectator*. Some of Sarah's contributions (identified by Professor Cary) include character sketches and comments on books, decorating, and nature. "Tree Planting" (October 1883) advises New England villagers to plant white birches, poplars, and mountain ashes in preference to maples and horse chestnuts as shade trees, and "The Colour Cure" (March 1882) explores the connection between colors and moods, an article that Sarah told Whittier made Annie Fields laugh "a good deal."

It is a tribute to Sarah's powers of concentration and to her dedication to her profession that she was able to write so much while shuttling between South Berwick, Manchester-by-the-Sea, and 148 Charles Street, making frequent visits to friends and relatives in other places, and receiving visitors frequently as well. Credit must also be given to her sister Mary and to her mother, who freed her from household duties in order to give her time to write at home, and to Annie Fields, whose hospitable, well-run households afforded the leisure she needed for her work.

The Charles Street house was not particularly convenient to entertain in, but this fact was of no significance to guests charmed by the stimulating talk and entertainment. The front door opened onto a reception room with dark-blue velvet furnishings and a gray rug. Flowers and paintings caught the eye of the guest who waited there; beyond was a large dining room with windows that looked out over a shady garden running down to the river. A thickly carpeted stairway led to the drawing room, which ran the length of the house. The kitchen was in the basement and the guest rooms on the third and fourth floors.

The long drawing room with its side alcoves was the heart of the house. The windows facing on Charles Street were thickly curtained, but the back windows opened out onto the deep garden and a view of the Charles River. Bookcases extended to the ceiling and a moss green carpet covered the floor. Priceless literary and art treasures filled every nook and cranny: manuscript cases held the original manuscripts of books written by famous authors, and portraits, busts, and framed autographed pictures filled the room. Henry James called 148 Charles Street a "waterside museum." Its riches included a charcoal sketch by William Hunt, a founding member of the Pre-Raphaelite Brotherhood; and a portrait of Alexander Pope painted by Thomas Hudson, a famous English portrait painter of the eighteenth century. Also on display were a volume of Pope that had been owned by Lincoln, a rare Blake, and (under glass) a lock of Keats's hair, which had been given to Annie Fields by the artist Joseph Severn. Beside it was a drawing of Keats done by Severn, who had been with

Keats when he died. Over a sofa hung a portrait of a youthful Dickens, while upstairs in one of the bedrooms was a self-portrait made by Thackeray during a visit to the Fieldses. It was a place, Willa Cather said, where the past lived on, where it was protected and cherished and given "sanctuary from the noisy push of the present."

In this sanctuary Annie's friends became Sarah's friends. Here James Russell Lowell read them a poem he had just finished and promised to give them the manuscript. And here Matthew Arnold sat by the fire one cold night reading "The Scholar Gypsy" to them. The Thomas Bailey Aldriches, who lived nearby on Beacon Hill, were frequent guests. Aldrich and Sarah, who were on familiar, bantering terms, often referred to the dignified residence as "148 Charley Street."

Saturday afternoons were the established time for receiving callers, but a famous stream of visitors also enjoyed breakfasts, luncheons, teas, and dinners, which might be followed with readings from Shakespeare, Milton, or Donne or by stimulating conversations about any topic under the sun. If Charles Eliot Norton was a guest, discussion might turn to the humanities or to the state of education. When Governor and Mrs. William Claflin were present, Massachusetts politics dominated the conversation. Annie faithfully recorded in her journal the quips and cranks of her illustrious guests—noting, for example, that when the "autocrat of the breakfast table," Dr. Oliver Wendell Holmes, found himself in the company of actors, even such a famous one as Joseph Jefferson, he addressed them condescendingly as "you gentlemen of the stage."

The best thing about 148 Charles Street for Sarah was not the constant stream of illustrious guests or the quietly elegant surroundings—although she relished these—but Annie herself, who possessed an incredibly rich store of memories. What tales she could tell of the long stays of Dickens when he was a young man eager to arrange skits and games with his good friend James Fields! And of Ralph Waldo Emerson, who refused to believe that Dickens was a sincere person, insisting that he had "too much talent for his genius." And of talking with Leigh Hunt about "poor Shelley." And of staying with the Brownings in Italy and one day meeting the Brownings's son, Pen, who complained he was tired of riding in the city. When Annie suggested he ride in the country, Pen replied that he couldn't do that since he and his pony were "one of the sights of Rome, you know."

As much as she loved the past, Annie was always eager to entertain new people and new ideas, and much as she cherished the friendships of the older writers and artists she and her husband had known, she was interested in new artists and new forms of art. Sarah's presence at 148 Charles Street came to be accepted and expected among Annie's friends, and invitations included both women just as letters to one invariably included messages and good wishes to the other. On December 31, 1884, Whittier wrote a note to "My dear friends Annie Fields and Sarah Jewett" to wish them a happy New Year and to thank them for their friendship, telling them, "You have done more than you can ever know to make my past year happy."

If she had set out to search for an ideal second home, Sarah could hardly have found a more agreeable haven than the hospitable Georgian home at 148 Charles Street that Henry James declared was "addicted to the cultivation of talk and wit."

Theodore Herman Jewett (Sarah's father)

Caroline Perry Jewett
(Sarah's mother)

Sarah Orne Jewett in the backyard of her neighbors,
the Neallys, Portland Street, South Berwick, Maine

Sarah and Mary Jewett

Carrie Eastman and son Theodore
(Stubby) around 1880

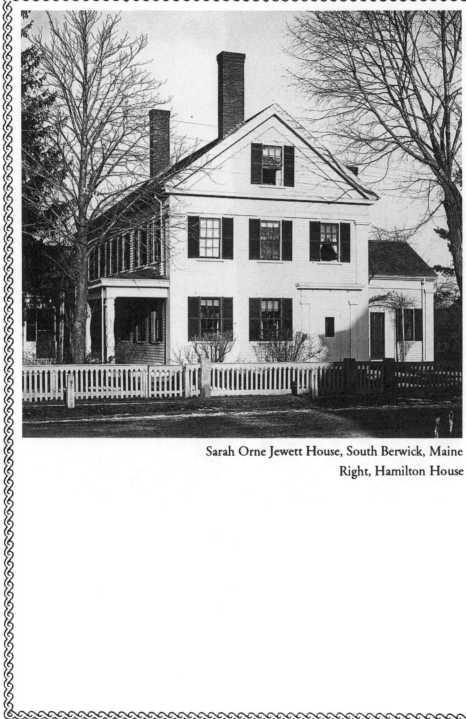

Sarah Orne Jewett House, South Berwick, Maine
Right, Hamilton House

Right, Sarah's writing desk, upstairs hall, Jewett home.
Below, Front hall, Jewett home, South Berwick

Sarah Orne Jewett in her early forties wearing crystal
lavalier given to her by Sarah Wyman Whitman and
admired by Tennyson.

Sarah's room, South Berwick (note portrait of Annie Fields on fireplace mantel)

Annie Adams Fields

Sarah Orne Jewett

The Drawing Room at 148 Charles Street, Boston

Sarah (left) and Annie

Sarah Orne Jewett

Kate Douglas Wiggin
(Mrs. G.C. Riggs) author of
Rebecca of Sunnybrook Farm

Celia Thaxter in her beloved garden

Madame LeBlanc

Mrs. Humphrey Ward

Harriet Beecher Stowe

Sarah Orne Jewett in doorway of Jewett home, South Berwick

Sarah Orne Jewett, Litt.D. awarded by Bowdoin College, 1901

◆

CHAPTER SEVEN

"A White Heron" and Other Tales

S ARAH'S THIRD NOVEL, *A Marsh Island* (1885), appeared a year after publication of *A Country Doctor*. Although the setting is as integral to the story as Thomas Hardy's Egdon Heath is to *The Return of the Native*, Sarah as usual was reluctant to be pinned down about her location. It was, she told a questioner, somewhere within the borders of Essex, and she declared, "Even I have never succeeded in finding the exact place!" Perhaps, she said, it was noticing an island farm from a train window in the coastal area of salt marshes between Newburyport and Manchester that first gave her a "hint of the book."

Whittier had been born on a farm in Haverhill, in Essex County, and he encouraged Sarah when she wrote to him that she was thinking about doing a "longish story" set in that general area. In the fall of 1883 she told the Quaker poet that the story was well begun in her head although she hadn't made the "first scratch" on a sheet of paper. She must have worked on the novel concurrently with *A Country Doctor*, since it was serialized in the *Atlantic* beginning with the January 1885 issue. Later that year Houghton Mifflin published it as a book.

Sarah's favorite motif of urban versus rural values runs

through *A Marsh Island*. This theme is expressed chiefly through a love triangle involving a dilettante landscape painter, the daughter of the farm family he boards with for the summer, and her faithful lover, a local metalworker-farmer. The landscape painter in the story faces the same problem Sarah faced: he loves nature and rural life but finds it limits his artistic ambitions and chances for professional development. His decision to return to the city parallels Sarah's own decision to spend a major share of her time in the intellectually stimulating environment of Boston.

Even critics who found the characters in *A Marsh Island* dull consistently praised it for the descriptions of the farm and the landscape and for the details of the daily life of the farmers as they harvest the salt hay and get it to market, gather apples and make cider, ritualistically sun their lard pots and stone jars, and attend Sunday evening socials.

Like Marjorie Kinnan Rawlings in the twentieth century, Sarah used her village neighbors and area natives in her best writing, and like Marjorie, who was emotionally bound to the Florida setting and people she depicted, she loved and identified with the Maine settings and people she described. Both writers preserve a time and a place and a people on the edge of inexorable change under the pressure of the modern world.

Literary World called *A Marsh Island* a "sweet and fragrant tale...full of sylvan loveliness." And *Cottage Hearth* described it as an "exquisite water-color." The book produced a "drowsy effect" on the *Critic*'s critic, but the reviewer for *Harper's* called it "an idyl," and he, too, referred to the scenes in the novel as "water-color sketches." More recent critics have found much to like about *A Marsh Island*. In *Pioneers and Caretakers; A Study of 9 American Women Novelists*, Louis Auchincloss calls the book "a charming, concentrated, well-balanced little novel," and says it is "all as it should be for the kind of story it is," but he also points out that it has a "slight" theme for a novel. After complaining of "lack of

psychological motivation" and "insufficiency of plot," Richard
Cary (*Sarah Orne Jewett*) comments that Sarah has achieved
a "sense of epic" in the lives of her farm folk, who "blend
into the soil and derive from it the strength and wisdom of
eternal evolution." Arthur Hobson Quinn (*American Fiction*)
sums up the essence of *A Marsh Island* when he says it is a
"prose poem of earth and water, but it is not a great novel."

The spring of 1885 saw the beginnings of a new friendship—one of the most richly satisfying of Sarah's life—with
a Frenchwoman, Madame Marie Thérèse Blanc. This friendship existed solely through correspondence for some eight
years before they finally met in Paris. Their acquaintance
came about through a review by Madame Blanc of Sarah's
A Country Doctor in *Revue des Deux Mondes* (February 1,
1885). Intrigued by Sarah's portrayal of a young woman's
struggle to be accepted as a doctor, Madame Blanc began her
review with a long exposition on women's emancipation. She
went on to include an analysis of *Deephaven* and three of
the collections of Sarah's short stories and sketches in addition to *A Country Doctor.*

The long essay-review is a perceptive examination of Sarah's
writing virtues—her ability to evoke Maine people and landscape and her "discernment full of benevolence"—and of her
shortcomings as a writer: a lack of inventiveness, the static
quality of her plots, and a tendency to digress. Although
Madame Blanc placed Sarah beneath George Eliot on the
writers' totem, saying that George Eliot possessed "all the gifts
of genius" while Sarah had only "the gentle seduction of
talent," she praised her highly as a pastoral essayist.

Pleased by this notice in France's leading literary periodical and impressed by the insight of the reviewer (who correctly
surmised the closeness of Sarah and her father), Sarah wrote
a note of appreciation to the author of the review, which was
signed M. Th. Bentzon, thanking "him" for "his" keen insight and understanding of her work. She was pleased to learn,

upon receiving Madam Blanc's reply, that the sympathetic reviewer was a woman.

Marie Thérèse Blanc's education and experience were unusual for a Frenchwoman in the nineteenth century and so were her intellectual pursuits and her personality. Under an English governess she had read Washington Irving at an early age and become fascinated with America. She was married at sixteen to a man chosen by her father and divorced at the age of nineteen, left with an infant to support. She turned to writing to earn an income, and with the encouragement of her friend George Sand, she began to publish fiction, essays, biographical sketches, and literary criticism. She also did translations, including such prominent American authors as Bret Harte, Thomas Bailey Aldrich, Sidney Lanier, Hamlin Garland, Thomas Nelson Page, and George Washington Cable. Blanc's interest in American local colorists and in women's rights made Sarah Orne Jewett doubly intriguing to her.

Although Madame Blanc was a pioneer in equal rights for women, she was also a realist and recognized that there was a prejudice against women writers—especially those who expressed strong opinions—among editors and the reading public in general. Accordingly she used her mother's maiden name, Thérèse Bentzon, shortened to Th. Bentzon, as her pen name. And it was this by-line that had led Sarah to think a man had written the review of her work. They soon discovered they had much in common, including a reverential love of the past and of nature, in addition to their literary interests. This was the beginning of a correspondence from which evolved a friendship that Madame Blanc called one of the "dearest affections of my life." Along with their letters, they exchanged pictures and looked forward eagerly to the time they could come face to face.

Madam Blanc's review had the effect of enlarging and enhancing Sarah Orne Jewett's reputation, and her translations of Sarah's work, beginning with "A Little Traveler," seven

months following the review, made it known to readers other
than her American-British followers. Over the years Sarah
would reciprocate by introducing Madame Blanc's work to
American editors and promoting it in every way she could.
Another result of the friendship was to increase Sarah's appreciation and study of George Sand's novels. Sand, who died
in 1876, wrote a series of romantic tales portraying the struggle
of women against the constraints of marriage and social
restrictions and another series portraying the idyllic quality
of country life, themes dear to Sarah's heart.

When Sarah wrote a story she feared was too romantic
to interest her editors, she asked Annie Fields, "What shall
I do with my 'White Heron' now she is written? She isn't a
very good magazine story, but I love her, and I mean to keep
her for the beginning of my next book."

Ironically the story Sarah didn't know what to do with
became her most popular short work. When it was published, along with eight other stories in a collection titled *A
White Heron and Other Stories*, the reviewer of *The Overland
Monthly* (October 1886) perceptively called it a "tiny classic."
It has been anthologized numerous times, translated into several languages—including Japanese, French, and Spanish—
and has been made into a film by the Learning Corporation
of America (1978). The story is a rich source for scholars, who
continue to mine it for its wealth of symbolism and allegory,
striking imagery, and autobiographical elements. Recently,
feminist criticism has tended to explore sexual connotations
and symbolism to a degree that probably would have amazed
Sarah.

The heroine of "A White Heron" is nine-year-old Sylvia,
who lives with her grandmother on an isolated farm deep
in the Maine woods. Formerly a city child, Sylvia has made
friends with the animals and trees and birds and, like Wordsworth, has become one with nature. Her grandmother says
"the wild creaturs counts her one o' themselves." One day a

charming young ornithologist comes into her world looking for a rare white heron (or snowy egret), which he plans to kill and stuff as a trophy. Sylvia is tempted to find the bird for him, not only because of his offer of a ten-dollar reward but also because she has fallen under the spell of his kindness and sympathy. During a day spent with him in the woods, he tells her many things about birds and their habits and gives her a jackknife, which she considers a great treasure. Although she doesn't like his gun or understand why he kills the birds he seems to like so much, she watches him with increasing admiration, and "the woman's heart, asleep in the child, was vaguely thrilled by a dream of love."

Early the next morning she climbs a tall pine tree to look for the heron's nest. The climb is dangerous and difficult, but having arrived at the top, trembling and triumphant, she feels as if she too could swoop and soar into the clouds like the hawks around her. Looking down, she sees the white heron float up from a dead hemlock like a feather on the breeze. Together they watch the golden dawn. She climbs down, eager to tell the young man about the nest in the dead hemlock, but when she remembers what she and the heron have experienced together, she cannot speak: "she cannot tell the heron's secret and give its life away."

Sarah would have known the snowy heron, as Sylvia did, to be a rare bird. She would also have been aware of the insatiable appetite of milliners for its feathers and the fashionable hobby among bird fanciers and scientists of gathering specimens. Late twentieth-century ecologists have pointed to "A White Heron" as one of the earliest stories with a theme of conservation and praised the insight of the author, who recognized that as the incursions of civilization destroyed the American frontier, certain species of birds were threatened with extinction.

From a feminist critical perspective, Sylvia's rejection of the temptation to please the young man who attracts her may be seen as a rejection of material and fleshly pleasures because of the need to be true to her own nature, which is inextricably tied to the nature around her. In sacrificing the heron, she would have sacrificed her own integrity.

Madame Blanc was one of the first to discuss naturalism in "A White Heron," in a laudatory essay in the *Revue des Deux Mondes* (September 1887). New England writer Mary E. Wilkins wrote to Sarah to say that she herself had never written anything as good as "A White Heron," which she compared to Tolstoy's "Two Deaths" in its appeal. *Literary World* (November 1886) called it the "purest and tenderest, the most idyllic of all Miss Jewett's works." And most critics chose the title story as being the best in the collection. *Harper's* (February 1887), however, termed three of the other stories in the group—"The Dulham Ladies," "Martha and Mary," and "Marsh Rosemary"—"exquisitely good."

Of the three, "The Dulham Ladies" has proved to be the most enduring. It is reminiscent of the humorous social satire of Elizabeth Gaskell's *Cranford*. Sarah used names with satirical Dickensian suggestiveness, and among the more exciting events in the small village of Dulham is the weekly sewing society meeting. The sisters Dobin are distressed when newcomers address them as "Dobbin" and explain (to no avail) that the name has one *b* and should be pronounced "Do-bin," adding that it probably evolved from the French *"D'Aubigne."* The sisters are extremely proud of their pedigree, which includes Greenaples and Hightrees of Boston, and of the fact that their mother had taken tea with Governor Clovenfoot on Beacon Street in company with an English lord (who was wearing the blue ribbon of the Knights of the Garter.) They are willing to share this brilliant experience of their forebear and to entertain the ladies of the sewing society with tales of their antecedants but are increasingly dismayed to find their precious anecdotes interrupted and ignored.

Realizing they may be a bit behind times, the sisters Dobin decide to modernize themselves and replenish their thinning locks by acquiring "frisettes," hairpieces to wear over their rising foreheads. They are outrageously conned and flattered by a cynical shopkeeper who foists off on the innocents two large and unbecoming hairpieces that have long been out of fashion. The younger townspeople are much amused over this display of foolish vanity, while the sisters' aging contemporaries, even though dismayed, are more compassionate in their reaction. Both attitudes are lost on the oblivious Dobin sisters, who are well pleased with themselves, feeling they have done their duty to society by observing the fashions of the day. Richard Cary considered this much-anthologized story one of Sarah's best. "For skill of organization, subtlety of characterization, and sensitivity to ethos," he said, "this story must be rated among Miss Jewett's truly memorable accomplishments."

Since his wife's death, Uncle William Jewett, a fond, indulgent uncle to the girls, had lived in the big house next door to Sarah, Mary, and their mother. He had long ago given up the W. I. store, which catered to the shipping trade, and he now dabbled in banking and real estate in addition to managing a drugstore. In 1886 Sarah wrote to Annie that she was worried about her Uncle William, whose health had been failing for some time. She wanted to hold time back and keep the two houses just as they were when she was a child, she told Annie. And she described a pleasant scene of his sitting by in the summer kitchen while the women of the family engaged in making currant wine. He talked cheerfully about what he meant to do next year to make more wine, but Sarah predicted sadly, "Poor hopeful human nature. It seems so utterly improbable that he will be here at all next year." She proved to be right—William Jewett died in 1887.

Happily for Sarah the two houses were kept as family homes. She and her mother and Mary moved into the big house, and Sister Carrie and her husband, Ned Eastman, and their son, Stubby (Theodore Jewett Eastman), took the house next door. Sarah delighted in having her nephew to play with, buy presents for, and encourage in his reading. She told Annie that just before the Fourth of July she had set Stubby and some of his friends to pulling weeds out of the grass at fifteen cents a hundred. By dinner (noon) they had gotten sixty-five cents out of her. On the Fourth, she enjoyed setting off firecrackers with the boys.

At this time some physical changes were made in the big house: dormers were added to the roof and the back garden was increased in size with trellises and flagstone walks. John Tucker did much of the heavy outside work, but both Mary and Sarah enjoyed working in the garden. Box hedge enclosed the garden, which was filled with petunias, larkspur, lilies, mignonette, hollyhocks, roses, peonies, asters, and flowering currant and snowberry bushes. The trellised arborway covered with honeysuckle was a pleasant place to have breakfast or tea. The yard became a showplace of South Berwick, and for its constant maintenance Mary undoubtedly gets most of the credit.

A White Heron and Other Stories is dedicated to "my dear sister Mary." Sarah frequently expressed her appreciation of Mary's efficient management of family business affairs, especially after their mother's health began to decline. Mary's writing was restricted mostly to business and personal letters, but she was also a voracious reader, and she and Sarah enjoyed discussing books. When Sarah and Mary were separated, they kept in close touch through daily letters keeping up this habit of constant correspondence, even after the telephone was available to them. Occasionally Sarah could persuade Mary to come to Boston or to Manchester with her, and when Mary became engrossed in her "works and ways," Sarah reminded her that even the president could take time to "go a-fishing."

With each publication Sarah's recognition grew, and her readers became eager to know more about her. In *Acts and Anecdotes of Authors* Charles Barrows reported that Miss

Jewett worked on her fiction in the afternoons and evenings and that her favorite recreation was horseback riding, which she recommended to women as a "most healthful and refreshing exercise." The next best thing, she told her interviewer, was a brisk walk. Other reporters inquired about her working habits. She told them that she wrote sporadically, sometimes turning out a 6,000- to 7,000-word sketch in a day and sometimes not writing at all for weeks except for letters and memoranda, although she was always thinking about her work.

She told Annie that one morning at church when she was "dreadfully bored" with the sermon, she had made up a "first rate story" in her head. Another time a hint from Whittier sparked the idea for the story "The Courting of Sister Wisby," which appeared in the *Atlantic Monthly* for May 1887. The power of her unconscious mind surprised her, and she marveled at how a glimpse of a place from a train window or of a person on a railroad platform could plant the germ of an idea that would incubate and eventually spring forth practically full-blown. "Good heavens!" she wrote Annie. "What a wonderful kind of chemistry it is that evolves all the details of a story and writes them presently in one flash of time!" For two weeks, she explained, she had been noticing certain things and having hints of character and suddenly one day the plan of the story came into her mind; in half an hour she had put all "the little words and ways into their places" and could read it off to herself like print. "Who does it?" she asked in wonder. "For I grow more and more sure that I don't!"

Although she became quite adept in marketing her work, it was never something she enjoyed, and once she told Annie that the business side of writing seemed "very noxious" to her. "I wonder if in heaven our best thoughts—poet's thoughts, especially—will not be flowers, somehow or some sort of beautiful live things that stand about and grow, and don't have to be chaffered over and bought and sold," she said.

Her stories were appearing regularly in the most prestigious magazines in America—the *Atlantic, Harper's,* and the *Century.* These magazines were carefully crafted, and a variety of fancy printing styles and elaborate illustrations enhanced the presentation of the stories.

The more she succeeded, the more she determined to improve, continuing to read widely in the classics and among contemporary writers. She was particularly attracted to Flaubert, who works she read in the original. Flaubert's success in *Madame Bovary* in making interesting the trivial commonplaces of the lives of simple, country people confirmed her inclination to follow that path. Over her desk at South Berwick she fastened two bits of advice from the French author. The first, to "*Écrire la vie ordinaire comme on ecrit l'histoire*" (to write the life of ordinary people as if one were writing history), had been her aim from the beginning of her career. And the second, also: "*C'est ne pas de faire rire, ni de faire pleurer, ni de vous mettre a fureur, mais d'agir a la façon de la nature, c'est a dire de faire rever*" (Not to make one's readers laugh or cry or become angry but, like nature, to make them dream). She attributed it to her French blood that she nibbled all around her stories "like a mouse," paring them to their essence.

A natural corollary to her success was that young (and old) writers asked her for advice, and if she felt they were serious about their work, she was generous in responding to their appeals. First, she told them, one must know what good work is before one can do good work of one's own. The suggestion that they read good stories over and over many times to understand why they are good was one she followed herself, with French and Russian storytellers as well as with English and American writers. Before sending their efforts out into the world, she urged them, they should study different magazines to learn their "personalities" and so better understand their needs. With slight variations, she frequently repeated her father's advice on not writing *about* people and things but telling them "just as they are." The most important thing she told aspiring writers was to *work* at their art, but she added that a divine spark was necessary for excellence: "the great messages and discoveries of literature come to us—they *write* us, and we do not control them in a certain sense," she admitted.

Although Sarah usually tried to avoid becoming involved in large public affairs, she occasionally was drawn into a cause. In the spring of 1887 she served as secretary for a committee to arrange an Authors' Reading in the Boston Museum to raise funds for a Longfellow Memorial and discovered the hazards involved in dealing with a group of writers. One of the authors she corresponded with was Mark Twain, who agreed to appear on the program if he could be first, as he had to catch a train to New Haven for another performance that same day. His reading was "English as She Is Taught," which later appeared in the *Century*.

Whittier, always shy about appearing in public, declined to perform but made a fifty-dollar contribution. Charles Eliot Norton acted as chairman for the program, which included (in addition to Mark Twain) Julia Ward Howe, Oliver Wendell Holmes, James Russell Lowell, Thomas Bailey Aldrich, William Dean Howells, and Edward Everett Hale. It was a memorable occasion and a huge success, with every seat in the museum filled, many standees, and a crowd that had to be turned away.

That same spring Sarah solicited Whittier to head a subscription that was being gotten up to build a house for Walt Whitman, who at sixty-seven was in poor health following a paralytic stroke. Whittier, who was not enamored of Whitman's *Leaves of Grass*, grumpily replied that he had helped when money was collected to buy Whitman a horse and carriage, "which is more than I ever had." He agreed, however, to add a "mite" to the collection, although he declined to have his name associated with it.

One day in 1886 Sarah wrote to Annie that she could hardly find room to write her letters as her table was so over-spread with papers for her current project. She was hard at work on a history of the Normans for G. P. Putnam's series "The Story of the Nations" for young readers. She enjoyed the research—reading history and myths and literature connected with the Vikings and the Normans. She relied heavily on Edward Augustus Freeman's gigantic five-volume *History of the Norman Conquest* and corresponded with Professor Freeman (at Oxford) about problems she encountered. The writing, so different from anything she had done, was not easy, but by November 1886 it was finished and she was dividing her time between indexing the book and dressmaking. *The Story of the Normans: Told Chiefly in Relation to Their Conquest of England*, published in 1887, is dedicated to Sarah's maternal grandfather, Dr. William Perry, of Exeter, then in his ninety-ninth year.

The Story of the Normans, which was popular in the United States and in England, ran to several editions in both countries and garnered some favorable reviews. The New Orleans *Daily Picayune* praised its "depth, comprehension and eloquence" in describing the "romantic and thrilling career of the Normans." And *Dial* called it a "narrative of blended symmetry and strength." The reviewer referred to the "quiet, earnest spirit, the scrupulous veracity, the careful construction, the finished style," concluding that it was "history with the charm of romance."

Modern reviews have not been as kind in their appraisals, criticizing particularly the author's blending of fact and legend and her insistence that the Normans possessed a superiority of character over the Saxons, whom they conquered. The original Northmen (Scandinavians) had better laws and government, she said, and better history, poetry, and social customs than did the Anglo-Saxons and Franks. And she declared that after the Vikings settled in the north of France and turned their energy to "better channels," they inspired "every new growth of the religion, language or manners, with their own splendid vitality."

Following the conquest of England, Sarah concluded, "much that has been best in English national life" has come from the Norman elements in it rather than the Saxon. However (and this is sometimes overlooked by critics) she pointed out the advantage of the mixture:

> It is the Norman graft upon the sturdy old Saxon tree that has borne best fruit among the nations— that has made the England of history, the England of great scholars and soldiers and sailors, the England of great men and women, of books and ships and gardens and pictures and songs!

She wrote that the "brighter, fiercer, more enthusiastic, and visionary nature" of the Normans mingled with the "stolid, dogged, prudent and resolute" nature of the Anglo-Saxons to create the English character. And it was this heritage, she said, that the English colonizers brought to America. In individual instances where the two did not mix, she claimed, it was easy to distinguish Norman from Saxon heritage.

In several of her subsequent stories she emphasized this theory. For example, in "The King of Folly Island" the main character is the son and heir of "the Old Vikings who had sailed that stormy coast and discovered its harborage and its vines five hundred years before Columbus was born in Italy." And in "A War Debt" the Bellamys' granddaughter appears to the protagonist, Tom, as "the newer and finer Norman among Saxons. She alone seemed to have that inheritance of swiftness of mind, of sureness of training." Tom himself is described as "straight and trim, like a Frenchman."

The Story of the Normans concludes: "Today the Northman, the Norman, and the Englishman, and a young nation on this western shore of the Atlantic are all kindred who, possessing a rich inheritance, should own the closest of kindred ties." But Sarah was well aware that all Americans did not share her Anglophilism. In *Country By-Ways* she had remarked that if an elderly New England lady were "suddenly dropped into the midst of provincial English society, she would be quite at home." But Sarah added that "west of the Hudson River that same lady would be lucky if she did not find herself behind the times, and almost a stranger and a foreigner."

In her masterpiece *The Country of the Pointed Firs*, however, Sarah shows that she remained a Francophile at heart. Of the most admirable character in the novel she says, "Mrs. Blackett was plainly of French descent, in both her appearance and her charming gifts, but this is not surprising when one has learned how large a proportion of the early settlers on this northern coast of New England were of Huguenot blood, and that it is the Norman Englishman, not the Saxon, who goes adventuring to a new world." And Mrs. Blackett's daughter, Mrs. Todd, tells the narrator, "They used to say in old times that our family came of very high folks in France."

In the late winter of 1888 Whittier and Sarah and Annie commiserated on various illnesses. Whittier and Sarah suffered recurrent bouts of painful and sometimes crippling rheumatism, and that particular February Whittier was incapacitated by neuralgia and Sarah by a bad cold. Sarah relayed a prescription sent to Whittier by Annie: a tablespoonful of rum and four lumps of sugar mixed into a glass of milk, to be drunk at eleven A.M. and ten P.M.

Annie's illness may have been flu. They enjoyed having a peat fire in Annie's room, and one evening James Russell Lowell came to sit with them and read a poem he had written for the *Atlantic* about Turner's painting of an old ship, "Turner's Old Temeraire." Sarah's description of Lowell reading to Annie delighted Whittier, who called it "a convalescent princess with her minstrel in attendance!" To complete their convalescences the two women decided to go to Florida.

Unlike Whittier, who consistently resisted the urgings of friends to visit in the South during the rigors of Northern winters, Sarah and Annie made several trips to resorts, including St. Augustine, where they stayed at the fashionable Hotel Ponce de Leon. Sarah also visited such popular spas as Poland Springs, Maine, and Hot Springs, Virginia, in search of relief from the arthritis that particularly affected her back and legs.

Every two or three years, during the last two decades of the nineteenth century, Houghton Mifflin published a collection of Sarah's short stories, and the offering for 1888 was *The King of Folly Island and Other People*. In the most skillfully told story in the collection, a simple tale called "Miss Tempy's Watchers," which is certainly one of Sarah's most static, two of Miss Tempy Dent's friends sit through the night in her kitchen, keeping a wake following her death. They pass the long hours knitting, eating a supper of tea and bread and butter with some of Miss Tempy's quince preserves, and discussing their dead friend. Through their revealing anecdotes the reader learns that the dead woman was sensitive, generous, and caring, and that her spiritual presence seems to pervade the house. In the end this presence has the effect of dissolving the differences that had separated the two watchers and causes each of them to resolve to live in the future with more charity.

When George Washington Cable read *The King of Folly Island*, he picked out the story "The Courting of Sister Wisby" for special praise. He told Sarah that it was "an exquisitely exact picture," adding, "It is the very snow-water of New England." And his letter closed with thanks "and a prayer" to her to write more.

The humorous tale "Law Lane" pleased many readers, with its Romeo and Juliet love story and Montague-Capulet feud, which is resolved by the good humor and ingenuity of Mrs. Powder, one of Sarah's lovable despots.

Other stories in the collection charmed or disenchanted reviewers according to their individual temperaments. The anonymous review in the *Epoch* fairly well summed up the general attitude: the critic complained that Sarah's writing lacked "that completeness of form and purpose that the ideal short story possesses." He added, however, that her characters and style were charming and her "keen and loving observation of nature and her minutest facts" praiseworthy. *The King of Folly Island* is dedicated to Whittier "With grateful affection."

Between long writing spells Sarah played with her friends. Alice Longfellow, a favorite of both Annie's and Sarah's, went with them and other Cambridge friends to enjoy winter sports in the White Mountains, not far from South Berwick. Sarah reported to Whittier that they had "a royal good time." They walked on the four feet of snow, through the firs and birches and beeches, on snowshoes and played like children in the snow, and she enjoyed taking Annie tobogganing, "for she never had coasted down a hill in her life, poor little town-y!"

In July 1889, Sarah accepted an invitation by Alice Long-fellow to visit Mouse Island in Boothbay Harbor. The wooded island had a mineral spring and Sarah, who found water cures helpful in relieving the pain of her arthritis, was glad to visit the rustic island with her friend. Much as she loved sports, Sarah found it hard to keep up with Alice, who was an ardent sportswoman. "She never gives in except at sailing in the sun," Sarah reported to Annie. "At rowing she never quails, and though I am tough I do sometimes ship my oars." Along with the rowing and sailing Sarah soaked in the atmosphere of the region: the fir balsams, spreading pastures, tiny inlets, and vast expanse of sea. It was a setting she would remember and return to again—and six years later make good use of in the work that would prove to be her masterpiece.

◆

CHAPTER EIGHT

"To know the world..."

ER FRIENDSHIP WITH the writer Celia Thaxter grew more dear to Sarah with the passing years. Like Sarah, Celia was deeply moved by nature and frequently anthropomorphized birds in her poems for children. She portrayed the kingfisher as mannish and haughty and described the "burgomaster gull" as a tyrant. For Celia nature was the source of her creativity and her greatest solace during an often difficult life. Her father, during her early years, kept the lighthouse on White Island, a tiny, rocky bit of land constantly battered by the Atlantic Ocean.

When Celia was twelve her father bought Hog Island, the largest of the Isles of Shoals, about nine miles off the coast of Portsmouth, New Hampshire. He renamed it Appledore and built a summer resort hotel there, which opened in 1848 and quickly became a favorite retreat for many well-known people in the art world. Among the distinguished frequent summer guests were Nathanial Hawthorne, Oliver Wendell Holmes, Harriet Beecher Stowe, James Whitcomb Riley, Ralph Waldo Emerson, Edwin Booth, Ole Bull, the violinist, and Annie and James T. Fields. Among the famous painters who visited often were William Morris Hunt and Childe Hassam, destined to become America's foremost Impressionist painter. Hassam would later do the pictures and illuminations for Celia's best-known book, *An Island Garden*.

At sixteen Celia married Levi Thaxter, her father's partner, who was also her tutor. Thaxter was a Harvard graduate but never seemed to find an occupation that suited him, although he tried teaching and gave successful public readings of Robert Browning's poetry. After an accident in which he nearly drowned, he preferred to live on the mainland. Celia returned to Appledore each summer season to help her parents and brothers run the hotel. The Thaxters had three sons, and in the 1870s, when Levi Thaxter's health began to fail, he moved to Florida with the two younger children. Celia kept with her Karl, the oldest son, who was mentally disturbed.

Celia had a cottage on Appledore for her own, and it was here that she created her famous garden. In the autumn, when she retreated to Portsmouth, she filled her windows with plants, and in April, she transported them to Appledore on the *Pinafore*, a small steam tug. With its decks filled with green leaves and blossoms, palms, and ferns and the sprouted seedlings carefully packed in baskets to keep them steady, the boat resembled a seaborne garden. Her cottage and glorious garden provided a haven for her many friends, including Sarah, Annie, and Whittier.

It was Whittier who pushed Celia into writing about her beloved islands. Impressed by her stories of the Shoals and the Shoalers and of the sea and the wind and shipwrecks, he gave her no peace until she wrote them down. "It is thy kismet," he told her. "Thee *must* do it!" Bowing to her fate, she wrote four essays for the *Atlantic*, which were then published as a book, *Among the Isles of Shoals*, to wide acclaim.

Celia wrote four sonnets on Beethoven, and the parlor of her cottage was often filled with his music, sometimes performed by internationally famous musicians. She enjoyed painting and sketching, as Sarah did, specializing in watercolors and in painting on china. The few remaining pieces of her work reveal exquisitely detailed birds, butterflies, shells, and flowers and grasses. She endowed flowers with human feelings and souls, again as Sarah did, and she wrote poems of praise and thanksgiving to them and to the birds that visited the Isles of Shoals. Her favorite bird, the sandpiper, inspired her most popular poems and gave her the nickname used by her family and friends. Her letters to Sarah (whom she addressed as Pinny or Owl) are often signed with a drawing of a sandpiper.

At 148 Charles Street, at the Jewett home in South Berwick, at Whittier's home in Amesbury, or in Celia's cottage on Appledore, Sarah, Annie, Whittier, and Celia were often together, and when they were absent from one another they reached out with long letters. "Does Sandpiper play with you, or has she married a ghost and therefore she cannot come?" Sarah asked Annie in a letter. The ghost referred to Celia's interest in psychic phenomena. For a time after her mother's death, Celia was overcome by inconsolable grief and explored avidly the possibility of communicating with the dead. Her absorption in mysticism grew until her faith in it was shattered by encounters with humbugs posing as mediums. Although Sarah was always more skeptical than Celia, she allowed herself to be drawn into dabbling in the popular pastime of fortune telling and enjoyed participating in chilling ghost-story sessions with her friends in the cozy parlor of the cottage on Appledore, while freezing winds rattled the windows.

Celia and Sarah discussed their writing and exchanged manuscripts for criticism. Both were enthusiastic pioneer conservationists, and the destruction of nature to satisfy the vanity and greed of human beings must have been a frequent topic of discussion between them. A year after the publication of *A White Heron and Other Stories*, Celia's essay condemning plume hunting, "Woman's Heartlessness" appeared in the *Audubon Magazine*. Sometime later the Pennsylvania Audubon Society reprinted it as a circular.

In 1890 Houghton Mifflin published three books by Sarah

Orne Jewett. The first, *Tales of New England*, consisted of eight stories from her previous collections. The second book, *Betty Leicester: A Story for Girls* (first published in install-ments in *St. Nicholas* as "A Bit of Color"), came to be con-sidered a classic in the children's literature of the nineteenth century. In the story Betty goes to stay with two kind but strait-laced aunts in Tideshead, a village very like South Ber-wick when Sarah was a teenager.

The fifteen-year-old heroine is patterned after Sarah her-self, and much that she says and thinks echoes the ideas recorded in Sarah's youthful diaries. Like Sarah, Betty has a worrisome conscience and wants to be good, but her in-dependent spirit rebels when the aunts treat her with typical Victorian moralizing. Betty, whose mother is dead, is close to her father and takes his teachings to heart just as Sarah did those of her father. Much that Dr. Jewett taught Sarah about human nature is evident in Betty's list of the principles she has absorbed from her father:

> Learn the right way to do things.
> Try to make yourself fit to live with other people.
> Remember every person stands in a different place from every other and so sees life from a different point of view.
> Remember nobody likes to be proved wrong.
> Be careful in what manner you say things to people that they do not want to hear.

Like her creator, Betty is fond of making good resolutions, finds it helpful to write them down, keeps notes on life in general, and thinks often and seriously about her responsi-bilities, but she also enjoys laughter and fun and being out of doors and feels a kinship with flowers and trees and animals. She is well trained in the proper manners for young women, but at times still likes to climb trees and fences. She has a talent for making friends and is always ready to enjoy whatever comes her way in the form of new experiences. The theme of the book is what Betty comes to realize: "that she herself must learn to throw herself heartily into her life just as it was." She also discovers happiness in trying to bring a bit of color into the gray lives of the elderly people of Tideshead.

Sarah told a young fan that the chapter called "Up Country" was her own favorite in the book. In this chapter Betty goes with Serena, one of her aunts' servants, to visit Serena's sister in another village some miles up country. As in Sarah's adult writing, there is authentic detailing of the local scenery and of the habits and speech of the individuals Betty encounters. The genuine goodness and humanity of Betty is seen in her ability to say and do exactly the right things to make the visit a happy one for the two old sisters and to enjoy herself in pleasing them.

An interesting sidelight to this chapter is that it contains the kernel of another story, "The Queen's Twin," which Sarah wrote ten years later and which became one of her most popular stories. Both Sarah and Betty idolized Queen Victoria, and Betty, who has witnessed Queen Victoria's Golden Jubilee, entertains the sisters with descriptions of the event. Betty denies being a "Britisher" but declares, "We're all English to start with, but with the glory of America added on." One of the sisters repeats a truism found in many of Sarah's stories: "Folks is folks... there ain't but a few kinds, neither, but they're put into all sorts of places, ain't they?"

The reviewer of *Cottage Hearth* found *Betty Leicester* worthy of a place beside *Little Women*. As usual, some critics complained of "very little plot," but even they found it "sweet and wholesome," "sunny and delightful," "genial," and "humorous." Sarah was especially pleased to receive a fan letter from Andrew Preston Peabody, minister, twice acting president of Harvard, editor of the *North American Review*, and prolific author. Dr. Peabody wrote that he, "a man of nearly fourscore," was impressed by her children's book.

Sarah dedicated *Betty Leicester* "With love to M. G. L.,

one of the first of Betty's friends." "M. G. L." was Mrs. James (Mary Greenwood) Lodge, who worked with Annie Fields in founding and operating the Associated Charities of Boston. Sarah nicknamed her "Marigold."

The popularity of *Betty Leicester* naturally made her editors eager to have more of the same sort, and Sarah did write one more book about Betty, a seasonal book, *Betty Leicester's English Christmas: A New Chapter of an Old Story*, published by Dodd, Mead in 1894.

The third book of Sarah's to appear in 1890, a collection of stories titled *Strangers and Wayfarers*, offered her readers a smorgasbord of themes and characters. Her deep sympathy for the problems of Irish immigrants to New England is shown in "The Luck of the Bogans." As Mike Bogan prepares to leave his native land, he carefully wraps a piece of Irish sod in his best Sunday handkerchief. Accompanied by his wife, Biddy Flaherty, and their son—"the luck of the Bogans"—Mike reaches America and opens a liquor store, which prospers. Ironically, the son eventually turns into a drunkard and is killed in a brawl in a bar. In a blind fury against fate, the agonized father destroys all the liquor bottles in his grogshop and smashes the liquor kegs.

Sarah's use of Irish dialect and her evocation of the flavor of the life of Irish immigrants is authentic, since the Irish workers in the Jewett households had always become friends of the family, and on her travels Sarah had carefully observed the Irish she met. She wrote several other stories about the Irish, but "The Luck of the Bogans," with its blending of humor and pathos, is probably the best.

Another story in this collection, "The Town Poor," reveals shady welfare practices. It may have been inspired by Annie Fields's experiences while performing charitable work. In the story two women friends decide to visit the "town poor," Ann and Mandanna Bray. Under the welfare system of the town, the destitute are placed in foster homes with the lowest bidders, who are then paid by the town to provide for their indigent guests. It is apparent to the visitors that the foster family that is supposed to be providing for the Bray sisters is virtually starving them, and they are distressed to find that the sisters live in circumstances so stringent that they have only one chair between the two of them. The visitors leave determined to force the town selectmen to correct the situation.

In "The Mistress of Sydenham Plantation" the relationship between the main characters is much like that between Hoke Coleburn and Mrs. Werthan in the 1988 play by Alfred Uhry, "Driving Miss Daisy." In Sarah's story, written one hundred years earlier, the former mistress of a plantation orders Peter, her one remaining servant, to take her on a tour of her estate, which has been turned into farms for former slaves. As the old servant faithfully goes through the mock inspection, Mistress Sydenham imagines that she sees her lost property and crumbling mansion as they were in the glory days of the past, for her mind, too, has been ravaged by the war and its aftershocks. The next day, Easter, Peter patiently helps his decrepit former mistress attend church. He has become the rock to which she can cling for survival amid the wreckage of her life.

In another story, "The White Rose Road," Sarah again sounds a lament so familiar in the late twentieth century. Pointing out that the once abundant salmon had nearly disappeared from her beloved Piscataqua River, she deplores the pollution caused by factories and sawmills. "Man has done his best to ruin the world he lives in," she grieves.

Although Sarah Orne Jewett and her contemporary writer of New England stories Mary Wilkins Freeman met only occasionally at literary gatherings, they exchanged letters highly appreciative of each other's talent. Literary critics insisted on calling them rivals and persisted in making comparisons. In a review of *Strangers and Wayfarers, Catholic World* (July 1891) said: "As a painter of New England life Miss Jewett is more subjective, more obviously reflective than her great rival in that field, Miss Wilkins." The reviewer added that although her stories lacked the "alertness" of those by Wilkins, her style was "charming." Horace Scudder in the *Atlantic Monthly* commented that both writers handled the New England dialect subtly, and he found "Miss Wilkins' humor more pungent, but Miss Jewett's more kindly and winning."

Strangers and Wayfarers is dedicated to "S. W., Painter of New England men and women, New England fields and shores." Sarah Wyman Whitman belonged to the talented coterie of friends that frequently gathered at 148 Charles Street. S.W., as her friends called her, was a high-spirited, emotional, devout, and multi-talented artist, specializing in designing stained-glass windows and painting. She did the cover decorations of several of Sarah's books, including *Strangers and Wayfarers*, and when Sarah decided to have a memorial window made for her father, her good friend Sarah Whitman was the artist she chose to design it.

Mrs. Jewett was a semi-invalid for the last ten years of her life. When her health began to fail more rapidly during the summer of 1890, Mary and Sarah stayed close to home, sharing in her care. Sarah remained in South Berwick during the winter of 1890–91, and her letters throughout the spring and summer refer to her mother's "serious illness." In September she told Horace Scudder that her mother's "weary illness still goes on." Between stints of looking after her mother and helping Mary with the household chores, Sarah worked on short stories and supervised the publication of a book for the centennial celebration of Berwick Academy. She also wrote the preface for the memorial booklet prepared for the occasion.

On August 12, 1891, James Russell Lowell died at Elmwood, the colonial house in Cambridge where Sarah had spent so many pleasant hours discussing books and writing with the famous poet, critic, and diplomat. In turn, Lowell had visited 148 Charles Street frequently, and it had been he who introduced Sarah to John Donne's poems, which she read with "perfect delight." Lowell liked to tease Sarah, mimicking her Maine accent and reminding her that the state of Maine was once merely a "deestrict" of Massachusetts. For Christmas 1890, Sarah had sent Lowell a rose-colored knife, which the poet in his thank-you note gallantly compared to the tempting roses in her cheeks.

In the spring of 1891, Sarah's publisher had asked Lowell to write a letter about Sarah's abilities as a writer to be used in connection with a collection of her stories that was going to be published in England. Lowell was seriously ill, and Sarah, thinking he had forgotten the request, did not mention it to him. But toward the end of April he wrote the letter and sent it to her with a note signed "Affectionately Yours." In the letter Lowell said of Sarah's stories, "Nothing more pleasingly characteristic of rural life in New England has been written. . . . They are properly idylls in prose." He praised her quiet pathos and subdued humor, saying she had wisely chosen to work within narrow limits, and he compared her to gem cutters and artists who made tiny woodcuts. Like these craftsmen, Lowell said, Sarah Orne Jewett made "small means suffice for great ends." Sarah was touched to learn that this letter for her was one of Lowell's last writing efforts.

The family hoped that the bright autumn weather would revive Mrs. Jewett's health, but on October 21, 1891, Caroline Frances Perry Jewett died, and the long, sad days and nights of watching were over. When she had traveled away from home to visit relatives and friends, Mrs. Jewett's letters to her daughters were filled with messages of loving concern for them, and Sarah tried to be a good daughter and always treated her mother with gentle kindness, but they did not share the close rapport she had had with her father. There is a hint of their relationship in a letter Sarah wrote to her "friend and playmate" Thomas Bailey Aldrich when his own mother died a few years later.

She knew how different this loss was, Sarah told him, from any other. "As long as one's mother lives the sense of being lovingly protected never fails, and one is always a child." Mentioning the strange sense of being alone in the world for the first time, she added that there follows a sense of having a larger life with the joining of both lives in one. "I never felt so near to my mother or kept such a sense of her love for me and mine for her as I have since she died," Sarah told Aldrich. "There are no bars of shyness or difference or inexpressiveness or carelessness; it seems as if I had never known my mother before."

At the time of Mrs. Jewett's death, Annie Fields, who came at once from Manchester, was a great source of comfort to the Jewett sisters. Among the many letters of condolence that poured in from their many friends was one from Whittier, who was himself in poor health and suffering from a bad cold. "In spirit I shall sit with you in your circle of mourning," he told Sarah. On December 17, 1891, Annie and Sarah went to Newburyport to help Whittier celebrate his birthday. Afterward he wrote to Annie, "The best thing on my birthday was to meet thee and our dear Sarah on the stairs, and the worst was that you went away so soon."

In February 1892, Annie and Sarah embarked on a second trip to Europe. They planned a long stay through the summer, exploring Italy, France, and England, taking the waters at spas, visiting European friends, and meeting up with American friends in various places. The voyage over was rough as their steamer, the *Werra*, pitched and rolled its way across the Atlantic. The first night out Sarah had a bad fall, suffering a blow on her head and two black eyes. But the ship's company was pleasant and Sarah finally got used to the pitching. Soon after they landed, news reached them that Sarah's brother-in-law, Ned Eastman, had died of peritonitis. Carrie selflessly wrote not of her own grief but of the distress she felt that the news might mar Sarah's trip.

In Venice the travelers met up with Mark Twain and his family and enjoyed the city, with its churches and mosaics and paintings, in their company. In a boat with red and orange and blue striped sails Sarah held the stern sheets as a breeze wafted them up the canal almost to the steps of the cathedral. After leisurely taking in the art and architecture and landscape of Italy, they moved on to France.

The highlight of the trip for Sarah was to be her first meeting with her longtime friend by correspondence, Madame Thérèse Blanc. When it came time to mount the stairs to Madame Blanc's apartment in Paris, Sarah's nerves failed her. "It is really taking a great risk to see so old a friend for the first time," she told Annie. "This dear and intimate friendship of ours may be in danger." But Annie kept Sarah from turning back, and they were ushered into Madame Blanc's salon, with its dainty white-and-gold Louis Seize furniture. Sarah found Madame Blanc "even more dear and kind and delightful" than she had expected from her letters. "There is no end to her friendliness," Sarah wrote to Alice Howe.

Madame Blanc entertained them, introduced them to her literary and aristocratic friends, and took them sightseeing around Paris and in the countryside. The French flowers (known and unknown) delighted Sarah as did the children, from whom she won smiles by a generous distribution of candy. Arriving at Chamonix at nightfall and seeing Mt. Blanc shining white in a full moon was one of their many unforgettable experiences under the French writer's guidance.

After settling into Madame Blanc's country home near Paris, they spent some weeks traveling to different places in France. Sarah particularly enjoyed their stay at Barbizon on the edge of the forest of Fontainebleau. In the daytime they explored the woods and after dinner they walked out on the plains and listed to the Angelus bell. Jean François Millet's own house was close to theirs, and the sound of the Angelus and the swish of a farmer's scythe cutting wheat made them look around expecting to see Millet's two figures with bent

heads. Their vine-covered old house opened onto a court-
yard that was also half farmyard, and Sarah was pleased to
find that "a nice piggy" lived in a little stone mansion close
by their gate. When it was time to travel on to England, it
was difficult to part with Madame Blanc, but their leave-
taking was cheered by her promise to come to stay at 148
Charles Street the next year and to visit New England with
them.

In London they spent eight hours one day listening to a
debate in the House of Commons, and they made the usual
tourist jaunts to Cambridge and Oxford. Matthew Arnold
had died three years earlier, but his family welcomed Annie
and Sarah and entertained them in the city and at their country homes. Sarah described to Sarah Whitman a delightful
day spent with Matthew Arnold's niece, Mrs. Humphrey
Ward. She was charmed with the writer, who at forty-one
was two years younger than Sarah. "She is brilliant and full
of charm, with a lovely simplicity and sincerity of manner,"
Sarah said. "I think of her with warmest affection." Sarah
reported to S.W. that they had watched one of the Wards'
young sons compete in a cricket match and enjoyed time in
the family's old-fashioned garden. Detecting Mrs. Ward's
inherited Arnold family sense of high purpose, Sarah correctly
predicted "Her life burns with a very fierce flame, and she
has not in the least done all that she can do."

On their way to Edinburgh Annie and Sarah stopped at
Whitby, where they visited several friends, including the du
Mauriers. George du Maurier, the grandfather of Daphne du
Maurier, had just published his first novel, *Peter Ibbetson*,
and was adding to the fame he had already acquired for his
graceful, satiric drawings in *Punch*. Sarah found him fascinating company. He showed them his drawings, sang old
French songs for them, and let Sarah romp with his fluffy
little terrier.

The highlight of their time in England was their visit with
Lord and Lady Tennyson at Aldworth, among the Surrey

hills. Tennyson complained of ill treatment by the newspapers and of reporters who wrote stupid things about him. He recited some of his poetry for them in his gruff voice. Then he peered with his dim eyes at a crystal lavaliere surrounded with silver leaves that Sarah was wearing. To Sarah Whitman, who had given the necklace to her, Sarah reported that Tennyson "looked at it over and over, fingered it, wondered much about it," and "thought to find things in it." He asked her if that was where she found her stories.

When news of the death of Tennyson arrived in America shortly after their return, Sarah wrote to Annie, "None of the great gifts I have ever had out of loving and being with you seems to me so great as having seen Tennyson." He seemed to her like a king in captivity, "one of the kings of old, of divine rights and sacred seclusions." And she was impressed by the great dignity and separateness of the life of England's famous Victorian poet.

Another death that fall touched Annie and Sarah more closely and left an unfillable void in their circle of close friends. John Greenleaf Whittier died on September 7 while they were still abroad. In him Sarah had had one of her most ardent admirers and a dearly beloved companion with whom she could share ideas and feelings about every subject under the sun. The previous year, when the Boston *Journal* published a page of "Tributes to Whittier" on the occasion of his eighty-fourth birthday, Sarah's tribute said, "The joy is ours of being sure that...he is growing yet, like one of our noblest forest trees, some great pine.... The roots of the great landmark cling fast to the strong New England ledges, but its green top, where singing birds come and go, is held high to the winds and sunshine in clearest air."

"One must know the world before one can know the parish," Sarah sometimes told aspiring writers, and she herself was the most avid of travelers and sensitive of observers. But after more than seven months abroad, it was sweet to be at home again for a while. Happy to be off the steamer, Sarah spent the first evening back at 148 Charles Street with Annie, enjoying the view looking out over the Charles River. The next day Sarah returned to South Berwick to her dear old home, which, she told a friend "seemed to put its arms round me."

There were, however, snakes even in paradise. One day Sarah wrote to Annie that out of a clear sky a man came to Mary with a plan for a syndicate to cut up and sell lots along the Piscataqua River bank. "Sometimes I get such a hunted feeling like the last wild thing that is left in the fields," Sarah lamented.

Sarah found there was great excitement in New England over the World's Columbian Exposition to be held in Chicago in 1893—a year later than originally planned—to celebrate the 400th anniversary of Christopher Columbus's landing in America. To capitalize on the chauvinism, Scribner's asked Sarah for a story for a patriotic number of their magazine in honor of the event.

Easterners flocked to the celebration, and along with them went Sarah, Annie, Carrie, and Stubby, and a friend—the author Susan Woolsey. They marveled at such wonders as the expansion engine, Pullman cars, and the Linotype machine. And they were thrilled by the first and largest Ferris wheel ever built in America. Its thirty-six glass-enclosed cars could each carry sixty people, for a total of 2,160 per ride. Sarah was especially interested in the architecture on display. "If I am not mistaken," she wrote to William Ward (her editor at *The Independent*), "the Chicago exposition will teach us to be more careful about our buildings—both in preserving the old ones and in building after better fashions." She proved to be right in that the Exposition marked a renewed interest in classic styles in America. Especially impressive at the fair were the buildings finished in fiber and plaster, which shone like white marble and gave the complex the name "The White City." The name was doubly appropriate since the fair used more electricity than the whole city of Chicago.

The vivacious and amusing Susan Chauncey Woolsey added greatly to the fun of the trip. She was a popular children's writer (under the pen name Susan Coolidge) and had become famous for her series of realistic stories about a girl named Katy. Since the titles of several of the stories begin with "What Katy Did...," they were often called the "Katy-did" series. Annie and Sarah frequently visited Susan Woolsey in Newport, and she was a welcome guest at 148 Charles Street when she came to Boston. William James reportedly called the irrepressible author a cross between an elephant and a butterfly. Sarah admired Susan's books and said of one of them, "I don't know a better book to give a child or a growing girl."

Phillips Brooks died the last week of January 1893, and Sarah wrote a sketch called "At the Funeral of Phillips Brooks," which appeared in "The Contributors' Club" section of the *Atlantic* in April 1893. The great preacher, who was rector of Trinity Church and Bishop of Massachusetts, had been a personal friend of Annie's and Sarah's, and his death brought shock and sorrow to them as well as to many others in Boston. In letters to friends, Sarah described the effect of his death on the city, with the mighty crowd of silent mourners around Trinity and the scene inside the church. Sarah Whitman had planned for great laurel wreaths to be placed on the plain black hangings and a magnificent one of red carnations and green on the front of the pulpit where Brooks had stood so often to deliver his resounding messages. To Sarah this wreath appeared to be "a victor's trophy," and she compared the procession of the coffin, covered with purple pall and white lilies and carried shoulder high up the aisle by tall, grave young men, to an old Greek festival. As the service ended, she told Alice Howe, the people began singing "For all thy saints who from their labours rest" with a burst of triumph but the voices stopped and stopped until there was hardly anyone left to sing at all, as they were all crying as if their hearts would break. His going, Sarah wrote, seemed to make a new Boston

with a lovely trail of light he had left behind, and her metaphor of his death and his legacy was one of the most
memorable written about the beloved minister. "It has been,"
she said, "like a great sunset that suddenly turned itself into
dawn."

The Jewett collection of short stories published by Houghton Mifflin in 1893 was *A Native of Winby and Other Tales*,
which contains two more of Sarah's Irish stories: "A Little
Captive Maid" and "Between Mass and Vespers." The title
story, "A Native of Winby," is a return-of-the-native tale about
the Honorable Joseph K. Laneway, who makes a sentimental journey to the village where he grew up. In this story Sarah
demonstrated clearly that she could probe the psyche of
men as well as of women. Joseph Laneway has achieved recognition as a general, a senator, and a millionaire and is torn
between his craving for the adulation of his village's popula-
tion and his longing to return to the innocent happiness of
his childhood days. His first sweetheart, Abby Hender, who
understands his ambivalence, helps him relive his youth by
preparing some of his favorite dishes and reminiscing with
him. She also understands his need for applause. "I'm real
glad they showed him proper respect," she comments when
he is given a proper political sendoff at the station. But she
thinks, "I had the best part of anybody."

The most popular story in the collection has always been
"The Flight of Betsey Lane." Betsey is one of Sarah's older
unmarried women who know how to make life rich and
adventuresome for themselves. A resident of the Byfleet Poorhouse, Betsey receives an unexpected gift of a hundred dollars.
She decides to use it on a trip to the Philadelphia Centennial—
a long-cherished secret wish. She hops a train, arrives at
the fair, and has a marvelous time, enjoying the wonders of the
West and the splendors of the East with calm satisfaction—
she had always known there was an amazing world outside

of Byfleet. Unlike the indifferent crowd that drifts restlessly through the grounds, Betsey is interested in everything and everybody. "What be you making here, dear?" she asks, and the demonstrator is happy to repond to the beaming grand-motherly questioner.

Through her outgoing friendliness Betsey meets an eye surgeon, who promises to come by and see what he can do for one of her friends at the Poorhouse who suffers from cataracts—or "upsightedness," as the residents call it. Betsey has a fine time buying gifts for all of her friends and returns to Byfleet feeling greatly enriched although she has only $1.35 in her pocket. She looks forward to being able to share her experience with her friends, promising them that she has enough to tell them to last for the rest of their days. "What's for the good o' one's for the good of all," she says.

In February 1893, Celia Thaxter wrote to thank Sarah for helping her with advice on a book she was writing about her garden on Appledore. Sandpiper wrote, "How good you are to help this old bird! All your suggestions I deeply prize & will most gratefully accept." She asked for permission to send the manuscript to Sarah again for one more "friendly smirch." Sarah was delighted to do anything she could to help her friend, whose health was deteriorating alarmingly and who called herself "the tiredest bird that ever scratched for worms."

Celia Thaxter's book, *An Island Garden*, was published by Houghton Mifflin in March 1894, with illustrations by Childe Hassam. Hassam's watercolor paintings and chapter headings were reproduced by an expensive and painstaking process called chronolithography, in which the lithographic artist might use as many as thirty stones to make one color reproduction of the original artwork. The gold-stamped floral design on the cover was the work of Sarah Whitman. The book has become a classic treasure for horticulturists and art lovers alike, and in 1988 Houghton Mifflin published a facsimile edition.

The book describes Celia's joys and frustrations in creating her fabulous island garden and expresses her delight in nature. Amid such practical hints as how to fight off slugs and sparrows and what to feed wallflowers are lyric passages of description. All the nuances of color, texture, shape, and aroma of various flowers are detailed. The very sight of a radiant circle of honeysuckle refreshed and lifted Celia's heart. And as for its odor, she writes, "it is like the spirit of romance, sweet as youth's tender dreams. It is summer's very soul." The rose was her favorite of all her beloved blossoms. A single rose gave her more delight than "a whole conservatory flushed with azaleas, and brilliant with forests of camellias and every precious exotic that blooms." Every day she wore a fresh rose pinned to her dress.

Like Sarah, Celia enjoyed playful whimsey and had a Peter Pan longing to return to childhood. And also like Sarah, she had a warm and outgoing friendliness that made people want to be around her. In Celia's flower-filled parlor, Whittier and Annie and Sarah had enjoyed many hours of rich entertainment. There were famous musicians to play Beethoven sonatas, Ole Bull telling Norwegian myths and playing his violin, William Dean Howells and Thomas Bailey Aldrich and James Russell Lowell to talk about writing, and John Singer Sargent, Childe Hassam, and other artists to talk art.

In the summer of 1894, Celia and Sarah rowed around the Isles of Shoals as Celia told tales of the history of the islands and the people who had lived and died there. Sarah told Annie, "She seemed to turn leaf after leaf of her history as if she had finished it and could read it like a book." Following her visit to Appledore, Sarah went to stay at Spring House in Richfield Springs, New York, to take the baths for her rheumatism. There she received a telegram telling her of the death of Celia Thaxter. Sarah was not well enough to travel to Appledore for the burial, but the description Annie sent her of Celia's funeral amid beds of her own flowers pleased her. She wrote to Annie, "Few losses can touch us so nearly as this. It is like having no more May or no more September in the year. Dear generous heart, unfaltering love, how we shall miss her now."

CHAPTER NINE

◆

Country of the
Pointed Firs

AS LABORS OF LOVE for their friend Celia Thaxter, Annie Fields collaborated in editing a collection of
Celia's letters, and Sarah prepared the Appledore
Edition of Celia's poems and wrote a four-page preface to
it. She also wrote a preface to Celia's *Stories and Poems for
Children*, published the year after her death. Sarah kept in
touch with the Thaxters' son John, who lived in the family
home at Kittery Point, Maine, and she tried to help John with
his writing, reading his manuscripts and writing him long
thoughtful letters of suggestions for improving them. Unfor-
tunately, although John worked hard at his writing, he failed
to find a publisher for his work.

In October 1894 the circle that met at 148 Charles Street
lost one more cherished member. Oliver Wendell Holmes
reached a graceful old age, bearing his years cheerfully and
drawing closer to his old friends. He spent many summers
in his cottage at Beverly Farms, which was near Gambrel
Cottage at Manchester-by-the-Sea. To tease his neighbors,
he datelined his letters "Beverly-by-the-Depot." A letter to
Annie Fields, written two years before he died, closed "with
affectionate regards and all sweet messages to Miss Jewett."
Holmes had made his mark as a physician as well as poet and

humorist. Independent-minded and forward-thinking, he had tried to gain admission for women to the Harvard Medical School, and he had supported liberal religious ideas. His lively mind and wide-ranging interests were greatly missed by his friends.

Sarah's next collection of stories, *The Life of Nancy* (Houghton Mifflin, 1895), includes "A War Debt," another story demonstrating Sarah's sympathy for ruined Southern aristocrats. Regrettably, it also contains stereotyped portraits of former slaves who behave irresponsibly.

A favorite and often reprinted story in the collection is "The Hiltons' Holiday," a simple story of a farmer who takes his children on a day-long trip to the city. The city is exciting and full of wonderful adventure, but there is a feeling of harmony with nature as the travelers return to the warmth and security of their home, where the mother is waiting to hear of their adventures and to feed them a satisfying supper.

In "All My Sad Captains" Sarah again goes back to her intimate knowledge of sea captains. Mrs. Lunn, an attractive widow, is courted by three old mariners past their prime and their well-remembered glory days. The awkward courting of the beached captains is funny and pathetic at the same time. When Rudyard Kipling received a copy of *The Life of Nancy* from Sarah, he wrote to her that he laughed over "Fame's Little Day," a story about a rustic couple who come to New York and through an impulse on the part of a young reporter come to believe that they are celebrities. Kipling said he read the sentimental story "The Only Rose" almost with tears, and he especially liked "All My Sad Captains," with its "perfect title." He told Sarah he was glad he had spent three winters in New England, as the experience enabled him to draw the full flavor out of her stories.

Kipling's favorite story in the collection, "The Guests of Miss Timms," is a comic tale that demonstrates Sarah's ability to use biting irony. Mrs. Persis Flagg, a pretentious, arrogant snob, persuades gentle Miss Pickett to go with her to visit Mrs. Timms in a nearby town. Although the invitation from Mrs. Timms has been vague and general, Mrs. Flagg is so sure their surprise visit will be welcomed with an invitation to spend the night that she has secretly packed overnight things in her large black bag. To their dismay, Mrs. Timms treats them with frigidly correct courtesy: she not only fails to ask them to spend the night, she also fails to provide any refreshment—much less the splendid dinner Mrs. Flagg has anticipated. At the earliest possible moment, Mrs. Timms ushers them out the door with obvious relief.

Disgruntled, Mrs. Flagg condescends to pay a visit to poor Nancy Fell, who is much below Mrs. Timms on the social scale. Good-hearted Nancy runs down her walk to open the gate for them and fixes them a simple feast of pork, dandelion greens, new biscuits, and potatoes. Her obvious pleasure in their unexpected visit and her generous hospitality force Mrs. Flagg to concede "'twas a real nice little dinner," although she adds that she herself doesn't "deem it necessary to cook potatoes when I'm goin' to have dandelion greens." And she adds, "She'll enjoy tellin' folks about our comin' over to see her." Mrs. Flagg's meanness is further demonstrated by the fact that she fails to give Nancy Fell the jelly she had brought with her as a gift for Mrs. Timms. The whole story is cleverly connected by the thread of another visit that the women observe. In the stagecoach they meet a woman who is also making an unexpected visit—to Mrs. Beckett, a woman she has met some time before at a conference. They observe the bewildered look on Mrs. Beckett's face when the visitor and her large trunk are deposited at her door by the stagecoach driver. As the stagecoach rolls on, Mrs. Flagg leans out the window and reports with pleasure, "She ain't got in yet," and they speculate that the woman will be on the return coach that evening. When they pass the Beckett house on their way home, however, they spy the visiting stranger sitting comfortably rocking by one of the front windows "in calm content."

And Mrs. Beckett stops the coach to ask the driver to send the woman's other trunk from the depot where it is stored. This incident, which foreshadows the rebuff by Mrs. Timms and recaps the warm welcome by Nancy Fell, gives unity and a pleasing completeness to the story.

In January 1896, when the temperature was ten degrees below zero in Boston, Annie and Sarah, along with the Thomas Bailey Aldriches and other friends, sailed on the yacht *Hermione* for a two-month cruise in the Caribbean. Annie Fields kept a thorough diary of the trip. On St. Valentine's Day she recorded that the President of the Republic of Haiti dined with them on the *Hermione*, and the talk included excited speculation over whether Cuba would revolt and win its freedom from Spanish rule.

In Nassau Sarah rejoiced to find herself in a warm world filled with flowers. Unhappily, however, storms made the cruise increasingly rough and most of the passengers, including Sarah, suffered such continual seasickness that they were glad to make any landfall. At Inagua a small boat carried them as close to shore as possible, and the captain then carried the women one by one to the beach. All except Sarah. Watching her chance, she deftly jumped and ran, reaching the beach damp but safe under her own power.

As the winter storms continued, all except Sarah voted to skip the Windward Islands, and the *Hermione* turned back to the mainland. Ensconced in the fashionable comfort of the Ponce de Leon Hotel in St. Augustine, they waited out the worst of the winter, returning to Boston at the end of March.

According to pattern, Sarah's relationship with Thomas Bailey Aldrich progressed from a formal editor-author relationship to a warm personal friendship. His wife, Lillian, also became Sarah's friend, and both Aldriches called her Sadie. During the time that Aldrich was editor of the *Atlantic*

Monthly (1881–1890), the Aldriches lived on Beacon Hill and exchanged frequent visits with Annie and Sarah. Sarah also visited them at their summer home in Ponkapog, Massachusetts, and exchanged whimsical letters with both of them. When Aldrich thought too much time had lapsed between her submissions, he wrote to her:

> Cute little spider down in Maine
> (All the time we need her)
> Spin some silvery webs again
> To catch the flying reader.

In addition to stints as an editor and literary critic for prestigious periodicals, Aldrich wrote poems reflecting the cultural atmosphere of New England, as well as essays, drama, and short stories. His use of surprise endings, as in the classic "Marjorie Daw," influenced the development of the short story, and his popular semi-autobiographical book, *The Story of a Bad Boy*, was a forerunner of Mark Twain's *Adventures of Tom Sawyer*. Both as an editor and as a writer, his warm appreciation of Sarah's writing was often expressed and deeply satisfying to her.

When the Aldriches rented a summer cottage at Tenants Harbor on the eastern shore of Maine, Sarah eagerly accepted their offer to visit. "I don't know when I have had four days of such real pleasure," Sarah wrote after she and Annie had spent an enjoyable time yachting and driving around the wooded point. Two months later Annie and Sarah returned to the area, taking a tiny cottage, The Anchorage, in Martinsville. In this quiet, serene retreat with its green spruces, gray rocks, and blue sea, Sarah began to develop in her mind the story line for *The Country of the Pointed Firs*.

Mary came to visit at The Anchorage and shared their activities of sailing, walking in the woods, and gathering mushrooms, wildflowers, and cranberries in the fields. The children of a neighboring family brought their mail from the village for fifteen cents a week and also sold them cunners and lobsters.

Although many readers insisted on identifying Martinsville as the setting of *The Country of the Pointed Firs*, Sarah as usual denied that her story was set in an actual location. But *The Country of the Pointed Firs* ran serially in the January through September issues of the *Atlantic* in 1896, and in August of 1896 Sarah and Stubby took a cruise down the Maine coast to Tenants Harbor. Explaining the trip to Mary, Sarah said, "It will serve me well to go down the coast *in this moment* . . . . I want to *put in* to some of the harbors, and see things fresh for my work. I shall set the 6th or 8th for having the *Pointed Firs* all finished up. I should like to take a fresh look at my Pointed Firs Country very much." The nearest she came to actually identifying Dunnet Landing (the village setting) was to say vaguely that it "must be somewhere along shore" between the region of Tenants Harbor and Boothbay. In 1919, when an illustrated edition of *Pointed Firs* was issued, the photographs for it were taken on St. George Peninsula, where Tenants Harbor and Martinsville are located.

Next door to The Anchorage lived Rosilla Batchelder, who in many ways resembled Almira Todd in *The Country of the Pointed Firs*. A resourceful, motherly provincial, Mrs. Batchelder proved to be a kind and helpful neighbor to Annie and Sarah. She gave them blackberries and flowers, and one day Sarah went on a cranberrying expedition with her. She was the wise woman of the neighborhood: "Everybody goes to Mrs. Batchelder for everything," Sarah told Mary and Carrie. When the illustrated edition of *Pointed Firs* was issued, Rosilla Batchelder's picture appeared in it.

Like Helen Denis and Kate Lancaster in *Deephaven*, the unnamed narrator in *Pointed Firs* comes from the city to spend the summer in a small rural village. But the sophisticated protagonist who visits Dunnet Landing is more understanding of the natives than the inexperienced and self-conscious young girls who vacation in Deephaven. During the twenty years separating the two books, Sarah had honed her writing skills, and she had absorbed many new experiences. *The Country of the Pointed Firs* both reflects and transcends her experiences during that time. Rereading the earlier book, Sarah commented that she felt like the grandmother of that author.

Underneath the simple surface tale of country people and their ways in *Pointed Firs* run deep undercurrents. The sea is the key to existence for the inhabitants of Dunnet Landing; there is a sense of timelessness and eternity connected with it and with the ancient pointed firs that march down to it. Interwoven into the story are supernatural elements and glancing references to antediluvian myths and legends. The narrator's landlady, Almira Todd, is an herbalist who understands the medicinal and mystical properties of the herbs in her "rustic pharmacopoeia" of a garden and of those that grow in the fields and woods. From wormwood, bloodroot, hys'sop, pennyroyal, tansy, lemon balm, and some two dozen other herbs she concocts potions to cure her neighbors' ills. The narrator is at first amused at Mrs. Todd's prescriptions but gradually falls under her spell. As her insight into Mrs. Todd's character deepens, she sees her as an almost mythological character—perfectly wise and good. Mrs. Todd makes clear the imagery of the pointed firs when she tells the narrator that trees which seem to grow right out of bare rock survive because their roots go down to a secret stream. "Every such tree has got its own livin' spring; there's folk made to match 'em," she says.

The novel progresses, as *Deephaven* does, through a series of meetings by the visitor with various characters in the little backward village. Like Deephaven, Dunnet Landing, with its decaying wharves and disabled schooners, is filled with eccentrics who have found various ways to survive, and the outlying islands, too, have their inhabitants with stories to tell. Captain Littlepage (whose name has inspired numerous symbolic interpretations by reviewers) is a foil to Mrs.

Blackett, Almira Todd's mother. This ancient mariner spins a tale of a ghostly "waiting place" somewhere between life and death where "fog-shaped" creatures blow about like cobwebs. The captain, who frequently quotes from *Paradise Lost*, believes that this uncharted place, two degrees farther north than ships have ever been, is where the answer to the meaning of life will be found. In his person he exemplifies the decline of the little seaport, which he says is at "low-water mark."

Mrs. Blackett, Almira Todd's mother, lives on Green Island with her shy fisherman son William. This optimistic eighty-six-year-old lives her simple life with a zest that refreshes and inspires all who meet her. The narrator finds it "impossible not to wish to stay on forever at Green Island." Another character who contrasts with Mrs. Blackett and her "golden chain of love and dependence with the community" is poor Joanna, who became a recluse on Shell-heap Island after a disastrous love affair. Poor Joanna is long dead, but not forgotten by the villagers, who respected her right to live her own life and kept a kind of secret watch over her, leaving her occasional gifts when they passed her lonely hermitage. The narrator makes a pilgrimage to Poor Joanna's island and finds a well-trodden path to her grave. She drinks from Poor Joanna's spring and muses that "in the life of each of us there is a place remote and islanded, and given to endless regret or secret happiness."

In a letter to Annie Fields, written in June 1885, Sarah revealed the prototype for Elijah Tilley, an old sailor in *Pointed Firs*, who knits and keeps his house as a shrine to his dead wife—whom he always refers to as "Poor dear!" Describing a day of playing on the beach at Wells, Sarah mentions to Annie meeting old D.B., who "sits at home and *knits stockings* and thinks on his early days as an able seaman in foreign parts." His wife had died two or three years ago, Sarah said, and he always referred to her as "Poor dear!" Eleven years later, Sarah transformed D.B. into Elijah Tilley in the chapter "Along Shore," with his story greatly embellished and expanded through incubation in her imagination.

Pointed Firs marks the climax of Sarah Orne Jewett's writing career. It contains, as Jewett scholar Margaret Farrand Thorp points out, "Almost the whole of New England, its landscape, its social changes, its people and their special qualities." Through it also run Sarah's favorite themes, clarified by years of investigation and refinement. Reverence for the past is balanced by the realization that if carried too far, it can lead to suffocation and stagnation. Captain Littlepage, the character who clings the hardest to Dunnet's lost grandeur, says, "The worst hae got to be best and rule everything." He is "offended" by bicycles and feels "we're all turned upside down and going back year by year." Almira Todd, with her unlimited understanding, says of him, "Oh, he used to be a beautiful man!"

Almira Todd, Sarah's supreme creation, is a powerful woman—physically and spiritually massive. Under Annie's influence, Sarah had continued to read and consider the myths of ancient Greece, and Mrs. Todd is gradually revealed to the narrator of *Pointed Firs* as a figure of mythic proportions. Because of the tragedy of her love story, the narrator compares her to Sophocles' Antigone. And because of her wisdom and knowledge of the use of arcane herbs she is described as a "priestess of experience," a "sibyl," and a "personification of some force of Nature."

But despite the universality of her character, Almira Todd is a very real woman. She hides her sentimentality by banging her pots and pans, making a joke, or finding an excuse to retreat. Completely in charge of her life, she tolerates and nurtures men, but sometimes finds them a nuisance. When she and the narrator set out for Green Island to visit Mrs. Todd's mother, she chooses to go in a small boat that they can manage themselves with the help of a young boy: "We don't want to carry no men folks havin' to be considered every minute an' takin' up all our time."

Green Island, where Mrs. Blackett, Almira Todd's mother,

lives with her fisherman son, is seen by the narrator as "a complete and tiny continent." The house where Mrs. Todd's mother lives stands on a hill, "high like a beacon," and the visitor finds it a place of peace and love and immediately feels a sympathetic communication with Mrs. Blackett, whose unselfconscious "exquisite" hospitality is irresistible. In the bedroom the narrator is invited to sit in Mrs. Blackett's thronelike rocking chair next to a window with "the prettiest view in the house." She notices the worn Bible on the lightstand and the owner's thimble beside a carefully folded thick-striped cotton shirt she is making for her son, and thinks of "those dear old fingers and their loving stitches" and "that heart which had made the most of everything that had need of love!"

The relationship between Mrs. Todd and her mother is expressed mostly through the many little thoughtful things they do for each other and through their admiration for each other's talents. Sarah may have had in mind her own relationship with her mother, which was not, until her mother's last illness, as perfect as she could have wished. Mother images dominate the description of the Bowden family reunion, the high point of *Pointed Firs*. The Bowden family house stands in its green fields like "a motherly brown hen waiting for the flock that came straying toward it from every direction." And Mrs. Todd proudly tells the narrator, "Mother's always the queen."

There is a mythic sense of universality in the reunion procession that resembles "ancient Greeks going to celebrate a victory, or to worship the gods of harvests in the grove above." In the unifying ritual, even the non-Bowden narrator feels included, and speaks of herself as one of the family: "We were no more a New England family celebrating its own existence and simple progress; we carried the tokens and inheritance of all such households from which this had descended, and were only the latest of our lines." Her inclusion is confirmed when she and Mrs. Todd share an early-apple pie: Mrs. Todd serves her the piece with *Bowden* written in icing on it, and she herself consumes the piece saying *Reunion.*

The demolishing and consuming of the great gingerbread replica of the old Bowden home is seen as "a pledge and token of loyalty" for the members of the tribe. Mrs. Blackett holds "court," and after the speeches and recitations of family history and poems written for the occasion, the narrator concludes, "Clannishness is an instinct of the heart." And as she hears repeated murmurs of "next summer" and sees how reluctant to part the clan members are, she understands the importance of their reunion ritual to them.

Sarah's favorite theme of city versus country finds its best expression in this novel, in which the narrator finds the inner peace she is seeking in the pastoral setting and in the lives of the women, who exhibit the wisdom and strength she would like to acquire. Like Thoreau's *Walden, Pointed Firs* is a nature lyric with all the notes in tune. Just as Thoreau saw what he looked at, so did Sarah. The beauty of Green Island, where Mrs. Blackett lives, is offset by the barrenness of Shell-heap Island, where poor Joanna lived her hermit life. And the decay of the dock area is as apparent as is the beauty of the woods and pastures. When Sarah describes a trout-fishing expedition the narrator goes on with William Blackett, it is evident that she is well acquainted with the ways of trout and brooks. At one point on this expedition she wanders through woods and pastures and finds a forsaken house and overgrown farm. Like Wordsworth—and like Sarah—she knows that this experience remembered in tranquillity will be the source of "many pleasures for future joy."

The Country of the Pointed Firs won instant acclaim and has continued to win high praise from critics down through the years. Some reviewers dwell on the author's precise use of language. When the narrator takes Captain Littlepage's arm she *sleeves* him. Solitary souls may *hive away* in their houses and *pray* visitors by their doorways. *Liable* as in "the weather is liable to bring visitors" or "They say large bows on top [of bonnets] is liable to be worn" is used for *likely* or *apt*. And puny folks *dwindle* away. *Master* is used as an adjective by the natives in its sense of exceedingly or exceptionally, as in a "master smart man" or "a master clever woman" or "a master long, rough road." And throughout the book, Sarah's talent for using metaphors effectively is exhibited in her comparisons drawn from mythological and sea imagery.

Other critics comment at length on the subtleties of her characterizations, such as the fiercely self-reliant women and the sad plight of the seafaring men whose memories are filled with long voyages to foreign shores where acquaintance with other lands and other laws enables them to see beyond the battle for town clerk in Dunnet Landing. Reviewing the book in the *Book Buyer* (October 1897), Alice Brown found it almost beyond praise. "You are simply bewildered by the richness and life-giving balm of this herby garden.... No such beautiful and perfect work has been done for many years; perhaps no such beautiful work has ever been done in America." The reviewer for *Academy* (March 13, 1897) called *Pointed Firs* an "epic of contentment." Sarah was compared favorably with Mary E. Wilkins, Mrs. Gaskell, and Jane Austen. A Chicago reviewer declared, "No American woman has equaled Miss Jewett in the possession of a characteristic literary style and none has ever rivaled her in the power of depicting the country life of New England." In the *Review of Reviews* (December 1896), Hamilton W. Mabie said the novel showed the author's "true and delicate art in all its quiet and enduring charm."

Sarah's friends, of course, were equally enthusiastic. Kipling, at the apex of his own career, wrote to praise her "perfect" tale. "It's immense—it is the very life. So many of the people of lesser sympathy have missed the lovely New England landscape, and the genuine New England nature," he told her, adding in a postscript, "I don't believe even you know how good that work is."

William James wrote praising the refreshing quality of

the book, which he said "has that incommunicable cleanness of the salt air when one first leaves town." His brother, Henry, referred to the book as "Sarah Orne Jewett's beautiful little quantum of achievement." Mary Ellen Chase, who read and loved *Pointed Firs* as a child, grew up to become herself a well-known writer of books about Maine. In an introduction to a 1968 edition of the book, she speaks of the rare sensitivity that set Sarah Orne Jewett apart "not only from all other Maine writers, but from many, if not most writers of all time and of many a place."

Willa Cather, in an introduction to a 1925 edition of *Pointed Firs*, placed the novel in company with *The Scarlet Letter* and *Huckleberry Finn* as one of the three books she predicted would achieve literary immortality. It was in a remark to Willa Cather, whom Sarah met during her last years, that she revealed the key to the excellence of the book: "The thing that teases the mind over and over for years and at last gets itself put down rightly on paper—whether little or great, it belongs to literature." Sarah was not consciously speaking of her masterpiece in her advice to the younger writer, but she could have been.

After *Pointed Firs* was published, Sarah wrote four more sketches set in Dunnet Landing and included some of the same characters. In posthumous editions these sketches have sometimes been included in the text and sometimes added after the original version. "The Queen's Twin," the most popular of these additional stories, is about Abby Martin, an elderly woman who thinks of herself as Queen Victoria's twin. Abby and Victoria were born on the same day and married on the same day to men named Albert. Abby named her first child Victoria, and when the next one was a boy her husband chose Albert (his own name) plus that of his brother Edward, and Abby was delighted when she heard that those were also names of the new little Prince of Wales. After that she waited to name her babies until she found out what the Queen had named hers. So both women had an Alfred and a daughter named Alice—whom both of them lost.

The high point of Abby Martin's life was the time she went on her husband's sailing ship up the Thames and got to see the Queen coming out of Buckingham Palace on her way to review her troops in a "beautiful carriage all shinin' gold." The Queen looked right at Abby "so pleasant and happy" as if she knew there was some bond between them. Since that day Abby felt as if the Queen were her special friend. Her best room is filled with newspaper and magazine pictures of Victoria all carefully framed, with fresh flowers placed daily in front of them. Abby's greatest treasure is the Queen's book on the Highlands, which she reads only on Sundays. Mrs. Todd, that wise oracle, tells Abby that her fancy that the Queen may come for a visit just shows how superior her imagination is. "The common things that happens outside 'em is all in all to most folks," she says, but for "folks that have any fancy in 'em, such beautiful dreams is the real part o' life." And as she and the narrator leave Abby on her lonely doorstep, Mrs. Todd comments, "It ain't as if we left her all alone!" After "The Queen's Twin" was printed in the English magazine *Cornhill*, Sarah was delighted to learn that Queen Victoria liked it.

Two of the additional four sketches concern Mrs. Todd's shy brother, William Blackett, and the marriage that is the culmination of his forty years of courting a country maiden. These sketches, "A Dunnet Shepherdess" and "William's Wedding," have the same carefully integrated background of sea and shore as the rest of *Pointed Firs*. There is gentle irony and great sympathy in the portraits of William, the ancient yet boyishly innocent beau, and his weatherworn, patient shepherdess sweetheart Esther. For four decades, while Esther has remained at home to help her crippled mother, William has made pretended fishing trips and managed to visit her once a year. When Esther's mother finally dies, the two innocent old lovers are married. In appropriate pastoral imagery, Esther carries in her arms a white lamb whose mother had died that morning, and the narrator thinks she has never seen "a young bride half so touching in her happiness."

The fourth Dunnet sketch, "The Foreigner," is considered by many critics to be one of Sarah's best stories. Strangely, however, after it was originally published in the *Atlantic Monthly* in August 1900, it was not reprinted until 1962. The framework for "The Foreigner" is a tale-within-a-tale, as Mrs. Todd on a stormy night recounts for the narrator the history of Eliza Tolland, a French Catholic, who has been made to feel an alien by the natives of the insular village. Mrs. Blackett urges her daughter, Mrs. Todd, to befriend the lonely stranger. As a result the two women become friends, and Eliza passes on to Mrs. Todd her knowledge of healing plants and herbs. On the night of Eliza's death, her mother appears to her (and to Mrs. Todd) to take her away, and Mrs. Todd says to Eliza, "You ain't never goin' to feel strange and lonesome no more." The idea for this transcendent scene may have come to Sarah from the death of Celia Thaxter, who was devoted to her mother, and whose brother said, "Mother came in the night and took sister away."

Sister Carrie's health, always fragile, seemed to improve during 1896, and Sarah and Mary rejoiced to see her so bright and well and full of eager plans for Theodore's entrance into college in the fall. Then after a visit to Exeter relatives in the spring of 1897, Carrie felt ill and was diagnosed as having an internal abscess. She was operated on by specialists from Boston, but the operation was too much for her weakened heart. She sank peacefully into a coma and died. Her unexpected death was a terrible shock to her sisters and to her seventeen-year-old son. Mary was named his official guardian, but both Sarah and Mary felt responsible for his care and welfare, and Stubby, as they still called him, was a great comfort and joy to them both as long as they lived.

In 1893 Sarah had dedicated *A Native of Winby* to

Caroline with these words: "To my dear younger sister: I have had many pleasures that were doubled because you shared them, and so I write your name at the beginning of this book." Speaking of her sister's death in a letter to Horace Scudder, Sarah again expressed her belief in metaphysical communication with the beloved dead: "One always seems to begin a new life in company with the soul that disappears into the 'world of light'—that goes away only to come nearer to one's heart than ever before," she wrote. "It all seems like transfiguration of the old way of loving and of friendship too." But to Grace Norton she wrote, "It is impossible to get over the feeling that something of me died and not the living brightness and affectionateness of my sister," for Carrie's cheerful physical presence was sorely missed, and the reality of their dwindling household depressed Sarah.

Madame Blanc provided a welcome distraction when she visited Gambrel Cottage at Manchester-by-the-Sea in the spring and then went to South Berwick for a long stay. Sarah led her friend on nature walks through her favorite haunts, introducing her to juniper and bayberry and scarlet columbines, which she scrambled over a wall to pick. One day, overcome by the wonder of being able to share her favorite places with her dear friend, Sarah exclaimed, "How did we come to be walking here together? I am made of this spot. But, You! How came this afternoon to be *ours*?" Madame Blanc could only smile in understanding and mutual wonder.

The French writer was determined to gather information for her French readers on many facets of American life. One of her interests was the Shakers, and Sarah, who had visited the Shaker colony in Alfred, Maine, offered to write to the leader of the group, her friend Elder Henry Green, a pleasant, well-read man and an excellent woodcarver. He welcomed the prospect of their visit, but though Alfred is only about twenty miles from South Berwick, in the southern area of Maine, getting there proved to be an ordeal. Torrential rains washed away the embankment supporting a railroad bridge, and when they attempted to drive by horse and carriage, they found that impractical because of road conditions. Finally they got to Alfred by train, taking a roundabout detour by way of Rochester, New Hampshire.

The visit was a great success, and Madame Blanc wrote a long account of it titled "Une Visite chez les Shakers," which appeared in *Revue des Deux Mondes* (November 15, 1897). She was impressed by the graciousness of the sisters and especially by Eldress Harriet N. Coolbroth who, she noted, "is related to Stonewall Jackson." Intrigued by the dress of the Shaker women, Madame Blanc bought herself a Shaker cloak, inspiring at least one of her Parisian friends to write to Elder Green to order one for herself.

The Shakers were interested in hearing Sarah tell of her trip to the West Indies. She discussed improvement in the Shaker schools with Elder Henry and left a gift for the library fund with him. Subsequently Sarah exchanged books with Elder Henry. One of the books she sent for the Shakers' library was Annie Fields's biography of Harriet Beecher Stowe. Over the years Sarah regularly purchased handmade items such as wooden workboxes from the Shaker colony for sale at the annual fairs held by the adult Bible class at Trinity Church, which was led by her friend Sarah Whitman.

Sarah often visited Charles Eliot Norton, editor and professor of literature at Harvard, and his daughters at Shady Hill, their Cambridge home. She became particularly good friends with Sara Norton and kept up a lively correspondence with her. On September 3, 1897, Sarah wrote to Sara Norton: "This is my birthday, and I am always nine years old." At forty-eight, she usually rode in carriages instead of on horseback, but she still enjoyed long walks, picnicking and outdoor winter sports. Her figure had filled out, and she had a queenly posture that made her seem imposing at first to strangers. Aware of this, she said deprecatingly that in reality she only came up to her shoulder. Some friends called her beautiful and others called her handsome, but all descriptions agree that she was an attractive woman. Her large brown eyes, abundant black hair tinged with gray, and fine features were enhanced by a sweetness of expression. Her usual dress was in the muted colors typical of her class: often she wore dark skirts and white waists with eyeglasses hanging from a black ribbon or attached to her lapel. Mary Ellen Chase, who met Sarah on Mary Ellen's thirteenth birthday in February 1900, always remembered the simple lavender dress with long sleeves and high waistline that her idol wore and the smile that transformed her features. The prophecy that Sarah made to the starry-eyed teenager that she would grow up to write good books about Maine remained a precious talisman in Mary Ellen Chase's memory.

In April 1898, Sarah and Annie set out on their third extended trip to Europe. The voyage over was long, and Sarah spent most of her time reading on the deck of the steamer. She liked arriving in Plymouth, where her thoughts turned to privateers who had sailed out of the harbor and to her grandfather who had been taken prisoner and shut up in the nearby wretched Dartmoor prison.

The train trip through Devonshire and Somerset fields of primroses and trees all in fresh April bloom and the song of blackbirds heard through the open window of their compartment enchanted Sarah. After ten days in London, sightseeing and visiting old friends, they left for Paris, also in its springtime beauty. They attended the hit play of the season, *Cyrano de Bergerac*, and visited Madame Blanc. Touring southern France, Sarah wrote enthusiastic descriptions to friends of golden lilies growing wild, of acres of white and scarlet poppies along roadsides, of fields of wild thyme, and of old mulberry trees looking rueful, "as if they thought it very hard to put out nice leaves every year with the other trees, only to have them picked for silkworms."

The highlight of several days spent at Avignon was a side

trip to visit the ruined château and exquisite old French garden in Grignan, where Madame de Sévigné (who immortalized Paris under Louis XIV in letters to her daughter) spent her last days. Sarah was thrilled to see the fig tree that Madame Sévigné wrote about still there and descendants of her wallflowers tumbling over the château walls. A bronze statue of the famous Frenchwoman in the marketplace of the tiny grim village, looking "so gay, so Parisian," struck Sarah as "perfectly incongruous."

In Provence they watched a *farandole* performed in an open arena. The colorful costumes of the dancers of different parishes, the grace and gaiety of the participants, and the lively music made a happy memory. Another unforgettable afternoon was spent with the poet Frédéric Mistral, famous for his epic poems, his passion for rehabilitating Provençal life, and his wide-brimmed black felt hat. Mistral and his wife spoke no English, but that was no handicap to conversation, as both Sarah and Annie spoke French fluently. They talked poetry and books and ate in the Provençal dining room, and they played with his little dog, named "Boufflo Beel" after the famous American performer, who had recently visited France. Sarah admired the Mistrals' pretty garden, and as they were leaving, their host and hostess filled their arms with roses and myrtle. Six years later, in 1905, Mistral would be awarded the Nobel Prize for his contributions to literature and philology.

In June the travelers went to Madame Blanc's country home for a long stay, and Sarah felt it was almost like coming home. At La Ferte sous Jouarre, about forty miles east of Paris, she was charmed by the big, walled garden filled with the sounds of a fountain and nightingales and by the view of the French countryside from her window: a long hill muffled in green trees and an old gray wall interrupted by weather-beaten red tilings of a roof and the sharp gable of an old farmhouse and by the sweet, far-off sounds of bells, "like a dream of bells," as the sound drifted across the Marne. In the old town of Jouarre, Sarah found that the square tower of the convent dated back to the time of Charlemagne, a discovery extremely pleasing to such an ardent history buff.

Most of the month of June was spent with Madame Blanc, with occasional side trips to Aix to visit the baths and to Grande Chartreuse, where Sarah slept in a cold convent cell and wondered if the cliffs overhead would tumble down during the night. Beyond Madame Blanc's garden a country lane opened up wonderful vistas. Sarah liked to take the basset hunting dogs of the household with her on her rambles. "It is much more exciting to know a new piece of country than to go to a new large town," she wrote to Sara Norton. Sarah was delighted when, through Madame Blanc, she became acquainted with some old French ladies with whom she could talk about French history. She became especially fond of a friend of Madame Blanc's mother, who was the widow of a famous soldier. The ancient woman lived alone in her large house, surrounded by old portraits, and was pleased to share her memories of courts and camps with her interested American visitor.

In July Mary and Stubby came to join Sarah and Annie, and Madame Blanc's nephew, Count Louis de Solms, undertook to show Theodore around Paris.

In England again Sarah fell in love with the Yorkshire country, riding and walking in the hills and on the moors among the heather and fern. She and Annie made a pilgrimage to Haworth and found it appealing but "dreadfully sad." The current vicar resented pilgrims to the Brontë family shrine, but Sarah told Sarah Whitman, "he didn't bite us." Although they had been advised that it would be a useless trip with nothing worth seeing, Sarah found the experience rewarding. She imagined the "little pale faces of those sisters at the vicarage windows" and looked with interest at the Black Bull Inn, where "the strange young brother used to comfort himself with light and laughter and country revelry, and break their hearts at the same time." It was also pleasant to renew their friendships with living literary acquaintances, such as

Mrs. Humphrey Ward and her daughter Dorothy and the Du Mauriers and to spend a day with the Rudyard Kiplings at Rottingdean on the coast.

Particularly memorable was a day spent with Henry James at Lamb House. Sarah and Annie took the train from London to Rye, where they found James waiting for them with a carriage. In five minutes they were at a green door with a brass knocker "wearing the air of impenetrable respectability," Annie wrote in her diary, "which is so well known in England." Smith, James's servant (who with his wife had been with the famous novelist for twenty years), opened the door to a house the travelers found severely plain, although they deemed it in the "best taste" and suitable for a scholar and private gentleman.

After they had been escorted upstairs to take off their hats, they descended to sit in the parlor overlooking a pretty garden with James and his secretary, Mr. McAlpine, whom Annie thought just the person to help Henry James, as he had a "bump of reverence" and appreciated his position and opportunity. Following a good luncheon, they explored the garden, and James showed them the small building that he laughingly called "The Temple of the Muse." It contained good writing tables for James and his secretary, a typewriter, and a few pictures, plus "excellent clear windows." Back in the parlor James told Sarah that he deeply and sincerely appreciated her work and reread it with increasing admiration. He questioned her about the setting of *The Country of the Pointed Firs* and complimented her on the language: "It is so absolutely true—not a word overdone—such elegance and exactness." The aging bachelor also gallantly expressed bewilderment at the miraculous youth of Annie and Sarah.

James took them by carriage to see the old city of Winchelsea, and then they all got into a train to go to Hastings. James brought along his aged black-and-tan terrier for a holiday, and at Hastings they enjoyed a ride along the esplanade. After tea and more talk they parted at the railway station, where James took a train back to Rye and Sarah and Annie returned to London with glowing memories of the warm hospitality shown them by the famous writer. In a notebook entry for February 19, 1899, Henry James acknowledged that Sarah Orne Jewett's story "A Lost Lover" in *Tales of New England* (which he termed "charming") had provided him with the germ of his story "Flickerbridge."

An undercurrent to their trip was the Spanish-American War, which was a constant topic of conversation and controversy during their stay in Europe. The excited reaction to the sinking of the U.S.S. Maine on February 15 had threatened to delay or cancel the trip altogether. Sarah, like many other Americans, had blamed the furor on petty politics, mercenary hopes, desires of naval personnel for promotions, and the "liking for a fight." But when war was formally declared in April and fighting actually begun, she changed her attitude. Writing to Sara Norton in June, she said that "such a war is to be laid at the door of progress" and compared the war to surgery that disgusts and frightens even as it cures. Like many others she had come to feel that American intervention was necessary to free Cuba from the tyranny of Spain, but she deplored the sensationalist journalism connected with the progress of the war and wished a few newspapers could be "drownded." Fortunately for Annie and Sarah, the fighting ended in August, well before their return trip.

CHAPTER TEN

◆

The Tory Lover

A FTER THEIR RETURN to New England, Sarah spent the next three months catching up on her voluminous correspondence and working on short stories. There was also time to play with Stubby (or Thidder, as Sarah sometimes addressed him in letters signed by "an ant"). Theodore had matured into a good-looking, cheerful young man who was a willing escort for his aunts, including Annie, whom he called "Aunt Annie." Sarah helped him choose his wardrobe and went with him to select curtains and rugs for his rooms in Cambridge.

In addition to taking him out for luncheons and tea, Sarah enjoyed going fishing and to football games with him. Together with Annie and Mary when she was in Boston, they went to lectures by Booker T. Washington and concerts by Paderewski and quite frequently to the theater. Sarah advised her nephew on his health, prescribing medicines for him when he was sick and urging him to have a good run every day to get the cotton out of his head from too long studying. He was often at 148 Charles Street for meals and to spend the night. In their letters to each other, Mary and Sarah referred to him as "our child," and proudly repeated compliments friends had made about him.

In January 1899 Sarah and Annie again boarded the *Hermione* with the Aldriches for a two-month cruise of the Bahamas. They spent a week in Nassau, which Sarah found charming, with its thatched-roof houses, women carrying large baskets of grapes and firewood on their heads, men riding little donkeys, and small black children wearing garments handed down to them by whites after they were outgrown. In letters to Sara Norton and Sarah Whitman she wrote glowing descriptions of wonderful new flowers, coconut trees, silk-cotton trees, and flaming flamingos. Port au Prince she thought "an awful scene of thriftlessness and silly pretense," but in Jamaica the new trees and flowers and the natives, with their bangles and turbans and strange eyes, charmed her. They returned to New England just ahead of the robins.

The last collection of stories by Sarah Orne Jewett to be published during her life was *The Queen's Twin and Other Stories*, which appeared in 1899. In addition to the two Dunnet Landing stories—"The Queen's Twin" and "A Dunnet Shepherdess"—it contained six other stories, including the highly praised "Martha's Lady," a story of a female friendship that was passionate and uplifting, as Sarah found many of her own relationships with her women friends to be. Helena and Martha are worlds apart socially—Helena is a lady and Martha is a maid—but they blossom through their mutual affection, and each is sustained by the knowledge that the other believes in her. Although Helena makes a brilliant match and has a happy marriage, her cousin, Miss Pyne, protests "in her heart" her decision to marry, "Helena was so equal to a happy independence," she thinks, "and even to the assistance of other lives grown strangely dependent upon her quick sympathies and instinctive decisions, that it was hard to let her sink her personality in the affairs of another." Clearly, she could have been speaking of the author herself, who had chosen a life of "happy independence" and who was guided by sympathy and instinct.

As usual, different stories in the collection appealed to different reviewers, but critics generally hailed the book and agreed with the reviewer of the *Outlook* (December 16, 1899), who praised her as a writer "who never attempts that which she cannot do." Sarah was especially pleased that "The Queen's Twin" won acclaim in England, where reviewers went out of their way to point out how the coincidences in the story between the proud recluse in New England and Queen Victoria might be possible.

At the end of the nineteenth century, Sarah's name was well known among publishers and her stories were popular among readers, so she felt confident in asking higher fees for her stories. In its April 6, 1899, issue *Life* magazine ran the following tribute:

> If I could look as she looks
> I wouldn't be bothered with books.
> If I could write as she writes
> My looks wouldn't vex me o' nights.
> But to write as she writes,
> And look as she looks,
> And charm as she charms—
> Who is there can do it,
> Save only Miss Jewett?

As her fame grew, so did the demands on her time. Requests for advice and support from individuals and groups multiplied. She responded warmly to fan letters, especially those that came from children about her juvenile books and stories, and she was generous in trying to help aspiring young writers, including John Thaxter, who worked prodigiously with little improvement.

She continued to take a lively interest in affairs in South Berwick, and she and Mary and Theodore served on a committee to administer the Fogg Memorial Library, which was housed in a wing of Berwick Academy and was the only public library in South Berwick. The local History Department of the Berwick Woman's Club held its regular meetings at the Jewett home, and Sarah tried to arouse interest in establishing a separate local historical society, although nothing came of this idea at the time.

In Boston Sarah co-hosted Annie Fields's Saturday afternoon receptions, and the two women were popular guests in the homes of the rich and well-known, particularly those who were connected with the arts. Their appearance at social functions rated notice in newspapers, and when they poured tea at an opening of an exhibition of John Singer Sargent's paintings, they drew as much attention as the art. In an article headlined "Tea More Popular Than Paintings," a reporter described Mrs. Fields's dress as "a black velvet gown relieved by a bit of exquisite lace" and noted that Miss Jewett was also dressed in black and wearing "a large, effective black hat with many nodding plumes."

In 1900 and 1901 trustees of the Public Library of Boston appointed Sarah a member of the Examining Committee to survey the library's resources. As chairman Sarah drafted and wrote the report of the subcommittee on books. Among other recommendations in the six-page report was one urging that children needed to be guided to the best books, including the classics and fairy tales. Another suggestion was that the library acquire Spanish, French, and German books and also that it should invest in travel books.

In January 1899 Annie had hired an automobile and driver one day to take them to a luncheon. They found it such an enjoyable adventure that from time to time they continued to hire cars for their transportation in and around the city. Another modern invention, a telephone, was installed at 148 Charles Street, and after one was also put into the Jewett home in South Berwick, Mary and Sarah sometimes spoke by telephone, usually only when they had a message of some urgency, as they preferred to continue their long practice of exchanging daily notes and letters. They had faith in the new means of communication, however, as they each bought stock in the Bell Telephone Company.

Among the many friends Sarah kept in touch with through long letters and visits was Alice Greenwood Howe, who had a cottage near Gambrel Cottage at Manchester-by-the-Sea. When *The Country of the Pointed Firs* was running serially in the *Atlantic*, Alice Howe had praised the sketches highly, and Sarah dedicated the book to her. The dedication was a surprise; Alice Howe knew about it only when she opened her copy.

After her mother's death, Sarah said: "it has been one of the best things in life to take up some of the old friendships that my mother had to let fall; there is a double sweetness in doing this; one feels so much of the pleasure of those who seem to see something of their lost companionship return." In addition to her mother's friends, many of Sarah's newer friends were also considerably older than she. Although there was a twenty-seven-year gap in the ages of Sarah and Mrs. Joseph (Susan Burley) Cabot, a close friendship grew between them. Mrs. Cabot kept a summer home, Misselwood, at Pride's Crossing, Beverly, Massachusetts, where Sarah visited her in the summer, and in the winter Sarah stayed several weeks in the elegant Beacon Street home of Mrs. Cabot. Toward the end of her life Mrs. Cabot was confined to her bed most of the time, but she was mentally alert and loved to play whist or backgammon in the evenings. "I sit in her room and talk and read and watch the sails go in and out of the harbor, and she speaks wisely from her comfortable great bed, while we have a comfortable sense of pleasure in being together," Sarah wrote to Sara Norton. Sarah dedicated *The Queen's Twin and Other Stories* to the aristocratic Mrs. Cabot, and when Mrs. Cabot died she left $20,000 from her large fortune to Sarah, along with a membership in the Boston Athenaeum.

In March 1900 Sarah and Annie set off on their fourth and final trip together to Europe. Traveling with them was

Mary Elizabeth Garrett, daughter of the president of the Baltimore & Ohio Railroad, who had a cottage at Dark Harbor, Maine, where Sarah visited. The crossing was rough, with gale winds that rolled them about in their berths and left water standing in their staterooms, and when they reached Naples they found spring was late and the weather disagreeably chilly. They enjoyed the museums, however, and made a trip to Pompeii. In a few days fig trees began to show green buds and the olives, Sarah wrote to Sara Norton, were "dark and splendid—as thick and warm and tufted as one of my own hills of pines."

Outside of Florence they had luncheon with Violet Paget, an English writer, who produced over thirty volumes of fiction, drama, and essays. She was a free spirit who wore short hair and tailored clothes and wrote under the pen name of Vernon Lee. The flowers along the banks of the villa's brook reminded Sarah of one of Botticelli's paintings, and she begged a little flowered Italian bowl of Miss Paget as a memento of the visit. They began a friendship that would grow mostly through correspondence, and enjoyed exchanging ideas about writing and about their mutual friend Madame Blanc.

From Brindisi the travelers took a steamer to Corfu and on to Greece, where they rode the train along the coast to Athens. They arrived at sunset, and their first impression of the Acropolis was of the great pillars of the Parthenon against the backdrop of the fiery sky. Although her formal education was limited, Sarah had studied on her own for many years and was well acquainted with Greek myths and legends. Now, seeing the wonderful marbles depicting the stories, row upon row, she told Sarah Whitman, "It is quite too much for a plain heart to bear," adding, "It isn't the least bit of use to try to write about those marbles, but they are simply the most human and affecting and beautiful things in the world." In the mornings they went to the museums and in the afternoons they visited the Acropolis, which enchanted Sarah with its setting of astonishingly blue sky and dazzling light, views of mountain ranges and far-off islands and ancient columns rising from springtime daisies and poppies.

Standing on Mars Hill, where St. Paul had preached his famous sermon, and visiting Corinth, she felt as if the biblical events were coming alive. They did a royal tour of Greece, traveling by coastal steamers or carriages. Despite being handicapped by an eye problem that forced her to cover one eye, wear black spectacles, and have guidebooks read to her, Sarah reveled in visiting places with magical names, such as Arcadia, Mycenae, Epidaurus, and Sparta. At Marathon she was duly impressed with the famous plain where the brave Athenian soldiers are buried, and in a letter to her cousin Alice Gilman she was equally enthusiastic over the brilliant carpet of wildflowers there—"little marigolds and big scarlet and purple anemones much larger than our pale ones, and two kinds of poppies and big blue forget-me-nots and tall stalks of asphodel...and pale purple gillyflowers all along the beach with our familiar beach peas."

From Contantinople she wrote to a girl who had sent her a fan letter after reading *Betty Leicester*. Her window, Sarah told her young reader, opened right out into the Arabian Nights: from it she could see all sorts of turbans and men with trays of sweetmeats and women with veils over their faces and the tops of mosques and minarets and queer companies of dogs that traveled about together and seemed to think they owned the city.

The finale of the three-month trip was a reunion with Madame Blanc at La Ferte and in Paris. They again enjoyed her bountiful hospitality and that of her aristocratic friends, such as Charlotte de Beaulaincourt, the daughter of the Maréchal de Castellane, who had served with distinction under both Napoleons. Madame Beaulaincourt was a friend of Empress Eugenie's, had a famous salon in Paris, and was the mentor of no less a genius than Marcel Proust, who modeled Madame de Villeparisis in *Remembrance of Things Past* after her. On their earlier trip in 1898, Sarah had been taken by Madame Blanc to visit the countess in her château near Paris, and she was pleased to have another opportunity to hear the tales of French history the aging woman had to tell.

When they returned to New England at the end of May, Sarah's eye was still troublesome. The first "foreign" letter she wrote was to Madame Blanc, and in it she mentioned that the *Atlantic* editors were urging her "almost irresistibly" to give them a long story for the next year. She had actually done a great deal of research toward such a book in the preceding three years, and for the year following her return from Europe she worked diligently on the writing of her last novel, *The Tory Lover.*

In June 1901 there were two pleasant interruptions in her working schedule. From Class Day to the commencement ceremony, she and Mary savored Theodore's graduation from Harvard. He received his A.B. *cum laude*, with a major in French, and their pleasure was increased by the fact that he had chosen to follow in his grandfather's footsteps and would enter Harvard Medical School in the fall.

The second notable event occurred during the 1901 Commencement at Bowdoin College, when Sarah Orne Jewett received the first degree of doctor of letters to be awarded by the school to a woman. She was thrilled by this honor from her father's alma mater. Sitting down to write Annie about the events of the day, she was so excited her pen "spluttered." She was especially touched at being so kindly welcomed by President Hyde and by the old chaplain's references to her father. "You can't think how nice it was to be the single sister of so many brothers at Bowdoin," she told Annie. The large audience applauded her twice with enthusiasm, and then there was the solemn satisfaction of walking in the procession in cap and gown and doctor's hood. "Mary was dear and lovely, and the great day was hers as much as mine, as you will know," Sarah concluded.

In gratitude to Bowdoin and as a permanent memorial

to honor her father, Sarah proposed to President Hyde that she commission her friend Sarah Whitman to design and fabricate a memorial window. The planning and execution took time and involved much correspondence, but finally on June 20, 1903, the stained-glass window was installed in Memorial Hall (now Pickard Theater), where it remains.

On July 10, 1901, Sarah wrote to her cousin Alice Gilman from Mrs. Cabot's place at Pride's Crossing that she had nearly completed *The Tory Lover* and was "almost too tired" after more than a year's steady hard work. She had been keeping at it both morning and afternoons and felt exhausted. Two days later she wrote Horace Scudder about the novel, telling him it was the culmination of the "dreams and hopes" of many a year. "I have always meant to do what I could about keeping some of the old Berwick flowers in bloom, and some of the names and places alive in memory," she told him, adding, "It has been the happiest year of work that ever came to me as well as the hardest."

The idea for such a book had teased her for many years. She had always been fascinated by the fact that John Paul Jones had recruited men in her home territory for his ship *Ranger*, which was built from New England wood on an island in the Piscataqua River. When Charles Dudley Warner (editor for *Harper's* and co-author with Mark Twain of *The Gilded Age*) visited her in South Berwick in the mid-1890s, he listened to her stories about the tensions between the people in her area who had had to choose whether to accept the Patriot cause or to remain loyal to Mother England. Having in mind that historical romances were becoming highly popular, he urged her to keep the idea for such a story about her area alive, telling her, "Even if your fires are banked up, keep the story fused in your mind." And this she had done.

She read copiously, devouring accounts of the American Revolutionary Period and everything she could find about John Paul Jones, including his logbooks. She had been absorbing since early childhood the stories told by her elders of the time when Berwick had an aristocracy. In her youth, she had often ridden the short distance from her home to the stately Hamilton Mansion at Pipe Stave landing on the Salmon Falls River, a tributary of the Piscataqua. After the death of Colonel Hamilton, in 1802, the beautiful old house fell upon hard times. For many years it was used as a farmhouse and for nearly a century it was handed down from family to family and sometimes treated more like a barn than a home. Sarah watched with increasing distress as it grew increasingly dilapidated. When it went up for sale in 1898, she interested one of her Boston friends, Mrs. Emily Tyson, in purchasing and restoring the house. After the restoration, Sarah again became a frequent guest in the historic home.

The Tory Lover begins in 1777 as Captain John Paul Jones lands at the Hamilton House wharf and is honored by Colonel Hamilton with a dinner attended by all the local dignitaries. In her dates (the Hamilton House was not built until 1787–88) and in the circumstances of some of her historical characters Sarah, like many other writers of historical romances, found it convenient to change facts to suit her purposes. In one instance, she was pleased to find that life imitates art.

She was aware that Lieutenant Samuel Wallingford of Dover, who had sailed with John Paul Jones, had been killed at sea. "But how could I write about him unless I kept him alive?" she asked Annie. She thought about the young man and his house and the members of his family whom she knew, and out of her imagination she renamed him Roger and made him a Tory whose sweetheart challenges him to do his duty and sign the Patriot's oath. To Sarah's amazement she found in papers sent her by a distant descendant of John Paul Jones proof that Wallingford *had* been a Tory who confessed to Jones that he had signed up for the sake of a lady and not from his own convictions. "Now how could I have guessed at his character, and what was likely to happen?" Sarah mused, adding, "Imagination is the only true thing in the world!"

In addition to using the Hamilton House and the Jewett house (along with its builder John Haggins), Sarah used other familiar landmarks and drew upon her intimate knowledge in describing the river and the surrounding countryside. Many autobiographical bits and pieces are woven into the fabric of the story. Roger Wallingford is confined in an English prison just as Sarah's own grandfather was, and her description of the prison has been praised for its realism. In addition to using historical persons such as John Paul Jones and Benjamin Franklin, Sarah brings in her own patriotic ancestor Nicholas Gilman as a character. Mary Hamilton, who is a splended horsewoman, has many of Sarah's traits, and her relationship with her wise mentor, Master Sullivan, is similar to the relationship Sarah had with Dr. Parsons at Mary's age.

In *The Tory Lover* Roger Wallingford changes his allegiance to please Mary Hamilton, his sweetheart, but his mother remains loyal to the crown. When her home is attacked by a mob of Patriots, she barely escapes. Thanks to the treachery of an enemy, Dickson, young Wallingford is accused of treason and ends up in Dartmoor Prison. Madam Wallingford and Mary Hamilton set out on the *Golden Dolphin* to search for Roger in England. After many narrow escapes and alarms, there is a happy ending: Dickson's treachery is discovered; Roger is freed; and he and Mary return together to New England with intimations of marriage. The novel has well-drawn scenes at sea, lovers' meetings, balls, dinner parties, mob scenes, and a prison scene, but it lacks the violence and romantic passion of other contemporary historical novels, such as Winston Churchill's *Richard Carvel*. This American writer, who was a graduate of the U.S. Naval Academy, also uses a hero who serves under John Paul Jones, and his popular book sold nearly a million copies.

The sales of *The Tory Lover* were less spectacular, but they were quite good for the time. By November 1901 it was in a fifth printing, with over 12,000 copies sold. Critics, at the time of its birth and down through the years, have tended to review *The Tory Lover* with ponderous seriousness, and it has been much maligned. Perceptive reviewers have pointed out the admirable workmanship of the book, which recreated the time, the place, and the people as well as the conflicts that tore family and friends apart during the Revolutionary period. It naturally suffered much in being constantly compared to *The Country of the Pointed Firs*, from which it was a complete departure. Critics who found the book praiseworthy usually qualified their praise by regretting that the author had strayed from her usual subject matter.

Sarah suffered the proverbial writer's despair over the gap between the dream and the reality. She wrote to Sara Norton: "I grow very melancholy if I fall to thinking of the distance between my poor story and the first dreams of it." As always, though, her optimistic nature and her belief in her integrity buoyed her and she added, "I believe that I have done it just as well as I could." In a letter to William Dean Howells she said that *The Tory Lover* was written "by heart" even better than *The Country of the Pointed Firs*, and that the two books held all her real knowledge and all her dreams about "my dear Berwick, York, Wells—the people I know and have heard about; the very dust of thought and association that made me!" But, she admitted, "one can't always say things as one should, when we care most; sometimes I write only the clumsy body, not the soul."

Praise from knowledgeable friends soothed her. One of these was Elizabeth Cabot Agassiz, biographer of her husband naturalist Jean Louis Agassiz and one of the founders of Radcliffe College, of which she served as president. When *The Tory Lover* first began to appear serially in the *Atlantic*, Mrs. Agassiz felt "doubtful" about it, but she told Sarah that she liked each number better than the last and came to take a great pleasure in the novel.

Horace Scudder wrote to applaud her "finely jointed workmanship." Many stories of the same general character, he told her, are "carpenter work; this is cabinet work of a

high order, and I marvel at the art which respects every particular, yet does not lose sight of the whole."

Most reviews of the novel, however, were and have continued to be less enthusiastic. Henry James, writing to thank
her for a copy of the book, expounded at length on his dislike
for "historic" novels, which he said are at best "all humbug."
He condescended to say she had handled her material "brave-
ly" and "firmly," but he urged her to go back to the "dear
Country of the Pointed Firs...that wants, misses, needs you."

In *Sarah Orne Jewett* Richard Cary concedes Sarah's pic-
torial art in scrupulously and lovingly portraying Berwick
during the Revolutionary era, but he faults her plot and
characterization and her inability to depict passion and violence. "*The Tory Lover*," Cary concludes "is the imprudence
of a thrush trying to roar like a lion."

Sarah reported to Madame Blanc in a letter written on
December 6, 1901, that she had had her usual bout of "la
grippe," which had put her behind in her work on some pro-
jected short stories. And she expressed excitement over a
coming visit to South Berwick by Julia Ward Howe and her
daughter, Laura Richards—both women prolific writers and
friends of Mary's and Sarah's. Laura Richards, who was just
one year younger than Sarah, had won acclaim for her story
Captain January, and was already well loved for her nonsense
verses for children. Mary had recruited Mrs. Howe to speak
to the Berwick Woman's Club, and the Somersworth (New
Hampshire) *Free Press* reported on December 13, 1901, that
Mrs. Howe spoke "of Whittier, the farmer boy, of Longfellow,
telling of his love for beautiful Fanny Appleton, many memories of Oliver Wendell Holmes and of James Russell Lowell as
'A Man's Man, not a Woman's Man.'" Before the speech, Mrs.
Howe's own momentous composition, "The Battle Hymn of
the Republic," was sung by the Reverend I. B. Mower. Mrs.
Howe and Laura Richards remained as guests in the Jewett
home for several days following the meeting.

In the early spring of 1902, Mrs. Humphrey Ward's daughter Dorothy came to South Berwick for a long visit of several weeks. Through Annie Fields Sarah had met the Ward family on trips to England, and she and Mrs. Ward had begun a pleasant friendship enhanced by frequent letters in which they discussed their current writing projects and commiserated with each other about their arthritis attacks. As usual when they had guests, Sarah helped Mary make plans for the entertainment and the meals. Lobster Newburgh, chicken, and Marlborough pie were among her suggestions for Dorothy Ward's visit. And she took pleasure in introducing her young English guest to the Maine that she had known only through Sarah's writings.

Another British visitor arrived in March to visit Annie and Sarah in Boston. Alice Meynell, poet and essayist, achieved such popularity in England that she was considered as a possible poet laureate upon the death of Tennyson. Mrs. Meynell, an energetic woman, bore her editor husband eight children while she continued to write prolifically and cultivated numerous friends in the literary world. In 1902 her volume of verse *Later Poems* enlarged her literary reputation, and she visited America. Annie and Sarah had discovered her poetry long before and had especially liked, Sarah told Sara Norton, the "reticence and restraint" of Alice Meynell's poems and essays. Sarah's friendship with this dynamic woman would brighten Sarah's last years.

On her fifty-third birthday, September 3, 1902, Sarah suffered a serious accident that cast a pall over her activities for the rest of her life and extinguished almost completely her ability to use the creative spark that continued to burn within her. On the afternoon of her birthday Sarah took her sister Mary and two friends for a carriage ride. Rebecca Young, treasurer of South Berwick's bank, sat in front with Sarah, and Mary and the other friend sat in the back. They took the route toward Old Berwick, a drive Sarah had made hundreds of times. But on this day the road on Place's Hill was covered with small loose stones. Partway down the hill the horse stepped on a rolling stone and fell, and Sarah and Rebecca were thrown out of the carriage over the horse's head. Rebecca was only bruised and Mary and her companion were not harmed, but Sarah suffered injuries to her head and spine from which she would never fully' recover.

For weeks she was hardly able to move, suffering from severe vertigo and violent headaches whenever she attempted to get out of bed. A few weeks after the accident she wrote to Tom Aldrich, "Perhaps you haven't heard what bad days I have fallen upon—or rather that I fell upon too hard a road the first of last month. I was thrown out of a high wagon and hurt my head a good deal and concussioned my spine, so that I am still not very well mended, and have to stay in bed or lie down nearly all the time."

Friends showered her with flowers, letters, and books, and in November she wrote to William Dean Howells to thank him for a book he had sent. Annie Fields had been seriously ill, Sarah told Howells, and added that he would understand how hard it had been not to be able to go to her. It was a great comfort to Sarah that Theodore, now in Harvard Medical School, frequently visited 148 Charles Street and sometimes stayed at night to help the nurses. As for her own condition, Sarah wrote with comic ruefulness, "The trouble was that I came down on my head and there is apparently some far greater offense in *half* breaking ones neck than in breaking it altogether." It was an added grief when John Tucker, faithful hostler and all-around handyman for the Jewett family for thirty years, died in December 1902.

Sarah saw several medical specialists, among them a woman doctor, a Dr. Dexter, who she thought was "an excellent practitioner." Her condition remained extremely difficult, however. Four months after the accident, she was still having attacks of acute pain in the back of her neck and spending the mornings in bed. And over a year later she continued to spend a good part of the day lying down or crept out into

the garden with a stick "walking zig-zag and swaying about."
She could read lying down and also write letters, but she was
unable to sit at her desk.

In an undated letter to Annie she admitted "an awful
feeling of despair rushes over me at the thought of doing any
more writing at all." It "fretted" her to think about copying
manuscripts and all the physical and mental effort connected
with writing. But with her usual optimism she told Annie,
"I shall be better by and by, and the stories will begin to write
themselves down again."

CHAPTER ELEVEN

◆

"The lilac bushes
still green"

ALTHOUGH IT WAS PAINFUL not to be able to write, Sarah had over the years provided herself with a network of friends who now gave her solace and distraction. One of these was Kate D. Riggs, who wrote books for children using her first name along with the name of her first husband, signing herself Kate Douglas Wiggin. In 1902, when *Rebecca of Sunnybrook Farm* surprised everyone by its instant popularity, Kate Riggs wrote Sarah to say that what pleased her most was that Sarah liked Rebecca, who was trudging along like a "stout, energetic little State O' Maine girl."

Before Sarah's accident, she had visited Kate Riggs in Hollis, Maine, and they had made short expeditions around the state together. But after Sarah was restricted by her infirmities, it was Kate who came to visit in South Berwick and at 148 Charles Street, offering friendship and encouragement. Between visits, she wrote jolly, friendly letters inquiring about Mary and Theodore, as well as the servants and the dogs and horses of the Jewett household. Mrs. Cabot was one of the mutual friends she and Sarah exchanged news of. When Bowdoin awarded Kate Wiggin an honorary doctorate, she wrote to President Hyde that deeply impressed as she was to be the daughter of Bowdoin, she was even prouder and happier to be Sarah Jewett's sister. And to Sarah she expressed the fervent hope that Sarah could attend the commencement to hold up her "feeble knees."

During the spring of 1903 the electric trolley lines of the Portsmouth, Dover, and York Street Railway added a branch line to South Berwick, and this brought more of Sarah's Boston and Newport friends to visit. William Dean Howells, now living in Kittery, blessed the trolley that took him to Berwick. One day he brought Henry James along for an afternoon of tea and talk. Sarah herself gradually began to make short trips, even though they cost her something in energy and pain. In a letter to Lizzie Gilman, Sarah compared herself to an old watch that stopped now and then and often ran down. When she had a little strength, the temptation to spend it was often too much for her and she quickly depleted her energy.

In February 1904, she managed to get to Boston, staying with Mrs. Cabot at 34 Beacon Street and then moving on to be with Annie at 148 Charles Street. She still had to husband her strength but was more able to think about business. She corresponded with Edward Garnett of London, who was promoting English editions of her works, and she wrote to Madame Blanc about a French translation of *The Tory Lover*, suggesting some corrections that should be made.

Although she was unable to write, some of her previously written short stories were published in the years following her accident. Two of these were Thanksgiving stories published in November 1902. "The Lost Turkey" is a children's story, published in *Youth's Companion*, and concerns an inadvertent act of kindness that ends a family feud. "Sister Peacham's Turn" (*Harper's Magazine*, November 1902) contrasts two elderly sisters, Mrs. Fellows—plump, outgoing, and good-natured—and Mrs. Peacham, who is thin, self-centered, and given to self-pity. In a battle of wits, Mrs. Fellows tricks Mrs. Peacham into taking her turn at preparing the Thanksgiving dinner and also into inviting the minister and his wife to join them. The activity of providing the hospitality and the compliments that follow bring Sister Peacham out of her self-imposed hermetic existence.

Sarah's children's story "Counted Out" appeared in *Youth's Companion* on December 24, 1903, and in May 1904 her short story "A Spring Sunday" appeared in *McClure's*. It is the story of Alonzo and Mary Ann Hallet, respectable and affluent city dwellers who play hooky from church one day in early spring and take a trolley ride to the little village where they began their married life. Through shared bittersweet memories of their young lives, when they were full of hopes and dreams and lost a dearly beloved little daughter, their love and faith in each other are revived. In the autumn of their lives the remembrance of the springtime of their youth has brought renewal.

Sarah's final story to be published during her life appeared in 1905. This story, "An Empty Purse: A Christmas Story," which had originally been published in the Boston *Evening Transcript* on December 21, 1895, was privately printed in 1905 for sale at the Christmas Fair at Trinity Chapel in Boston. It is one of several of Sarah's stories that follow biblical themes. Miss Debby Gaines, another of Sarah's indomitable spinsters, sets out to make Christmas the best she has ever had, despite having lost her small store of money saved for the occasion. She mends her own warm quilted petticoat to give to an old woman at the poorhouse, and she spends the day taking care of a sick child for a harassed young widow so the woman can take another child to visit grandparents. In contrast to Debby Gaines is wealthy Mrs. Rivers, whose standards at the beginning of the story are strictly gold and silver. Observing the happiness that Debby achieves in giving of herself, Mrs. Rivers rethinks her own materialism and comes to appreciate the joy of giving the gift of love.

A poem, "The Gloucester Mother," by Sarah appeared in *McClure's* in October 1908 and enjoyed a brief popularity. It is told by a mother who wakes in the night troubled by thoughts of people lost at sea—they do not, she thinks, rest quietly as do those buried on land. "How dark, how dark and cold / And fearful in the waves, / Are tired folk who lie not still / And quiet in their graves / In moving waters deep / That will not let men sleep." Much better, she believes, to lie under flowers a thousand springs, and she prays:

> God bless them all who die at sea!
> If they must sleep in restless waves,
> God make them dream they are ashore
> With grass above their graves!

In 1904 and again in 1905 Annie Fields went to Europe and Sarah enjoyed her travels vicariously. She had many "dumpy" days when pain forced her to lie around dozing fitfully. Different treatments were tried, including different medicines and the application of heat and wetness, but the only therapy that brought lasting relief was the most difficult one—keeping quiet in body and in mind. In the summer of 1905 a friend, Helen Bigelow Merriman, artist and author of books and articles on painters and painting, offered Sarah the use of the family home, Stonehurst, at Intervale, New Hampshire. In this large, comfortable house set on a wooded estate, Sarah spent quiet weeks with only a nurse for company. As her doctors had forbidden writing or reading, she tried to be content with crocheting and being read to by her nurse.

In September Sarah went alone with a nurse to take the waters at Poland Spring, Maine. Watching the antics of the *nouveau riche* who came to the spa amused her. There were all sorts of "terrible rich and splendid westerners and southerners" whose jewels and gowns were "a wonder" that dazzled her eyes, she told Annie. They reminded her of her wise old grandfather Perry's saying, "Oh, they're not people, they're nothing but a pack of images!" Occasionally she saw real people such as two "dear old ladies," sitting together at a table, that made her feel she must stop and speak.

Gradually her vertigo subsided and she began to enjoy her usual eclectic reading. She devoured Henry James's latest stories and enjoyed rereading Austen and Turgenev. She felt great sympathy for this stranger whose instincts seemed so like her own. Describing Turgenev's writing to Charles Miner Thompson, who had written a critique of her work for the *Atlantic*, she quoted from the preface of the book *Rudin:*

There was in him [Turgenev] such a love of light, sunshine and living human poetry, such an organic aversion of all that is ugly, or coarse, or discordant, that he made himself almost exclusively the poet of the gentler side of human nature. On the fringe of his pictures, or in their background, just for the sake of contrast, he will show us the vices, the cruelties, even the mire of life. But he cannot stay in these gloomy regions, and he hastens back to the realms of the sun and flowers, or to the poetical moonlight of melancholy.

William Dean Howells earlier had perceptively seen a likeness between Sarah's writing and Turgenev's, and now she was pleased to have time to read more of the writer and see the likeness herself. She also enjoyed reading Owen Wister, whose *The Virginian* and other western stories were becoming popular.

In 1904, when Sarah Wyman Whitman died, Sarah felt the loss of her friend deeply. In August 1903 she had written to Sarah, addressing her as "Dear Old Fellow," expressing pleasure that S.W. and Annie had been together during the summer and regret that the dread of being jolted on a train made her afraid to undertake a visit to her friend. One of Sarah's last literary endeavors was to edit Sarah Whitman's letters for publication. Many of the letters had been written to Sarah Jewett herself, and the responsibility of making it a book worthy of their friendship weighed upon her. She begged her collaborator, Frances Parkman, not to let the letters be chopped up into fragments and so lose the art that went into writing them.

Keeping in touch with her relatives and friends by letters had to serve as a substitute for the writing Sarah was incapable of doing, as any attempt to write creatively increased her feeling of vertigo. "My wits get blurred over easily," she told Alice Meynell. When people said to her, "Can't you write a little?" she could only tell them that she lacked the sense of balance so important to being able to create a story. To Dorothy Ward, she described her illness as being a "long pull," but she could only pull for a short while at a time and then had to give up and take to her bed for a long period of rest.

In the summer of 1906 Sarah made a long visit to Mrs. Cabot at Pride's Crossing. She especially enjoyed the Watteau Fête, with its shepherds and nymphs and real sheep and lambs in procession and dance. "I have really come back to some sense of pleasure in life," she told Sara Norton, "though I feel like a dissected map with a few pieces gone." When they had no visitors, she and Mrs. Cabot read some of their old favorite books together.

Sarah's three remaining grandaunts died in 1906, and characteristically she deliberately chose to take a positive attitude. She told her friend Mary Ellen Chase that she remembered their houses, where she had been so often warmly welcomed as "dear and beautiful and full of kindness" with a thankful heart. "It was wonderful," she added, "to have kept them all so long." On one of her good days, Sarah and Mary took the trolley trip to her Aunt Anne's house near Portsmouth. A caretaker let them into the house where they had so often visited as children and which Sarah had used as the setting for her story "Lady Ferry." In the yard still stood the old familiar pear tree with its harvest dropped on the grass as if even then Aunt Anne would not let them go away empty-handed.

Despite two attacks of influenza during the winter and

spring of 1907, Sarah was well enough by summer to accept an invitation to stay with her sister Mary at the cottage of Mary Cabot Wheelwright's family at Mt. Desert, Maine. Mary Cabot Wheelwright (1878–1958), the only daughter of Sarah Perkins Cabot and Andrew Cunningham Wheelwright of Boston and Northeast Harbor, used her inherited wealth to further her deepest interests—art and music. She helped found and direct the Museum of Navajo Ceremonial Art in Santa Fe, New Mexico, and the South End Music School in Boston. Sarah enjoyed sailing on the Wheelwright family yacht, the *Hesper.* It sailed, she told her friend Louisa Dresel, like a swallow, adding, "I don't like to joggle on a steam boat half so well as to sail free."

The fragrance of the woods and the salt air of the pointed-firs country in the Boothbay area revived old memories and aroused new hope. She felt that she might begin to write again, if she could find just the right place with the "right kind of quietness." But her muse refused to cooperate. "Why should writing be the most difficult thing now when I spent all my life once in doing it?" she mournfully wrote to Sarah Wheelwright, but quickly added, "Let us not discuss these things," and went on to thank Mrs. Wheelwright for a lovely visit.

Louisa Dresel, to whom Sarah wrote about this visit, was another resident of Beacon Hill and a frequent visitor to 148 Charles Street. Letters between Louisa and Sarah reveal that they also met frequently at Manchester and at Cove Hill, the Dresel family cottage on Massachusetts Bay. Dr. Richard Cary's description of Louisa Loring Dresel as "one of that great breed of literate, talented, austerely sophisticated women of genteel upbringing that proliferated around metropolitan Boston in the last decades of the last century" is offset by Annie Fields's characterization in a note to Sarah: "Loulie is bigger and more disastrous than ever! She is happier and kinder than ever, too." Their letters are full of chat about artists and art exhibits, since painting was Louisa's great love, and a field that Sarah continued to dabble in all her life. On trips abroad they wrote each other long, colorful descriptions and freely expressed their feelings. They felt free to tell each other their delight in childlike play—riding a bicycle and scooting downhill on a boy's sled. And they frequently exchanged gifts—books, pictures, jewelry, and amusing Christmas stockings stuffed with prunes, frizzy wigs, toy cats, and shamrocks. Sarah also discussed her work in progress with Louisa, keeping her apprised of both the agony and the ecstasy.

Sarah was saddened by news of the death of Madame Blanc in 1907. She wrote to their mutual friend Violet Paget (Vernon Lee) describing her sense of loss. "Every way I turn I find one of her letters, in a book, in a desk, as if she still put them into my hand and tried to speak in that way." Sarah told Miss Paget, "I shall always be missing her as new things and new days come and go without her, but the old days—nine years writing before we met and fifteen years since—are mine with all she was and all the friendship gave me." The following year she thanked the English author for sending her a copy of *The Sentimental Traveller*, telling her that the chapter on Madame Blanc and La Ferte was "first in my heart."

Just as winter turned toward spring in 1908, Mrs. Louis Brandeis came to tea one afternoon at 148 Charles Street. Mrs. Brandeis (whose husband would be appointed to the U.S. Supreme Court by Woodrow Wilson) was a near neighbor and an old friend of both Annie and Sarah. On this day she took the liberty of bringing along a young journalist and author named Willa Cather, who had begun to make her mark as a poet and writer of fiction. In *Not Under Forty* Willa Cather recorded her impression of the visit. "Sometimes entering a new door can make a great change in one's life," she wrote. Although Annie Fields was over seventy, she did not appear old to Willa. "I had seldom heard so young, so merry, so musical a laugh," she said. She found Annie Fields reclining on a green sofa and Sarah Jewett sitting across the low tea table from her, looking much like the youthful picture of herself in the card game called "Authors" that Willa had played as a child, except that her figure was fuller and her hair sprinkled with gray. Sarah was, Willa recognized, "a lady, in the old high sense. It was in her face and figure, in her carriage, her smile, her voice, her way of greeting one. There was an ease, a graciousness, a light touch in conversation, a delicate unobtrusive wit."

As the atmosphere of the house enveloped her, the young author felt the ugliness of the world to be securely shut out. "It was indeed the peace of the past, where the tawdry and cheap have been eliminated and the enduring things have taken their proper, happy places," she remembered. Mrs. Brandeis asked that Willa be shown some of the treasures of the house, but the starry-eyed young visitor had "no eyes for the treasures"—she was too intent upon her hostesses.

Annie and Sarah were as intrigued by Willa Cather as she was by them, and they gathered her into the circle of friends who were always welcome at 148 Charles Street and at Thunderbolt Hill at Manchester-by-the-Sea. Willa Cather's friendship with Annie Fields remained constant from their first meeting until Annie's death in 1915, and through Annie Willa came to know many important people in the literary world.

Although Sarah and Willa had only sixteen months to know each other, their friendship was instant and intense. Willa soon realized that underneath that ladylike exterior lay a realistic and innate capability and happily for her a willingness to take infinite pains to help an aspiring young author. During the brief time remaining to her, Sarah gave her new friend invaluable encouragement and advice. The meeting could not have come at a more propitious time for Willa Cather, who had recently come to Boston to work on assignment for *McClure's*.

Sarah read Willa's stories and praised much that she found in them, but pointed out to her that she was not using her "uncommon equipment"—that is, her backgrounds in Nebraska, in Virginia, and in newspaper and magazine offices, to the best advantage. "I want you to be surer of your backgrounds," Sarah told her, and she advised Willa, "Find your own quiet centre of life, and write from that to the world." "You must write to the human heart, the great consciousness that all humanity goes to make up," she warned. "Otherwise what might be strength in a writer is only crudeness, and what might be insight is only observation; sentiment falls into sentimentality—you can write about life, but never write life itself."

During Willa's visits to 148 Charles Street, Manchester-by-the-Sea, and South Berwick, the two women discovered they had much in common in their backgrounds. As children both had been drawn to older people and had grown up listening to tales of bygone days. What the sea was for Sarah, the prairie was for Willa—an endless source of fascination and an inspiration. Just as Sarah had grown up with an understanding of the divided loyalties of her family during the Revolutionary War, Willa had grown up with the ambiguity of the divided loyalties of her recent ancestors during the Civil War. Both women had considered becoming doctors, and both had restless natures, traveling and moving about a great deal. Most significantly, they shared a deep seriousness about their chosen work that would result in each of them being recognized as a pioneer in her chosen arena.

Not only did Willa send her stories in progress to Sarah for the older writer's perceptive comments, but she also encouraged Sarah to write something for *McClure's*. And Sarah tried hard to respond. "No story yet...but I do not despair," she wrote in August 1908. "I begin to dare to think I could get something done for you, and it should be for you," she promised.

When their mutual friend Charles Eliot Norton died in

October 1908, Sarah wrote to Howells, "What a dear friend—what a helper and teacher he has been! But how he has made us value the dust of which we are made, and how the springs of friendship quickly washed away everything but some fairy gold when we were with him." And she urged Howells to visit Sally Norton (Charles Eliot's daughter) as often as he could, as he was sure to be one of her "truest comforts." The previous fall in the *Atlantic* Howells had reminisced about his days as editor of the magazine in an article called "Recollections of an *Atlantic* Editorship." It had been his good luck, he wrote, to encourage Sarah Jewett in "the free movement, unfettered by the limits of plot, and keeping only to the reality, which no other eye than hers has seen so subtly, so humorously, so touchingly."

After a visit from Willa Cather to South Berwick in November 1908, Sarah felt too weak to make the half-hour drive to the station with her and wrote ruefully of her disappointment at being too "bankrupt" of strength to sit up long enough to make the short trip and enjoy another few minutes of talk. In mid-December Sarah used up a large chunk of her waning strength in writing Willa a long letter of advice, in which she pointed out specific ways that some of Willa's short stories might be improved. Bluntly, she told the younger writer that her writing was being hindered by "such incessant, important, responsible work as you have in your hands now." And she stressed the impossibility of meeting the heavy duties of editorship and being able to find time and energy for allowing her creative gifts to mature as they should. Sarah warned her that if she didn't have the time and quiet to perfect her work, she would be writing things five years from then that were not much better than at the beginning of her career. "To work in silence and with all one's heart, that is the writer's lot; he is the only artist who must be a solitary, and yet needs the widest outlook upon the world."

On her visits to South Berwick, Willa became good friends with Mary Jewett, and after Sarah's death, she visited Mary for periods of recuperation from her restless, busy life, finding peace and comfort in sitting at Sarah's desk and in her beloved garden. She dedicated *O Pioneers!* to Sarah's memory, and in 1925 she wrote a laudatory preface to *The Best Stories of Sarah Orne Jewett*, in which she distinguished between the writing of a creative artist and the work of a reporter. "A reporter," she said, "can write equally well about everything that is presented to his view, but a creative writer can do his best only with what lies within the range and character of his talent." An artist's genius is defined by noting his limitations, she wrote. Sarah Orne Jewett's stories, she noted, have "much to do with fisher-folk and seaside villages; with juniper pastures and lonely farms, neat gray country houses and delightful, well-seasoned old men and women. That, when one thinks of it in a flash, is New England."

Although she could no longer gather her creative forces to compose stories and sketches, Sarah wrote creative passages in letters. In January 1909, she described a sleigh ride along the frozen Piscataqua River to the house of a friend, Fanny Morse. The snow, she wrote, was "very white and thinly spread like the nicest frosting over the fields, and the pine-woods as black as they could be." There were tracks of "every sort of little beastie. They seemed to have been *all out* on visits and errands and going *such* distances on their little paws and claws; somehow it looks too much for a mouse to go half a mile along the road or across a field. Think how a hawk would see him!" She could identify every track but one that showed its maker to have long claws and a tail than never lifted. Finally she decided upon a big old rat who had come up from an old wharf by the riverside. The letter ended with an admonishment to her friend to take her time in recuperating from a recent illness and ended, "I have had such drear times trying to play well when I *wasn't!*"

What strength she could gather, Sarah spent. In January 1909 she gave a reading of "The Hiltons' Holiday" to an audience of 150 girls at Simmons College in Boston and stayed on afterward to meet and talk with all the girls who were from Maine.

During February she seemed to be making one of her "pulls" into better health, but in early March she suffered a stroke that left her paralyzed on one side, although her mind was still clear. She was in Boston, and Mary came hurrying to 148 Charles Street to be with her sister, and a corps of nurses was hired to take care of her.

As usual, Sarah made the best of a bad situation and established a sympathetic rapport with her young, inexperienced night nurse, Florence Dunnack. When Sarah discovered the nurse had grown up in Maine and knew anemones and dogtooth violets and trailing arbutus and had heard Julia Ward Howe read her "Battle Hymn of the Republic," they had endless material to talk about. The young nurse never forgot the interest her illustrious patient took in her nor her kindness and humor that relieved the somberness of the sickroom.

After the snow melted and the days warmed, it was decided to move Sarah back to South Berwick to continue her recuperation. Complicated arrangements were made for a special railroad car to take her home. Down the stairs that had echoed to the footsteps of Thackeray, Dickens, and Whittier she was carried, past the drawing room window overlooking the Charles, past her empty writing desk and past a long mirror that reflected the dining room where she and Annie had enjoyed so many excellent dinners in the company of friends such as Longfellow and Holmes. At the end of the train trip Sarah and her nurses were transported by ambulance to the big house on the village square where Sarah had been born.

There servants, family, and friends surrounded Sarah and gave her every attention they could think of. She sent her nurses out with the family driver, who had instructions to show them the view from some of her favorite vantage points. And when they returned, sometimes laden with wildflowers, she questioned them eagerly about every detail of the people, the places, the trees, the creatures, and the flowers they had seen.

As spring flowers came and went, the gardener made offerings to Sarah of lilies of the valley and pansies and other blossoms. Occasionally she felt well enough to move about the house in a wheelchair or to sit mutely by her old desk at the upstairs window overlooking the busy town square. On good days she received calls from neighbors and friends, but she rejected talk of illness and overt offers of sympathy. She and Annie kept in close touch by telephone and letters, and when she had advanced enough to be able to take a few steps, she thought of going back to Boston. Sarah told Annie that she knew she couldn't manage the stairs at 148 Charles Street, but she thought if she stayed at the Parker House, where there was an elevator, she could get along all right.

On May 20 she began a note to Annie, making plans to return to Boston. When the note, unfinished and unsigned (written in almost illegible slanted handwriting), reached Annie, she wrote across the bottom of it, "My courage and hope ended with this note." Annie had always known Sarah as a great planner, who constantly used her ingenuity to devise schemes to cheer her own path and the paths of others, so when Annie read, "Dear, I do not know what to do with me!" she truly despaired.

A few short weeks later, on the twenty-third of June, Sarah suffered another cerebral hemorrhage and died the following day at 6:40 in the evening. She was fifty-nine years old. The next morning Mary sent a note to Louisa Dresel at Cove Hill: "Dear Loulie, Dear Sarah went away from us yesterday afternoon just as the sun was setting. It was so peaceful that we hardly knew the moment of the passing, and I am so thankful for the blessed release for her."

Some years earlier Sarah had told a reporter who was interviewing her in the Jewett home in South Berwick, "I was born here and I hope to die here leaving the lilac bushes still green, and all the chairs in their places." Her plan had come true.

◆
Afterword

ANNIE FIELDS SURVIVED SARAH by nearly six years. She spent two years collecting and editing a book of Sarah's letters. The arrangement must have been a formidable task, as Sarah rarely put a date on her letters, preferring to head them "Tuesday evening" or "Sunday morning." Obviously some of the letters are misplaced chronologically, and some are cropped and edited to eliminate personal references and some of the nicknames and affectionate "little language" Sarah used so freely. But just as obviously the book, published in 1911, is a labor of love. And as Annie points out in the preface, the letters show, above all, "the portrait of a friend and the power that lies in friendship to sustain the giver as well as the receiver." When Annie Fields died in 1915, the hospitable doors of 148 Charles Street closed forever, and it wasn't long before bulldozers leveled the historic structure to make way for a parking garage.

Mary Jewett survived Sarah by twenty-one years, becoming more and more the *grande dame* of South Berwick. She was much involved in the affairs of the village and spent her time doing good works for a wide variety of causes and organizations, including the District Nursing Association, the York County Children's Aid Society, the New Hampshire and

Maine Historical Societies, and Berwick Academy. Regularly Mary made new clothes for Sarah's doll, and when Mary died, the doll was buried in her grave.

Theodore Eastman died following an operation just six months after his Aunt Mary—on March 9, 1931. He had become a well-known physician in Boston and was on the staff of the Massachusetts General Hospital. In his will he left the Jewett home in South Berwick to the Society for the Preservation of New England Antiquities of Boston, along with $20,000 to be used for its upkeep. Theodore, who had remained a bachelor, inherited a sizable fortune from his two aunts. His will provided various generous bequests to family servants and to relatives, with the residue of his estate going to Berwick Academy.

In addition to the Sarah Orne Jewett House, SPNEA owns and maintains the Hamilton House in South Berwick (which Sarah used as a setting in *The Tory Lover*). Both houses are well kept up and open to the public from June 1 through October 15.

In 1987 in a Boston bank vault, two copies of the Constitution, with scribbled notes and doodles by Nicholas Gilman, Sarah's illustrious ancestor (who was a New Hampshire delegate to the Constitutional Convention), were discovered. Gilman's clapboard home in Exeter, New Hampshire, is a museum where, as late as mid-1991, valuable historical treasures continue to turn up. Among these are a drawing by Paul Revere of the Boston Massacre, papers signed by Louis XVI and Lafayette, and a ring with a lock of George Washington's hair.

Celia Thaxter's cottage on Appledore Island burned to the ground in 1914, and her fabled garden fell on hard times, filling up with poison ivy and scrubby vegetation. But happily Cornell University, which operates Appledore Island as a research station, has restored her garden according to the descriptions by Celia and Childe Hassam in *An Island Garden*. Today the replica of her garden blooms from early spring until late fall with the same flowers she describes so lovingly in the book. In 1990–91 the National Museum of American Art in Washington, D.C., sponsored a showing of Childe Hassam's paintings of the garden entitled "Childe Hassam: An Island Garden Revisited."

Sarah entrusted her unprinted papers and unfinished manuscripts to Annie Fields and to her sister Mary. In 1916 Mary asked Mark A. DeWolfe Howe, a friend of Annie's and Sarah's, to collect and publish some of Sarah's poems. The resulting volume, simply entitled *Verses*, contains nineteen of her poems, including the two she wrote to her father soon after his death. The title page states that the book (printed by the Merrymount Press of Boston) is "Printed for Her Friends." Sarah herself never felt that she expressed herself in poetry as well as she did in prose, and critics have agreed with her, although twelve of these poems had been published previously in magazines.

In 1956 Professor Richard Cary of Colby College edited a volume of Sarah Orne Jewett's letters, in 1967 he compiled an enlarged and revised edition of some of her correspondence, and in 1971 he edited a volume of forty-four of Sarah's stories (*The Uncollected Short Stories of Sarah Orne Jewett*), which had not appeared in the eleven anthologies of her published works, although the majority of them had appeared in magazines or newspapers.

In 1910 Houghton Mifflin Company of Boston and Constable & Company of London brought out a uniform edition of her work in seven volumes with two choices of bindings— red cloth and blue leather. The set includes *Deephaven, A Country Doctor, Tales of New England, A Native of Winby, The Life of Nancy, The Country of the Pointed Firs*, and *The Queen's Twin*. Since then her stories have continued to be published separately and in anthologies and literary histories. Other nations have continued to discover the universal values in Sarah Orne Jewett's deceptively simple tales. Her stories have been translated into German, Japanese, Spanish and French.

Critics have often compared Sarah to Thoreau, who was also a pioneer ecologist, a mystic, and a transcendentalist with a prevailing sense of the past. Although he died when she was only thirteen, she would certainly have been acquainted with his works and ideas. She is less often compared to Ralph Waldo Emerson, whom she knew in his old age and for whom she had great respect, amounting almost to awe. His mystic idealism—"Nature is the incarnation of thought. The world is the mind precipitated"—was her philosophy also. And the ideas Emerson expressed in "Self-Reliance" were also those that guided her life. Resolutely, she chose the paths she would follow in her career and in her life. As far as it was possible, she made her own decisions and controlled her own destiny.

In an essay published in the *Atlantic Monthly* (October 1904), Charles Miner Thompson poetically and aptly characterized Sarah Orne Jewett and her writing. "I always think of her," he said, "as of one who, hearing New England accused of being a bleak land without beauty, passes confidently over the snow, and by the gray rock, and past the dark fir tree, to a southern bank, and there, brushing away the decayed leaves, triumphantly shows to the fault-finder a spray of the trailing arbutus." That "fragrant, retiring, exquisite flower," he said, symbolized her own "modest and delightful art."

Sarah Orne Jewett explored the ethos of New England and preserved forever an important segment of its history along with the homely details of a vanished way of life, including patterns of speech, behavior, and thought. In her writing and in her life she exemplified qualities of simplicity, serenity, sincerity, and sympathy, along with a wise optimism. She was secure in her belief that after the long chill of winter, the warmth of spring will follow in the lives of men as in nature.

♦

Selected
Bibliography

The following chronological listing of published works by Sarah Orne Jewett does not include some of her juvenile writing and some of her newspaper and magazine stories and articles.

Published Works by Sarah Orne Jewett

Deephaven. Boston: James R. Osgood and Company, 1877.
Play Days: A Book of Stories for Children. Houghton, Osgood and Company, 1878.
　　(Contents: "Discontent," "The Water Dolly," "Prissy's Visit," "My Friend the Housekeeper," "Marigold House," "Nancy's Doll," "The Best China Saucer," "The Desert Islanders," "Half-Done Polly," "Woodchucks," "The Kitten's Ghost," "The Pepper-Owl," "The Shipwrecked Buttons," "The Yellow Kitten," "Patty's Dull Christmas," "Beyond the Toll-Gate.")
Old Friends and New. Boston: Houghton, Osgood and Company, 1879.
　　(Contents: "A Lost Lover," "A Sorrowful Guest," "A Late Supper," "Mr. Bruce," "Miss Sydney's Flowers," "Lady Ferry," "A Bit of Shore Life.")

Country By-Ways. Boston: Houghton, Mifflin and Company, 1881.
> (Contents: "River Driftwood," "Andrew's Fortune," "An October Ride," "From a Mournful Villager," "An Autumn Holiday," "A Winter Drive," "Good Luck: A Girl's Story," "Miss Becky's Pilgrimage.")

The Mate of the Daylight, and Friends Ashore. Boston: Houghton, Mifflin and Company, 1884.
> (Contents: "The Mate of the Daylight," "A Landless Farmer," "A New Parishioner," "An Only Son," "Miss Debby's Neighbors," "Tom's Husband," "The Confession of a House-Breaker," "A Little Traveler.")

A Country Doctor. Boston: Houghton, Mifflin and Company, 1884.

A Marsh Island. Boston: Houghton, Mifflin and Company, 1885.

A White Heron and Other Stories. Boston: Houghton, Mifflin and Company, 1886.
> (Contents: "A White Heron," "The Gray Man," "Farmer Finch," "Marsh Rosemary," "The Dulham Ladies," "A Business Man," "Mary and Martha," "The News from Petersham" "The Two Browns.")

The Story of the Normans, Told Chiefly in Relation to Their Conquest of England. New York: G.P. Putnam's Sons, 1887.

"My School Days." *The Berwick Scholar*, October, 1887.

The King of Folly Island and Other People. Boston: Houghton, Mifflin and Company, 1888.
> (Contents: "The King of Folly Island," "The Courting of Sister Wisby," "The Landscape Chamber," "Law Lane," "Miss Peck's Promotion," "Miss Tempy's Watchers," "A Village Shop," "Mère Pochette.")

"A Plea for Front Yards." *The Berwick Scholar*, December 1888.

"Unlearned Lessons." *The Berwick Scholar*, February 1889.

Betty Leicester: A Story for Girls. Boston: Houghton, Mifflin and Company, 1890.

Tales of New England. Boston: Houghton, Mifflin and Company, 1890.
(Contents: "Miss Tempy's Watchers," "The Dulham Ladies," "An Only Son," "Marsh Rosemary," "A White Heron," "Law Lane," "A Lost Lover," "The Courting of Sister Wisby.")

Strangers and Wayfarers. Boston: Houghton, Mifflin and Company, 1890.
(Contents: "A Winter Courtship," "The Mistress of Sydenham Plantation," "The Town Poor," "The Quest of Mr. Teaby," "The Luck of the Bogans," "Fair Day," "Going to Shrewsbury," "The Taking of Captain Ball," "By the Morning Boat," "In Dark New England Days," "The White Rose Road.")

"Looking Back on Girlhood." *Youth's Companion*, January 7, 1892.

A Native of Winby and Other Tales. Boston: Houghton, Mifflin and Company, 1893.
(Contents: "A Native of Winby," "Decoration Day," "Jim's Little Woman," "The Failure of David Berry," "The Passing of Sister Barsett," "Miss Esther's Guest," "The Flight of Betsey Lane," "Between Mass and Vespers," "A Little Captive Maid.")

Betty Leicester's English Xmas: A New Chapter of an Old Story. New York: Dodd, Mead & Co., 1894. Published as *Betty Leicester's Christmas* by Houghton, Mifflin and Company, 1899.

"The Old Town of Berwick." *The New England Magazine*, 1894, pp. 585–609.

Introduction to *Human Documents: Portraits and Biographies of Eminent Men.* New York: S. S. McClure, 1895.

The Life Of Nancy. Boston: Houghton, Mifflin and Company, 1895.
(Contents: "The Life Of Nancy," "Fame's Little Day,"

"A War Debt," "The Hiltons' Holiday," "The Only Rose,"
"A Second Spring," "Little French Mary," "The Guests
of Mrs. Timms," "A Neighbor's Landmark," "All My Sad
Captains.")

The Country of the Pointed Firs. Boston: Houghton, Mifflin
and Company, 1896.

The Queen's Twin and Other Stories. Boston: Houghton, Mif-
flin and Company, 1899.
(Contents: "The Queen's Twin," "A Dunnet Shepherdess,"
"Where's Nora?" "Bold Words at the Bridge," "Martha's
Lady," "The Coon Dog," "Aunt Cynthy Dallett," "The
Night Before Thanksgiving.")

The Tory Lover. Boston: Houghton, Mifflin and Company,
1901.

An Empty Purse: A Christmas Story. Boston: The Merrymount Press, 1905.

Letters of Sarah Orne Jewett. Boston: Houghton, Mifflin and
Company, 1911. Edited by Annie Fields.

Verses. Boston: Merrymount Press, 1916.

Sarah Orne Jewett Letters. Waterville, ME: Colby College
Press, 1956. Edited by Richard Cary.

Sarah Orne Jewett Letters. Enlarged and revised. Waterville,
ME: Colby College Press, 1967. Edited by Richard Cary.

The Uncollected Short Stories of Sarah Orne Jewett. Edited
with introduction by Richard Cary. Waterville, ME: Col-
by College Press, 1971.
(Contents: "Jenny Garrow's Lovers," "The Girl With the
Cannon Dresses," "The Orchard's Grandmother," "Paper
Roses," "Stolen Pleasures," "Hallowell's Pretty Sister," "A
Guest at Home," "A Dark Carpet," "The Hare and the
Tortoise," "Miss Manning's Minister," "The Becket Girls'
Tree," "A Visit Next Door," "A Garden Story," "A
Christmas Guest," "The Growtown 'Bugle,'" "The New
Methuselah," "Mrs. Parkins's Christmas Eve," "A Finan-
cial Failure: The Story of a New England Wooing," "A
Way Station," "Peg's Little Chair," "An Every-Day Girl,"

"Peach-tree Joe," "Told in the Tavern," "In a Country Practice," "A Dark Night," "An Empty Purse," "A Change of Heart," "A Village Patriot," "A Pinch of Salt," "The First Sunday in June," "The Gray Mills of Farley," "The Parshley Celebration," "A Landlocked Sailor," "The Stage Tavern," "The Foreigner," "Elleneen," "The Green Bonnet: A Story of Easter Day," "A Born Farmer," "The Green Bowl," "The Honey Tree," "The Spur of the Moment," "Sister Peacham's Turn," "The Lost Turkey," "A Spring Sunday.")

Unpublished Sources

I have examined letters, transcripts, manuscripts, notes, journals, diaries, genealogical material, and pictures in the following libraries and archives:

Alderman Library, Special Collections, University of Virginia, Charlottesville, Virginia.

Dimond Library, Special Collections, University of New Hampshire, Durham, New Hampshire.

Hawthorne-Longfellow Library, Special Collections, Bowdoin College, Brunswick, Maine.

Houghton Reading Room, The Houghton Library, Harvard University, Cambridge, Massachusetts.

The Maine Women Writers Collection, Westbrook College, Portland, Maine.

Manuscripts and Special Collections Library, Maine Historical Society, Portland, Maine.

Miller Library, Special Collections, Colby College, Waterville, Maine.

Rare Books and Manuscripts Library, Columbia University Libraries, Columbia University, New York, New York.

Society for the Preservation of New England Antiquities Archives, Boston, Massachusetts.

Dissertations and Theses on Sarah Orne Jewett

Bishop, Ferman. "The Mind and Art of Sarah Orne Jewett." Doctoral dissertation, University of Wisconsin, 1955.

Collins, Michael Francis. "Humor in the Art of Sarah Orne Jewett." Master's thesis, University of North Carolina, 1964.

Donahue, Marie Agnes. "Sarah Orne Jewett: New England Realist." Master's thesis, University of New Hampshire, 1955.

Frost, John Eldridge. "Sarah Orne Jewett." Doctoral dissertation, New York University, 1953.

Fultz, Mary Catherine. "The Narrative Art of Sarah Orne Jewett." Doctoral dissertation, University of Virginia, 1967.

Horn, Robert L. "Universality in the Fiction of Sarah Orne Jewett." Doctoral dissertation, University of Wisconsin, 1968.

Jones, Mary Ellen. "Deephaven to Poker Flat: A Study in Regional Characteristics in Selected Fiction of Sarah Orne Jewett and Bret Harte." Master's thesis, Duke University, 1959.

Magowan, Robin. "The Art of Personal Narrative: Sand, Fromentin, Jewett." Doctoral dissertation, Yale University, 1964.

Schaefer, Anita Jeanne. "Three Significant Motifs in the New England Stories and Sketches of Sarah Orne Jewett." Doctoral dissertation, Florida State University, 1976.

Trafton, Burton Weston Floyd, Jr. "Little Kingdom Down East: A Psychological Perspective on the World of a Gifted Child, Sarah Orne Jewett, 1849–1909." Master's thesis, University of New Hampshire, 1957.

Weigant, Leo Augustus. "The Manners Tradition and Regional Fiction in Nineteenth Century America." Doctoral dissertation, Duke University, 1970.

Williams, Sister Mary, C.S.J. "The Pastoral in New England

Local Color: Celia Thaxter, Sarah Orne Jewett, and Alice Brown." Doctoral dissertation, Stanford University, 1972.

Selected Secondary Sources

Ammons, Elizabeth. "The Shape of Violence in Jewett's 'A White Heron.'" *Colby Library Quarterly*, March 1986, pp. 6–16.

Auchincloss, Louis. "Sarah Orne Jewett," in *Pioneers and Caretakers*. Minneapolis: University of Minnesota Press, 1965.

Baker, Carlos. "Delineation of Life and Character." Robert E. Spiller, et al., eds. in *Literary History of the United States*. New York: Macmillan: 1974, I, 845–48; II, 602–4, 946–47, 1242–43.

Bender, Bert. "'To Calm and Uplift 'Against the Dark': Sarah Orne Jewett's Lyric Narratives." *Colby Library Quarterly*, December 1975, pp. 217–20.

Berthoff, Warner. "The Art of Jewett's Pointed Firs." *New England Quarterly*, March 1959, pp. 31–53.

Bishop, Ferman. "Henry James Criticizes *The Tory Lover*." *American Literature*, May 1955, pp. 262–64.

———"Sarah Orne Jewett's Ideas of Race." *New England Quarterly*, June 1957, pp. 243–49.

———*The Sense of the Past in Sarah Orne Jewett*. Wichita, Kan.: University of Wichita, 1959. (University of Wichita Bulletin, vol. 39, no. 1; *University Studies*, no. 41).

Blanc, Marie Thérèse (Th. Bentzon). "Le Roman de la femme-médicin." *Revue des Deux Mondes* 67 (Feb. 1, 1885): 598–632. Translation in Richard Cary, *Appreciation of Sarah Orne Jewett*.

Boggio-Sola, Jean. "The Poetic Realism of Sarah Orne Jewett." *Colby Library Quarterly*, June 1965, pp. 74–87.

Bowditch, Mrs. Ernest. "The Jewett Library." *Colby Library Quarterly*, December 1961, pp. 357–64.

Brenzo, Richard. "Sarah Orne Jewett's 'A White Heron.'" *Colby Library Quarterly*, March 1978, pp. 36–41.

Brown, Frank Chosteau. "The Interior Details and Furnishings of the Sarah Orne Jewett Dwelling Built by John Haggins in 1774, at South Berwick, Maine." *Pencil Points*, February 1940, pp. 97–112.

Buchan, Alexander McIntosh. "'Our Dear Sarah'; An Essay on Sarah Orne Jewett." St. Louis, Washington University, 1953. *Washington University Studies, Language and Literature*, no. 24, St. Louis, MO, 1953.

Carter, Everett. *Howells and the Age of Realism*. New York: J. B. Lippincott, 1954.

Cary, Richard, ed. *Appreciation of Sarah Orne Jewett: 29 Interpretive Essays*. Waterville, Maine: Colby College Press, 1973.

———"Jewett and the Gilman Women." *Colby Library Quarterly*, March 1960, pp. 94–103.

———"Jewett's Literary Canons." *Colby Library Quarterly*, June 1965, pp. 82–87.

———"Jewett, Tarkington, and the Maine Line." *Colby Library Quarterly*, February 1956, pp. 89–95.

———"Jewett on Writing Short Stories." *Colby Library Quarterly*, June, 1964, pp. 425–40.

———"Jewett's Cousins Charles and Charlie." *Colby Library Quarterly*, September 1959, pp. 48–58.

———"Miss Jewett and Madame Blanc." *Colby Library Quarterly*, September 1967, pp. 467–88.

———"The Multicolored Spirit of Celia Thaxter." *Colby Library Quarterly*, December 1964, pp. 512–36.

———"The Other Face of Jewett's Coin." *American Literary Realism*, Fall 1969, pp. 263–70.

———*Sarah Orne Jewett*. United States Authors Series, no. 19. New York: Twayne Publishers, Inc., 1962.

———"The Rise, Decline, and Rise of Sarah Orne Jewett." *Colby Library Quarterly*, December 1972, pp. 650–63.

———"Sarah Orne Jewett (1849–1909)." *American Literary*

Realism, Fall 1967, pp. 61–66.

———"Sarah Orne Jewett and the Rich Tradition." *Colby Library Quarterly*, November 1957, pp. 205–17.

———"Some Bibliographic Ghosts of Sarah Orne Jewett." *Colby Library Quarterly*, September 1968, pp. 139–45.

———"Violet Paget to Sarah Orne Jewett." *Colby Library Quarterly*, December 1970, pp. 235–43.

Cather, Willa. *Not Under Forty*. New York: Knopf, 1953.

———Preface to *The Best Short Stories of Sarah Orne Jewett*. 2 vols. Boston: Houghton, Mifflin and Company, 1925.

Chapman, Edward M. "The New England of Sarah Orne Jewett." *Yale Review*, October 1913, pp. 157–72.

Chase, Mary Ellen. Review of "A White Heron" in *New York Times Book Review*, October 13, 1963, p. 30.

———"Sarah Orne Jewett as a Social Historian." *Prairie Schooner*, Fall 1962, pp. 321–37.

Cook, Blanche Wiesen. "Female Support Networks and Political Activism: Lillian Wald, Crystal Eastman, Emma Goldman." *Chrysalis*, no. 3 (1977), p. 48.

Donahue, Marie. "Celia Thaxter's Island World." *Down East*, August 1976, pp. 72–75, 98–99.

———Introduction to *The Tory Lover*. South Berwick: The Old Berwick Historical Society, 1975, pp. vii–ix.

———"Of Pennyroyal and *Pointed Firs*." *Maine Digest*, Winter 1970, pp. 76–82.

———"Sarah Orne Jewett's 'Dear Old House and Home'" *Down East*, August 1977, pp. 62–67.

Donovan, Josephine. "Nan Prince and the Golden Apples." *Colby Library Quarterly*, March 1986, pp. 17–27.

———*Sarah Orne Jewett*. New York: Ungar, 1981.

———"The Unpublished Love Poetry of Sarah Orne Jewett." *Frontiers: A Journal of Women Studies*, January 1980, pp. 26–31.

Faderman, Lillian. *Surpassing the Love of Man: Romantic Friendship Between Women from the Renaissance to the Present*. New York: William Morrow, 1981.

Fike, Francis. "An Interpretation of *Pointed Firs.*" *New England Quarterly*, December 1961, pp. 478–91.

Folsom, Marcia McClintock. "Tact Is a Kind of Mind-Reading: Empathic Style in Sarah Orne Jewett's The Country of the Pointed Firs." *Colby Library Quarterly* 18 (1982): 66–78.

Frost, John Eldridge. "The Letters of Sarah Orne Jewett." *Colby Library Quarterly*, September 1959, pp. 38–45.

———*Sarah Orne Jewett.* Kittery Point, ME: Gundalow Club, 1960.

———"Sarah Orne Jewett Bibliography: 1949–1963." *Colby Library Quarterly*, June 1964, pp. 405–17.

Green, David Bonnell, ed. *The World of Dunnet Landing: A Sarah Orne Jewett Collection.* Lincoln: University of Nebraska Press, 1962.

Held, George. "Heart to Heart with Nature: Ways of Looking at 'A White Heron.'" *Colby Library Quarterly*, March 1982, pp. 55–65.

Hobbs, Glenda. "Pure and Passionate: Female Friendship in Sarah Orne Jewett's 'Martha's Lady.'" *Studies in Short Fiction* 17 (1980): 21–29.

Hollis, C. Carroll. "Letters of Sarah Orne Jewett to Anna Laurens Dawes." *Colby Library Quarterly*, September 1968, pp. 97–138.

Horn, Robert L. "The Power of Jewett's *Deephaven.*" *Colby Library Quarterly*, December 1972, pp. 617–31.

Hovet, Theodore. "'Once Upon a Time': Sarah Orne Jewett's 'A White Heron.'" *Studies in Short Fiction*, Winter 1978, pp. 63–68.

Howe, Julia Ward, ed. *Representative Women of New England.* Boston: New England Historical Publishing Company, 1904.

Howe, Mark A. DeWolfe. *Memories of a Hostess: A Chronicle of Eminent Friendships Drawn Chiefly from the Diaries of Mrs. James T. Fields.* Boston: Atlantic Monthly Press, 1922.

————*Who Lived Here?: A Baker's Dozen of Historic New England Houses and Their Occupants.* Boston: Little Brown and Company, 1952.

Howells, William Dean. *"Deephaven." Atlantic Monthly* 34 (1877): 759.

————"Recollections of an Atlantic Editorship." *Atlantic Monthly*, November 1907, pp. 594–606.

"In Memoriam: Sarah Orne Jewett." *Colby Library Quarterly*, September 1959, pp. 37–38.

James, Henry. "Mr. and Mrs. James T. Fields." *Atlantic Monthly*, July 1915, pp. 21–31.

Jewett, Fredericke Clarke. *History and Genealogy of the Jewetts of America.* 2 vols. New York: Grafton Press, 1908. 2: 647–50.

Jewett, Theodore H. "Elements of Success in the Medical Profession." Introductory Lecture Delivered Before the Students of the Medical Department of Bowdoin College, February 21, 1867. Portland: B. Thurston, 1869.

Johes, Katherine T. "From Stowe's Eagle Island to Jewett's 'A White Heron.'" *Colby Library Quarterly*, December 1974, pp. 515–21.

Kraus, Mary C. "Sarah Orne Jewett and Temporal Continuity." *Colby Library Quarterly*, September 1979, pp. 157–74.

Levy, Babette May. "Mutations in New England Local Color." *New England Quarterly*, September 1946, pp. 338–58.

Lucey, William L. "We New Englanders..." *Records of the American Catholic Historical Society of Philadelphia*, March, June 1959, pp. 58–64.

Magowan, Robin. "Pastoral and the Art of Landscape in *The Country of the Pointed Firs.*" *New England Quarterly*, June 1963, pp. 229–40.

Master Smart Women; A Portrait of Sarah Orne Jewett. Based on the film by Jane Morrison in collaboration with Peter Namuth. Text by Cynthia Keyworth. Unity, ME: North Country Press, 1988.

Matthiessen, Francis Otto. "A Bibliography of Sarah Orne Jewett." *Colby Library Quarterly*, November 1949, pp. 198–201.

———*Sarah Orne Jewett*. Boston: Houghton Mifflin Company, 1929.

Mawer, Randall R. "Setting as Symbol in Jewett's A Marsh Island." *Colby Library Journal*, June 1976, pp. 83–90.

More, Paul Elmer. "A Writer of New England." *Nation*, October 27, 1910, pp. 386–87.

Morison, Samuel Eliot. *John Paul Jones: A Sailor's Biography*. Boston: Little, Brown, 1959.

Nagel, Gwen L. *Critical Essays on Sarah Orne Jewett*. Boston: G. K. Hall, 1984.

Nagel, Gwen L. and James Nagel, comps. *Sarah Orne Jewett: A Reference Guide*. Boston: G. K. Hall, 1978.

Noyes, Sylvia Gray. "Mrs. Almira Todd, Herbalist-Conjurer." *Colby Library Journal*, December 1972, pp. 643–49.

Nye, George P. "Jewett and the Juvenile Critics." *Colby Library Quarterly*, September 1959, pp. 45–48.

Patterson, David. "James and Jewett." *Colby Library Quarterly*, February 1953, p. 152.

Philips, David E. "Maine's Most Brilliant Storyteller." *Down East*, December 1984, n.p.

Pratt, Annis. "Women and Nature in Modern Fiction." *Contemporary Literature*, Fall 1972, pp. 476–90.

Quinn, Arthur Hobson. *American Fiction*. New York: Appleton-Century, 1936.

Renza, Louis A. *"A White Heron" and the Question of Minor Literature*. Madison: University of Wisconsin Press, 1984.

Rhode, Robert D. "Sarah Orne Jewett and 'The Palpable Present Intimate.'" *Colby Library Quarterly*, September 1968, pp. 146–55.

Richards, Laura E. *Stepping Westward*. New York: Appleton, 1931, pp. 361–72.

Robinson, Phyllis. *Willa: The Life of Willa Cather*. Garden City, N.Y.: Doubleday, 1983.

Shackford, Martha Hale. "Sarah Orne Jewett." *Sewanee Review*, January 1922, pp. 20–26.

Sherman, Sarah Way. *Sarah Orne Jewett: An American Persephone*. Hanover and London: University Press of New England for University of New Hampshire, 1989.

Short, Clarice. "Studies in Gentleness." *Western Humanities Review*, Autumn 1957, pp. 387–93.

Smith, Eleanor M. "The Literary Relationship of Sarah Orne Jewett and Willa Sibert Cather." *New England Quarterly*, December 1956, pp. 472–92.

Spofford, Harriet Prescott. *A Little Book of Friends*. Boston: Little Brown, 1916.

Stackpole, Everett. *The First Permanent Settlement in Maine*. Excerpt from *Spague's Journal of Maine History* v 14 (no. 4). (Prepared for the meeting of the Piscataqua Pioneers at South Berwick, August 18, 1926.)

Stevenson, Catherine Barnes. "The Double Consciousness of the Narrator in Sarah Orne Jewett's Fiction." *Colby Library Quarterly*, March 1975, pp. 1–12.

Stowe, Harriet Beecher. *The Pearl of Orr's Island*. Hartford, Conn.: The Stowe-Day Foundation, 1979.

Thaxter, Celia. *An Island Garden*. Boston: Houghton Mifflin, 1988.

Thaxter, Rosamond. *Sandpiper: The Life of Celia Thaxter*. Sanbornville, N.H.: Wake-Brook House, 1962.

"Theodore Herman Jewett, M.D., of South Berwick." *Transactions of the Maine Medical Association, 1877–1879*, pp. 680–84. Portland: Stephen Berry, Printer, 1879.

Thompson, Charles Miner. "The Art of Miss Jewett." *Atlantic Monthly*, October 1904, pp. 485–97.

Thorp, Margaret F. *Sarah Orne Jewett*. University of Minnesota Pamphlets on American Writers, no. 61. Minneapolis: University of Minnesota Press, 1966.

Toth, Susan Allen. "Sarah Orne Jewett and Friends: A Community of Interest." *Studies in Short Fiction*, Summer 1972, pp. 223–41.

——"The Value of Age in the Fiction of Sarah Orne Jewett." *Studies in Short Fiction*, Summer 1971, pp. 433–41.

Trafton, Burton W.F., Jr. "Hamilton House, South Berwick, Maine." *Antiques*, May 1960, pp. 486–89.

——"Home Town Girl." *Yankee*, March 1950, pp. 34–35, 39, 71–72.

Waggoner, Hyatt H. "The Unity of *The Country of the Pointed Firs.*" *Twentieth Century Literature*, July 1959, pp. 67–73.

Weber, Carl J. "New England Through French Eyes Fifty Years Ago." *New England Quarterly*, September 1947, pp. 385–96.

——"Sarah Orne Jewett's First Story." *New England Quarterly*, March 1946, pp. 85–90.

——"Whittier and Sarah Orne Jewett." *New England Quarterly*, September 1945, pp. 401–7.

Weber, Clara, and Carl Weber. *A Bibliography of the Published Writings of Sarah Orne Jewett*. Waterville, ME: Colby College Press, 1949.

West, Rebecca. Introduction to *The Only Rose and Other Stories*. London: Jonathan Cape, 1937, pp. 7–14.

Westbrook, Perry D. *Acres of Flint: Writers of Rural New England, 1870–1900*. Metuchen, N.J.: Scarecrow Press, 1951. Revised Edition: 1981.

Wood, Ann Douglas. "The Literature of Impoverishment: The Women Local Colorists in American 1865–1914." *Women's Studies*, 1972, pp. 3–46.

Newspapers

Bangor (Maine) *Daily Commercial*, February 24, 1912; December 20, 1901.

Boston *Evening Transcript*, June 25, 1909; May 16, 1925.

Boston *Journal*, June 27, 1909; June 30, 1901.

Boston Sunday Herald, July 14, 1901.

Hartford *Daily Times*, April 22, 1895.

Kennebec (Maine) *Daily Journal*, August 31, 1901.

Lewiston (Maine) *Journal*, June 25, 1909; May 18, 1935; June 7, 1936; August 5, 1939; November 24, 1956; June 7, 1958.

New York Times, June 25, 1909; April 19, 1926; October 5, 1931.

Philadelphia *Press*, August 18, 1895.

Portland (Maine) *Daily Press*, February 18, 1910.

Portland (Maine) *Telegram*, April 26, 1931; April 28, 1931; April 14, 1940; April 28, 1940; October 4, 1942; September 2, 1973; August 30, 1981.

San Francisco *Bulletin*; September 13, 1895.

◆
Index

Academy magazine, 170
Acts and Anecdotes of Authors
  (Charles Barrows), 129-130
Adventures of Tom Sawyer (Twain), 163
Agassiz, Elizabeth Cabot, 192
Aldrich, Lillian (Mrs. Thomas Bailey),
  162-163, 182
Aldrich, Thomas Bailey, 67, 124, 147-48;
  and Appledore, 156; and friendship
  with SOJ, 162-163, 182; and Holmes
  reception, 90; and Longfellow
  Reading, 132; and 148 Charles St.,
  118; travels of, with SOJ, 162, 182
Alfred (Maine), 174-175
"All My Sad Captains," 160
American Fiction (Quinn), 123
American Society for Psychic
  Research, 98
Amesbury, Mass., 112
Among the Isles of Shoals (Celia
  Thaxter), 140
Amsterdam, 102
Anchorage, The (Maine), 163
Andersen, Hans Christian, 38, 54, 82
Angelus (Millet), 149-150
"Apology, An," 49
Appledore Island (Maine), 139, 140,
  141, 155, 156, 214-215 *See also* Isles
  of Shoals
Arabian Nights, 39
Arnold, Matthew, 91, 118, 150
"Asquam House" (Holderness, N.H.),
  110
Associated Charities of Boston, 92, 144
Athens, Greece, 186

Atlantic Monthly, 54-55, 67, 68, 91,
  131, 153
"At the Funeral of Phillips Brooks," 153
Auchincloss, Louis, 122
Audubon Magazine, 141
Austen, Jane, 39, 170, 201
"Autumn Holiday, An," 94

Balzac, Honoré de, 59
Barbizon (France), 149-150
Barrows, Charles, 129
Batchelder, Rosilla, 164
"Battle Hymn of the Republic," 193, 209
Baudelaire, Charles, 59
Beacon Hill (Boston), 118, 163, 185,
  198, 203
Beecher, Henry Ward, 58
Beethoven, 140, 156
Bell Telephone Co., 184-185
Bentzon, M. Th., 123-124. *See also*
  Blanc, Marie Thérèse
Berwick (ship), 21
Berwick Academy, 37-38, 42-43, 46,
  146, 183-184, 212
Berwick Woman's Club, 184, 193
"Best China Saucer, The," 82
Best Stories of Sarah Orne Jewett, 12,
  208
Betty Leicester, 142-144, 187
Betty Leicester's English Christmas, 144
"Between Mass and Vespers," 154
Beverly (Mass.), 159, 185
Birckhead, Kate, 63
"Bit of Color, A," 142
"Bit of Shore Life, A," 88

Blake, William, 117
Blanc, Marie Thérèse, 124; death of, 204; and friendship with SOJ, 123, 124, 149; hospitality of, 149-150, 176-178, 187-188; and visit to New England, 174-175; and writing of SOJ, 123-124, 198
Book Buyer, 170
Booth, Edwin, 51, 91, 101, 139
Boothbay Harbor (Maine), 96, 137, 164, 203
Boston, 44, 104, 181
Boston Athenaeum, 185
Boston *Evening Transcript*, 199
Boston *Journal*, 66, 151
"Boston marriages," 108
Boston Public Library, 184
Bowdoin College (Brunswick, Maine), 21, 188-189, 197-198
Brandeis, Mrs. Louis, 204, 205
British gum, 22
Brontë Family, 178
Brooks, Phillips, 51, 58, 61, 153-154
Brooks, Van Wyck, 69
Brown, Alice, 170
Browning, Pen, 119
Browning, Robert, 140
Bull, Ole, 101, 139, 156
Burt, Cicely, 49

Cable, George Washington, 124, 136
Cabot, Mrs. Joseph (Susan Burley), 185, 189, 197, 198, 202
Cambridge, Mass., 59, 146
Canada, 47-48
Capote, Truman, 13
Captain January (Richards), 193
Cary, Richard, 13-14, 39, 203; and *A Country Doctor*, 116; and "The Dulham Ladies," 128; and *A Marsh Island*, 123; and "Mr. Bruce," 55; and SOJ letters and stories, 213; and "Tom's Husband," 111; and *The Tory Lover*, 193
Cather, Willa, 13, 32, 105, 118; and *Country of the Pointed Firs*, 12, 171; and Fields, Annie, 91-92, 103, 204-205; description of SOJ by, 103, 205; and friendship with SOJ, 205-208
Catholic World, 145-146
Cato (slave), 43
Century Magazine, 111, 131
Cervantes, 39
Charles River, Mass., 117, 152
Chase, Mary Ellen, 171, 176, 202
Churchill, Winston (American writer), 191

Church of New Jerusalem, 59
Cincinnati, Ohio, 48-49
Cincinnati Gazette, 73
Civil War, 20, 42-43, 108
Claflin, Gov. William, 83, 118
Claflin, Mrs. William, 83, 118
Colby College (Waterville, Maine), 60
Cologne, Germany, 102
"The Colour Cure," 116
Concord, Mass., 72
Congregational Church (South Berwick), 71-72
Conservation, 11, 94-95, 126, 141. *See also* Ecology
Constable & Co. (London), 213
Constantinople, 187
"Contributor's Club," *Atlantic Monthly*, 116, 153
Cook, Blanche Wiesen, 105
Coolbroth, Harriet N., Eldress, 175
Cornell University, 212
Cottage Hearth, 122, 143
"Counted Out," 199
Country By-Ways, 35, 97, 135; dedication to father, 93; reviews of, 95; themes in, 36, 44, 53, 93-95
Country Doctor, A, 36, 111, 112-116, 121, 123, 213
Country of the Pointed Firs, The, 32, 163, 213, 192, 193; characters in, 32, 76, 77, 104, 135, 164-169; dedication of, 185; language in, 169-170; reviews of, 169-171; setting of, 164; themes in, 167-169
"Courting of Sister Wisby, The," 136
Crabby (dog), 41, 52
Craigie House (Cambridge, Mass.), 95-96
Cranford (Gaskell), 127
Critic, The, 122
Critical Essays on Sarah Orne Jewett, 14
Cuba, 162, 180
Cushing, Elizabeth, 31-33
Cyrano de Bergerac (play), 153, 176

Daily Picayune (New Orleans), 133
Dark Harbor, Maine, 186
Dartmoor Prison, 176, 191
Dawes, Anna Laurens, 71, 73, 107
de Beaulaincourt, Charlotte, 187
de Castellane, Maréchal, 187
Deephaven (fictional town), 69, 74-75
Deephaven, 73-81, 213; characters in, 32, 75-78, 164, 165; publication of, 57; reviews of, 79-80, 123; setting of, 74-75; writing of, 71
"Deephaven Cronies," 69

"Deephaven Excursions," 69
de Sévigné, Madame, 177
de Solms, Louis, Count, 178
Dexter, Dr., 195
Dial, 133
Dickens, Charles, 91, 101, 108-109, 118, 119
"Discontent," 81
Doctor Breen's Practice (Howells), 115
Doctor Zay (Phelps), 115
Dodd, Mead, 144
Doe, Edith Haven, 44, 51
Donovan, Josephine, 14, 106
Dresel, Louisa, 203, 210
"Driving Miss Daisy," (Uhry), 145
"Dulham Ladies, The," 127-128
du Maurier, George, 150, 179
"Dunluce Castle," 100
Dunnack, Florence, 209
Dunnet Landing, 164, 165, 171
"Dunnet Shepherdess, A," 172, 182

"Eagle Trees, The," 97
Eastman, Caroline Jewett (sister), 87, 128, 148, 152, 173-174. *See also* Jewett, Caroline Augusta
Eastman, Edwin C. (brother-in-law), 87, 148
Eastman, Theodore Jewett (nephew), 13, 128 129, 152, 195; and aunts, 173, 181; death of, 214; and Fogg Memorial Library, 183; in France, 178; and Harvard graduation, 188
Ecology, 11, 94-95, 126. *See also* Conservation
Eclectic, 79
Eliot, A. C. (pen name), 47, 54, 66
Eliot, Alice (pen name), 47, 66
Eliot, George, 39, 123
Eliot, Maine, 66
Embargo Act of 1807, 20
Emerson, Ellen, 72
Emerson, Ralph Waldo, 59, 72, 91, 118-119, 139, 214
Emerson School for Girls (Boston), 91
"Empty Purse, An," 199
England, 101, 150, 176, 178
"English as She is Taught," (Twain), 132
Epoch, 137
Essex County, Mass., 121
Exeter, New Hampshire, 22, 23, 24, 33-34, 46, 104, 212

Faderman, Lillian, 111
"Fame's Little Day," 160
Fielding, Henry, 39
Fields, Annie (Mrs. James T.), 72, 90, 95, 148, 184, 200; and Willa Cather, 91-92, 205; and charity work, 92, 110, 144; and death of husband, 92-93; description of, 91-92, 103, 204-205; and Louisa Dresel, 203; early life of, 91-92; illnesses of, 135, 195; relationship with SOJ, 14, 98, 102, 210, 213; and SOJ letters, 213; and Stowe biography, 175; and Celia Thaxter, 139, 140, 156, 159; and travels with SOJ, 99-102, 136, 148, 152, 162, 176, 185-188; and visit to South Berwick, 99
Fields, James Thomas, 54, 67, 90-91, 98-99; and *Atlantic Monthly*, 54; death of 92-93; and Dickens, 101; and Annie Fields, 91, 104; and Celia Thaxter, 139
Fields, Osgood & Co., 91
Flag of Our Union, The, 47
Flaubert, Gustave, 131
"Flickerbridge," (Henry James), 180
"Flight of Betsey Lane, The," 32, 154-155
Fogg Memorial Library, South Berwick, 160
"Foreigner, The," 173
France, 149, 176-178
Franklin, Benjamin, 191
Freeman, Dr., 50
Freeman, Edward Augustus, 133
Freeman, Mary E. Wilkins, 12, 88, 127, 145-146, 170
Free Press (Somersworth, N.H.), 193
Freud, 108
"From a Mournful Villager," 94
Frost, John Eldridge, 13
Fuller, Margaret, 31

Gad's Hill (England), 101
Gambrel Cottage (Mass.), 103, 159, 174, 185. *See also* Manchester-By-The-Sea (Mass.)
Garland, Hamlin, 124
Garnett, Edward, 198
Garrett, Mary Elizabeth, 186
Gaskell, Elizabeth, 127, 170
Giant's Causeway (Ireland), 100
The Gilded Age (Twain), 189
Gilman, Edward (ancestor), 24
Gilman, Nelly (cousin), 45-46
Gilman, Nicholas (great-granduncle), 24, 46, 191, 212
"Girl with the Cannon Dresses, The," 66
"Gloucester Mother, The," 199-200
"Godspeed," (Whittier), 99
Gordon, Grace, 51, 64
Grande Chartreuse, France, 178

Great Expectations (Dickens), 48
Greece, 186-187
Green, Henry, Elder, 174-175
"Guests of Miss Timms, The," 160-162
Guptill's Woods, 52

Haggins, John ("Tilly"), 20-21, 30, 191
Hale, Edward Everett, 132
Halliburton, Georgina, 63-64, 107
Hamilton House, 190, 191, 212
Hannah (servant), 102
Hardy, Thomas, 121
Harper's Magazine, 45, 90, 96, 97, 100, 122, 127, 131
Harte, Bret, 124
Hassam, Childe, 139-140, 155, 156, 212-213
Hatch, George, 76
Haverhill, Mass., 121
Haworth, England, 178
Hawthorne, Nathanial, 88, 91, 139
Hayes, Mary, 52
Heidelberg, Germany, 102
Hermione (yacht), 162, 182
Hilborn (servant), 102
"Hilton's Holiday, The," 160, 208
Hingham, Mass., 24
History of the Norman Conquest (E. A. Freeman), 133
Holland, 102
Hollis, Maine, 197
Holmes, Oliver Wendell, 91, 193; and actors, 118; and Appledore, 139; *Atlantic* reception for, 90; death of, 159; and friendship with SOJ, 159-160; and Longfellow Reading, 132
Homer, Winslow, 91
Hot Springs, Maine, 136
Houghton, Mifflin & Co., 73, 136, 213
"How I Became a Progressive" (Theodore Roosevelt), 12
Howe, Alice Greenwood, 185
Howe, Mrs. Julia Ward, 90, 132, 193, 209
Howe, Mark DeWolfe, 215
Howells, William Dean, 54, 67, 90, 115; at Appledore, 156; and *Deephaven*, 69, 73, 80; and Longfellow Reading, 132; and *Mate of the Daylight*, 111; and relationship with SOJ, 68, 97, 195, 198; and SOJ's writing, 201, 207
Huckleberry Finn, 12, 171
Hudson, Thomas, 117
Hunt, Leigh, 119
Hunt, William Morris, 117, 139

Inagua, 162
Independent, The, 62, 81

Indians, 25, 64
Interlaken, 102
Intervale, N. H., 200
Ireland, 100-101
Island Garden, An (Celia Thaxter), 140, 155-156, 212-213
Isle of Wight, 101
Isles of Shoals, 44, 96, 139, 140, 141, 156. *See also* Appledore
Italy, 149, 186

Jamaica, 182
James, Henry, 68, 103, 198, 201; and *Country of the Pointed Firs*, 171, 179, 193; and description of 148 Charles St., 117, 119; hospitality of, 179-180; and *The Tory Lover*, 193
James, William, 98, 153, 170-171
Jefferson, Joseph, 118
Jefferson Medical College (Philadelphia), 22
"Jenny Garrow's Lovers," 40, 47
Jewett, Augusta (aunt-in-law), 29, 30
Jewett, Caroline Augusta (sister), 30, 58, 87, 128. *See also* Eastman, Caroline Jewett
Jewett, Caroline Frances (Perry) (mother), 25, 58, 99, 117, 128; character of, 31; death of, 147; friendships of, 185; illness of, 146; marriage of, 24; and reading, 39; and relationship with SOJ, 147-148
Jewett, Eliza Sleeper (step-grandmother), 31
Jewett, Mary Rice (sister), 13, 37, 50, 54, 65, 71, 83, 128; at Anchorage, 163; birth of, 24; and Willa Cather, 208; domesticity of, 58, 117, 129; and Fogg Library, 183; in France, 178; later years, 211-212; and nephew, 87, 181; nickname of, 107; and relationship with SOJ, 49, 98, 105, 108, 129, 184, 202; scholarship of, 38
Jewett, Mary Rice (step-grandmother), 26-28
Jewett, Sarah Orne, 64, 194-196, 200-201; ancestry of, 19, 27, 29, 33; anglophilism of, 143; birth of, 24; and Blanc, Madame, 123-125; and Willa Cather, 205-208; childhood of, 23, 26-36; childlike traits in, 97-98, 113, 204; and clothes 45, 176; and conservation, 11, 94-95, 126, 141; death of, 210; descriptions of, 41, 103, 175-176; domesticity of, 58, 105; and ecology, 11, 94-95, 126; education of, 37-39; and father, 19,

Jewett, Sarah Orne (continued)
34-36, 50, 84-85; and feminist
critics, 104-111, 125; and Annie Fields,
91-93, 103-110; friendships of, 44,
49-51, 52, 63-64, 104-105, 123, 124,
182; and gardening, 129; hobbies
of, 47; humor in, 39-40, 51-52, 65, 146,
160-162; illnesses of, 34, 41, 52, 57,
72-73, 187, 193, 203, arthritis: 34,
41, 52, 73, 97, 135, 136, 137, 156,
194; and Irish stories, 144; and lesbian issue, 103-110; and Longfellow
reading, 132; love poems of, 106; and
marriage, 105, 109, 110-111, 114,
115; moralizing of, 62, 79, 81-82,
89-90, 97, 142; and mother, 146-148;
and nature, 26, 35, 42, 52-53, 66,
88, 94-95, 112, 125, 126, 127; and
nephew, 87, 128-129, 181; nicknames
of, 63, 106-107, 141; pen names of,
47; and psychic phenomena, 98-99,
141, 173, 174; reading of, 35, 38-39,
45, 48, 51; and religion, 49, 58-63,
71-72; and Shakers, 174-175; and
slavery, 43; social life of, 44, 46-47,
48-51, 71, 72, 105, 181; and Spanish–
American War, 157; and sports, 41-42,
65, 130, 137; and Celia Thaxter, 98,
139, 140, 159; and themes in writing,
11-12, 116, 121-122; travels of, 47-48,
99-102, 136, 148, 162, 176, 185-188;
and Whitman subscription, 132;
and women's rights, 11, 113-114,
123, 124; on writing, 54, 67-68,
130-132, 189, 206, 207; works of:
see specific works
Jewett, Sarah Orne (Sally) (paternal
grandmother), 26-27
Jewett, Theodore Furber (paternal grandfather), 19-21, 28, 31, 110
Jewett, Theodore Herman (father), 25,
44, 46, 65, 87, 98; and Civil War, 43;
and *A Country Doctor*, 112-113; early
life of, 21-22; death of, 36, 83-85;
illnesses of, 64, 83; influence on
SOJ, 19, 33-36, 50, 142; marriage
of, 24; and Swedenborgianism, 61
Jewett, William (uncle), 20, 29, 44, 128
Jewett House, South Berwick, 20-21,
69, 75, 191, 210, 212
Joe (dog), 41, 52
Johns, Barbara A., 115
Jones, John Paul, 29, 189, 190, 191

"Katydid" books (Coolidge), 153
Keats, John, 117-118
"King of Folly Island, The," 134, 136-137

Kipling, Rudyard, 160, 170, 179
Kittery, Maine, 25, 29, 68, 159, 198

"Lady Ferry," 33, 88, 202
Lafayette, 29, 32, 212
La Ferte, Jouarre, France, 177-178
Lamb, Charles, 48, 63
Lanier, Sidney, 124
Later Poems (Alice Meynell), 194
"Late Supper, A," 12, 89
Lathrop, George, 111
"Law Lane," 136
Lawrence, D. H., 106
Learning Corporation of America, 125
Leaves of Grass (Whitman), 132
Lee, Vernon, 186, 204
Lesbianism, 105-109
Leslie, Dr. Horace Granville, 112
Lewis, Dr. Winslow, 22
Life, 183
Life of Nancy, The, 160-162, 213
Lily (friend), 62
Literary World, 79, 90, 111, 122, 127
Little Boar's Head, N.H., 59
"Little Captive Maid, A," 154
"Little Traveler, A," 124-125
Little Women (Alcott), 51, 56, 143
Lodge, Mrs. James (Mary Green-
wood), 143-144
London, 102
Long, Mary Olivia Gilman (aunt), 46
Longfellow, Alice, 96, 137
Longfellow, Henry Wadsworth, 91,
95-96, 98, 193
Longfellow, Samuel, 96
Longfellow Memorial Reading, 132
"Lost Lover, A," 180
"Lost Turkey, The," 198
Louis XVI, 212
Louisbourg, Siege of, 29
Lowell, James Russell, 67, 91, 193;
death of, 146-147; and Longfellow
Reading, 132; and 148 Charles
Street, 118, 135
Lucerne, 102
"Luck of the Bogans, The," 144

Mabie, Hamilton W., 170
Macauley, Thomas, 48
Madame Bovary, 131
Manchester-by-the-Sea (Mass.), 103, 159,
174, 185. *See also* Gambrel Cottage
Marie Antoinette, 23, 49
"Marjorie Daw," (Aldrich), 163
Marsh Island, A, 121-123
"Marsh Rosemary," 127
"Martha and Mary," 127

"Martha's Lady," 182
Martinsville (Maine), 163
Mason, Ellen, 63
Mate of the Daylight, 110-111
Matthiessen, Francis O., 13
McClure's, 199, 205, 206
Merriman, Helen Bigelow, 200
Merry's Museum, 62
Meynell, Alice, 194
Millet, Jean François, 149
Mills, John Stuart, 31
Misselwood (Mass.), 162
Misses Raynes' School, The, 30
"Miss Sydney's Flowers," 89-90
"Miss Tempy's Watchers," 136
"Mr. Bruce," 31, 55, 68, 89
Mistral, Frédéric, 177
"Mistress of Sydenham Plantation,
The," 145
Morse, Fanny, 208
Mount Agamenticus, 94
Mt. Desert, Maine, 203
Mouse Island, Maine, 137
Museum of Navajo Ceremonial Art
(Santa Fe, N.M.), 203
Mystery of Edwin Drood, The
(Dickens), 101

Nagel, Gwen L., 14
"Nancy's Doll," 82
Nassau, 162, 182
Nation, The, 68, 95
National Museum of American Art
(Washington, D.C.), 213
"Native of Winby, A.," 154, 173-174, 213
Newburyport, Mass., 148
New Church Philosophy, 60-63, 97, 113
New England: Indian Summer
(Brooks), 69
Free Press (New Hampshire), 170
Newichawannock Falls, 25
New York, 44
New York Times, 79, 114-115
North American Review, 45, 143
Norton, Charles Eliot, 118, 132, 175, 207
Norton, Sara, 175, 207
Norway, 101-102
Not Under Forty (Cather), 91, 204
Nubble Light (Neddick Point, Maine), 77

"October Ride, An," 53, 81, 93
Old Corner Bookstore (Boston), 91
Old Friends and New, 88, 90
Old Kensington (Lady Ritchie), 101
Oldtown Folks (Harriet Beecher
Stowe), 107
"Old Town of Berwick, The," 11
Oliphant, Margaret, 39

Oliver Twist (Dickens), 48
148 Charles St., 91, 99, 103, 105,
117-119, 147, 152, 181, 211
Oneida Indians, 64
"Only Rose, The," 160
"On Star Island," 96
"On Rosees," 30
O Pioneers! (Cather), 208
Osgood, James R., 73, 80, 81
Ouida (Marie Louise de la Ramée), 48
Our Young Folks, 47, 62
Outlook, The, 183
Overland Monthly, The, 125

Paderewski, 181
Page, Thomas Nelson, 124
Paget, Violet (Vernon Lee), 186, 204
Paris, 102
Parkman, Frances, 202
Parsons, Theophilus, 13, 58, 63, 64, 65,
82; and *A Country Doctor*, 113; death
of, 96-97; and death of Dr. Jewett,
84; and *Deephaven*, 73, 78-79; and
"Miss Sydney's Flowers," 89; and
relationship with SOJ, 59-61, 62,
98, 104; and *The Tory Lover*, 191
"Patty's Dull Christmas," 82
Peabody, Andrew Preston, 143
Pearl of Orr's Island, The (Harriet
Beecher Stowe), 40
Pennsylvania Audubon Society, 141
"Pepper-Owl, The," 82
Perry, Abigail Gilman, 23
Perry, Caroline Frances. *See* Jewett,
Caroline Frances
Perry, John Taylor (uncle), 48, 73
Perry, Sarah (aunt), 48
Perry, William (maternal grand-
father), 22-23, 24, 133, 200
Peter Ibbetson (George du Maurier), 150
Phelps, Elizabeth Stuart, 115
Philadelphia Centennial (1876), 72
Pioneers and Caretakers (Auchincloss),
122
Piscataqua River, 20, 25, 53-54, 93,
145, 152, 189, 208
Plato, 14, 67
Play Days, 31, 81-83
Poland Spring, Maine, 136, 200
Ponce de Leon Hotel, St. Augustine,
Florida, 136, 162
Ponkapog, Mass., 163
Pool, Ernest Hillhouse, 107
Pope, Alexander, 117
Port au Prince, Haiti, 182
Portland, Maine, 43, 44, 45
Portsmouth, N.H., 20, 44, 140, 202

Powderhouse Hill, South Berwick, 37
Pray, Lizzie (servant), 102
Proust, Marcel, 187
Provence, France, 154
Punch, 150
Putnam, G. P., 133

Quampeagan (South Berwick), 25
"Queen of Sheba," 99, 102
Queen's Twin, The and Other Stories,
    104, 182, 185, 213
"Queen's Twin, The," 143, 171-172,
    182, 183
Queen Victoria, 104, 143, 171-172, 183
Quinn, Arthur Hobson, 123

Radcliffe College, 192
Ramée, Marie Louise de la (Ouida), 48
Ranger (ship), 189
Rawlings, Marjorie Kinnan, 12, 122
Reade, Charles, 101
Rebecca of Sunnybrook Farm (Kate
    Douglas Wiggin), 197
Remembrance of Things Past (Proust),
    187
Return of the Native (Hardy), 121
Revere, Paul, 212
Review of Reviews, 170
Revolutionary War, 29, 190, 192
Revue des Deux Mondes (Madame
    Blanc), 123, 127, 175
Rice, Cora Lee, 106
Richard Carvel (Winston Churchill), 191
Richards, Laura, 193
Richfield Springs, New York, 156
Riggs, Kate D. (Kate Douglas Wiggin),
    197-198
Riley, James Whitcomb, 139
Ritchie, Anne Thackeray, 101
"River Driftwood," 53, 93
Riverside Magazine for Young People,
    54, 55, 62, 66, 67
River Society, The, 20-21
Rollinsford, N.H., 44, 52
Roman, Judith, 106-107, 111
Rome, 102
Roosevelt, Theodore, 12
Rossetti, Christina, 101
Rotterdam, 102
Rudin (Turgenev), 201
Rye, N.H., 59

St. Augustine, Florida, 136, 162
St. George Peninsula, Maine, 164
St. John's Episcopal Church (Ports-
    mouth, N.H.), 58, 71
St. Nicholas (magazine), 62, 81, 142
Salmon Falls River, Maine, 20, 190

Sand, George, 124, 125
*Sarah Orne Jewett: A Reference
    Guide*, 14
Sarah Orne Jewett (Cary), 123, 193
Sarah Orne Jewett (Donovan), 14
Sarah Orne Jewett (Matthiessen), 13
*Sarah Orne Jewett: An American
    Persephone* (Sherman), 104, 107-108
Sargent, John Singer, 91, 156, 184
Saturday Review (London), 79, 83, 115
Scarlet Letter, The (Hawthorne), 12, 171
"Scholar Gypsy, The," (Arnold), 118
Scribner's Magazine, 152
Scudder, Horace, 55, 67, 95; and *Old
    Friends and New*, 90; and *Play Days*,
    82-83; and *Strangers and Wayfarers*,
    146; and *The Tory Lover*, 192-193
"Self-Reliance" (Emerson), 214
Sentimental Traveller, The (Vernon
    Lee), 204
Severn, Joseph, 117-118
Shakers, 174-175
Sheila (horse), 81, 94
Shelley, Percy Bysshe, 119
Sherman, Sarah Way, 107-108
"Shipwrecked Buttons, The," 31, 54,
    66, 82
Shore House, The, 68, 69
Simmons College (Boston), 209
"Sister Peacham's Turn," 108
Smollett, Tobias, 39
Society for the Preservation of New
    England Antiquities, 212
"Sorrowful Guest, A," 88
South Berwick, Maine, 75, 103, 105,
    152, 174, 183-184, 209-210 and
    Country By-Ways, 93-95; history of,
    20-21, 25; social life in, 46
South End Music School (Boston), 203
Spain, 180
Spanish-American War, 180
"Spring Sunday, A," 199
Sterne, Laurence, 39
Stories and Poems for Children (Celia
    Thaxter), 159
Story of a Bad Boy, The (Aldrich), 163
"Story of the Nations, The," 133
Story of the Normans, The, 133-135
Stowe, Harriet Beecher, 40, 58, 107,
    139, 175
Strangers and Wayfarers, 144-146
Swedenborg, Emanual, 58-59, 72
Swedenborgianism, 13, 58-61, 94, 97, 113
Sweet, Sarah O. (pen name), 66
Switzerland, 102

Tales of New England, 142, 180, 213

Tenants Harbor, Maine, 163, 164
Tennyson, Alfred Lord, 48, 101, 150-151
Terry, Ellen, 101
Thackeray, William Makepeace, 91, 108-109, 118
Thaxter, Celia, 139, 159; and conservation, 141; death of, 156; and garden, 155, 212-213; illness of, 155; and nature, 139; and nickname, 107; and psychic phenomena, 98, 141, 173; writings of, 140, 155
Thaxter, John, 159, 183
Thaxter, Karl, 140
Thaxter, Levi, 140
Thompson, Charles Miner, 201, 214
Thoreau, Henry David, 72, 169, 214
Throp, Margaret Farrand, 167
Thunderbolt Hill (Mass.), 103. *See also* Gambrel Cottage
Ticknor and Fields, 91
Tolstoy, Leo, 127
"Tom's Husband," 110
"To My Father," 85, 213
Tory Lover, The, 43, 188-193, 198
"Town Poor, The," 144-145
"Tree Planting," 116
"Tributes to Whittier," 151
Trinity Episcopal Church (Boston), 51, 58, 94, 153, 175, 199
Tucker, John, 94, 102, 129, 195
Turgenev, Ivan, 201
"Turner's Old Temeraire," (Lowell), 135
Twain, Mark, 68, 132, 149, 163, 189
"Two Deaths," (Tolstoy), 127
Tyson, Emily, 190

Uhry, Alfred, 145
"Uncle Peter's Tragedy," 54
Uncollected Short Stories of Sarah Orne Jewett, The, 213
Under the Olive (Annie Fields), 93
Under Two Flags (Ouida), 48
"*Une Visite Chez les Shakers*," (Madame Blanc), 175
U.S. Marine Hospital (Chelsea, Maine), 22
U.S.S. Maine, 180
"Unpublished Love Poems of Sarah Orne Jewett," 106
"Up Country," 143

Venice, 102
Verses, 213
Virginian, The (Owen Wister), 201

Walden (Thoreau), 169
Walker, Charlie, 50

Wallingford, Lt. Samuel, 190-191
Walton, Izaac, 39
Walworth, Ella, 51, 56, 64, 71
"War Debt, A," 134, 160
War of 1812, 20
Ward, Dorothy, 179, 194
Ward, Mrs. Humphrey, 150, 179, 194
Ward, William Hayes, 62
Warner, Charles Dudley, 90, 189
Washington, Booker T., 181
Washington, George, 212
Washington, D.C., 83
Water Babies (Kingsley), 48
Wells, Maine, 58, 64, 75, 76
W. I. (West Indies) Store, 21, 128
Wheelwright, Mary Cabot, 203
Wheelwright, Sarah, 179
White Heron and Other Stories, A, 125-126, 127, 129, 141
White Mountains, Vermont, 83, 137
"White Rose Road, The," 145
Whitman, Sarah Wyman, 146, 151, 153, 155, 175, 189, 201-202
Whitman, Walt, 132
Whittier, John Greenleaf, 45, 105, 109-110, 119, 121, 135, 193; and "The Courting of Sister Wisby," 130; death of, 151; and death of Mrs. Jewett, 148; and *Deephaven*, 81; and "Dunluce Castle," 100; and Fieldses, 91; friendship with SOJ, 80, 96-97, 98, 99, 104, 148, 151; and Holmes Reception, 90; and *The King of Folly Island*, 137; and Longfellow Reading, 132; and *A Marsh Island*, 102; and Celia Thaxter, 140, 141, 156; and Whitman, 132
Wide Awake, 62
Wiggin, Kate Douglas, 197-198
Wilkins, Mary E. *See* Freeman, Mary E. Wilkins
"William's Wedding," 172-173
"Winter Courtship, A," 39
"Winter Drive," 35, 94
Wister, Owen, 201
"Woman's Heartlessness" (Celia Thaxter), 141
Women's Rights, 11, 113-114, 123, 124
Woolsey, Sarah Chauncey, 152-153
Wordsworth, William, 169
World's Columbian Exposition (Chicago), 152

Yeats, William Butler, 59
"Yellow Kitten, The," 82
York, Maine, 75
Young, Rebecca, 194-195
Youth's Companion, 198, 199